Ambedkar's Philosophy on Religion and Morality

Ambedkar's Philosophy on Religion and Morality

Dr Seshagiri Rao Regulagadda

KALPAZ

ISBN: 978-93-5128-187-0

Price: ₹ 1050

First Published, 2016

Published by

Kalpaz Publications
C-30, Satyawati Nagar,
Delhi – 110052
E-mail: kalpaz@hotmail.com
Ph.: 9212142040

Printed at: G. Print Process, Delhi

Cataloging in Publication Data—DK
Courtesy: D.K. Agencies (P) Ltd. <docinfo@dkagencies.com>

Regulagadda, Seshagiri Rao, author.
Ambedkar's philosophy on religion and morality / Dr Seshagiri Rao Regulagadda.
pages cm
Includes bibliographical references.
ISBN 9789351281870

1. Ambedkar, B. R. (Bhimrao Ramji), 1891-1956—Philosophy. 2. India—Religion. 3. Ethics—India. I. Title.

DS481.A43R44 2016 DDC 200.954 23

Contents

Introduction

Since the period of the Enlightenment, the relation between morality and religion has been the subject of more general philosophical analysis, as distinct from its treatment in the hands of theologian. The general understanding is that as systems of thoughts, morality and religion both are considered very close to the essential nature of philosophy.[1] Philosophy gives its main thrust to the normative ideas. Descriptive realm tells us what the going is on at present. How can one make judgment about the descriptive realm? How can one take a certain attitude towards the descriptive realm? A close analysis reveals that human attitude not only matters descriptive realm, it also contains normative bite. Human activities precisely contain attitudes, judgments towards certain given circumstances. The explanations of human activity of rejecting or receiving with normative claim necessarily presuppose norms.

Systems of Morality and Religion precisely are attempts to describe the acts or craving of humans which clearly includes the normative claims. Religion can be visualised as normative claim in the sense it is an attempt to visualise the ideal concepts. And morality mainly discusses the ideal values. Altogether philosophy is an attempt to sketch the normative ideas in the realm of knowledge, reality, ethics, aesthetics, religion etc, in a justified manner. And philosophical analysis of religion and morality tell us how justifiably we can talk about the ideal values and concepts. In the realm of religion and morality normative idea is almost identified with ideal nature.[2] But what is the problem with the ideal nature is ideality that often loses its relevance because it is always considered as a kind of leap from the empirical realm. And only a philosophical analysis can reveal how much the so called ideal systems are necessary for the life or how much problematic the duality of empirical and ideal or how much each does contribute one another.

Moreover, philosophical analysis provides adequate justification for ideas in the systems of religion and morality. Analysis of Western religion and morality reveals that it is mainly anthropocentric; it mainly revolves around the human relations.[3] God is constituted in the position of father and humans are considered as sons or daughters of the father. And all other specification is worked out by developing this model. Morality is worked by looking on the idea of how children should behave with parents. It mainly emphasises that humans, all other creatures are the creations of God, and the supremacy of one absolute God over the all creations is emphasised in the Semitic religions.

Contrary to the Semitic tradition, the Indian tradition is the Vedic Hindu tradition mainly revolves around the ideas of Vedas and Upanishads. Thus, the pronouncements of those texts are considered as sacred and ideal and, the only remaining task to provide arguments in favour of it. Here argument does not cross the limits, which Vedas drew. However, in heterodox tradition, inquiry is without any presuppositions. That result in the amazing arguments regarding religion and morality. Especially Buddhism is a system, which is predominantly ethical but excludes the concept of God and Jainism does not provide any categorical difference between God and Human.

In this context, the main aim of this dissertation is to trace the philosophical perspective of Ambedkar with special reference to his philosophical ideas of Religion and Morality, which in turn would pave the way for practical responses to the problem of different ideology in the Indian society. Unlike many other social scientists, Ambedkar did not reject the role of religion as product of mainstream thinking. He clearly understood the deep role that religion can play in the society. At the same time he understood how inadequate the religion in its present form is to do such role in society. Therefore, Ambedkar's attempts are to reformulate the religion and morality on the basis of humanity. Ambedkar's understood that the attempts of Buddha were also on the similar lines. According to Ambedkar's morality is the basic need of humanity, and of a healthy society. And he criticised Hinduism for de-linking their religious ideas from the moral basis. Hinduism does not consider the religious and moral ideas as corrective force against the evils of society. Instead, Hinduism often mixes with the illness of society and often produces new illness of inequality. Buddhism considers morality and religion as firmly rooted on equality and humanity which stems from human mind.

First Chapter deals with the concepts of religion, morality and philosophy and their interrelatedness. The definitions provided on the notion of truth do not have unanimity. There is much disparity regarding the definition of truth. The notion of truth plays a crucial role in all of these definitions. Some philosophical doctrines completely deny the space of religion and theology by terming it as spurious or meaningless. Logical positivism is the best example for this one. But some other philosophical systems stand on the other extreme by completely accommodating mysticism. There are philosophical shifts which focus from the abstract concepts to the question of existence, for example: Existentialism. These shifts have also their own impacts. The commitment towards something is an undeniable fact in the human existence. Moreover, religion forms this commitment, i.e., the necessary basis of all human activities. Later, it also discusses the conceptions of morality and philosophy. Moral philosophy is concerned with what people think and ought to think in deciding what is the right course of action, or is what to be done, or is one that will lead to something that is good. For this reason, moral philosophy is divided into two parts, meta-ethics and normative ethics. Whereas the latter is primarily concerned with the way people ought to conduct their lives, the former addresses questions such as 'Are there any objective truths of morality. Philosophy of Religion is a theoretical study and therefore a philosopher of religion makes an analysis of the concept of religion. The Philosophy of religion is a second order idea that means it is thinking about philosophy. Theologians are concerned mainly with the first order question such as whether God exists or not, whether the God is benevolent or not etc.

The Second Chapter of the thesis deals with the conception of religion and morality in the Semitic tradition. In this analytical survey, the philosophical conceptions of three religions: Judaism, Christianity, Islam, and the place of morality dealt. As we know all these three religions are related very much with each other. In origin, Christianity was an outgrowth and a transformation of Judaism, so much so that the Christian religion makes absolutely no sense at all apart from Judaism. Earliest Christianity emerged from the Jewish-influenced belief that God had appointed Jesus to be the *Messiah*, one who would deliver God's people from injustice. In Islam religion also, the faith that Muhammad proclaimed was not presented as being a new faith; rather it was presented as being restoration of an earlier monistic faith, as practised by Abraham and others that had subsequently been corrupted by distortions. In particular, according to the *Qu'ran*, both the Jews and Christians, who claimed to be the true descendants of Abraham, had introduced deviations. This interrelations and close historical contexts make their ideas similar.

The fundamental elements of the message were monotheism that there is only one God. Although there is great diversity within Judaism, most Jewish traditions share a common sense of history and perhaps of time. It is the shared experience and understanding of past, present and future, which often seen as key elements holding Judaism together. Judaism, by the very first five fundamental beliefs could be categorised as a monotheistic religion. There have been considerable debates about the nature of god. However, the non-corporeality of god is the popular interpretation. Judaism advocates a unique relation between God and world. In this statement, God, who is the Creator of the universe and who has chosen Israel in love? Judaism is highly concerned about the practical aspects of the principles which they hold. Perhaps the best-known of the ethical teachings of the Bible is the so-called 'Ten Commandments' But the Jewish morality is not simply based on the Biblical texts, rabbinic texts also contribute much to it. Jewish ethics, defines the ethical principles by presupposing the will of human being to choose to be good and bad. Man contains both the elements of heavenly and earthly. The choice of human being helps man to develop one of these aspects.

The main aspects of Christian ethics can be concluded as follows. 'If you have seen your brother, you have seen your Lord.' The fellow human being is considered as the lord. The teaching of Jesus paves the foundation of Christian ethics, in spite of the presence of commandments and rules in the Old Testament. In the conception of God, distinguishing mark of Christianity is concept of Trinity. Christianity also asserts God as creator of world. "This doctrine asserted that God is three in one and one in three, God as the father, Holy Spirit and Son (Jesus Christ)." Christians believe that the Messiah had come: while Jews believe that Messiah is yet to come.

In Third Chapter, moral-religious concepts of Indian religions especially with *Vedic* tradition, Buddhism, Jainism and Hinduism are discussed. It is often claimed that the *Vedic* tradition avoids existence of unique God, and promotes Polytheism. This claim certainly unjustified, for all through the *Rig Veda* illuminates the sense of all-pervasive divine presence, immanent in humanity and nature, unifying the universe. The real is one; the learned call it by various names: *Agni, Yama*. It is not merely that the gods are one, but that the whole of the universe in its physical, material and natural aspect is permeated by one divine presence. However, in Buddhist conception, at least in its original philosophy, we cannot find the conception of God, since it denies the existence of God and upholds the principle of Impermanence. According to the Buddha, reality, whether of external things or the psychophysical totality of human individuals, consists in a succession and concatenation of microseconds called *dhamma*s. In Mahayana Tradition, Buddha is elevated into the status of God. However, *Hinayana* tradition denies god in doctrine. Buddha is only a preacher, a guide to truth. According to them, all things are momentary. However, it believes in the absolute existence of dharma. In Jainism, in some sense we can say that they allow the existence of God, but the conception of God is entirely different in comparison with other religions. Jainism does not believe in an entity or being such as God, which is quite distinct from world. For Jainism, God is only embodied souls like men and animals. Hinduism also believes in one God. The creator aspect of *Brahman* is called *Brahma*; the preserver aspect, Vishnu; and the destroyer aspect Shiva or *Maheshwara*. These three form the so-called Hindu Trinity. Different powers or glories of God are personified through imagination and called Deities in Hinduism. Deities are not so many gods; they are personified expressions of the different powers and glories of the one and only God. It also considers God in the impersonal aspects also. The major philosophical distinction in the Hindu thought is *Saguna Brahman* and *Nirguna Brahman*. Trinity is the part of the *Saguna Brahman*.

The Fourth Chapter mainly discusses Ambedkar's critique of the Semitic and Indic religion. Ambedkar's analysis and criticism mainly concentrate on the nature of Indic religion. It is because he understood and analysed religion only in sole relation with the social aspects. The question of social equality and the problem of caste is the major concern of his analysis. While Ambedkar's appreciates the democratic, egalitarian aspect of Buddhism, he criticises Hinduism for its attempts to provide justification to the present hierarchical order of the society. Ambedkar's understood that caste and its division is not only evil, which intrudes into Hinduism, but he analyses that caste and its division is the very part and the basis of the Hindu Religion.

The rationality and the scientific method of Buddhism were favoured in Ambedkar's conception and he appreciated its rejection of the speculative notion of God and Soul. But in Buddhism he found morality as the centre of religion. Ambedkar makes such a morality the basis of religion, which he construes as *Dhamma*. He was sympathetic towards other religion like Christianity, Judaism and Jainism. He criticises Jainism by holding Buddhist, position that there is no need to take such a strict position to the principle of *Ahimsa.*

The Fifth Chapter deals with the Ambedkar's view on religion. Ambedkar sincerely thinks that religion is quite necessary for the social life. On one hand he denies the existence and need of the supernatural ideas but at the same time he affirms the necessity of religion. From this point it is clear that for him, God is not the centre of religion. *Dhamma* or Moral principles are the centre of religion and implementation of moral principles in this social life is the crux of the problem of religion in social life. It builds up the person. It is a powerful driving force for human activity and it instill hope. Only religion can satisfy the human being who is not satisfied with material things. Its ethical power can prevent social evils, crimes and atrocities, Religion alone can cultivate equality, liberty and fraternity and the enforcement of justice and order. In addition, Ambedkar notes that not all the religions have the same kind of moral principles. Some are *liberative* and *oppressive*. *Oppressive* religion always will be with irrational elements. Only a rational religion can provide a *liberative* outlook. Ambedkar equates *Dhamma* is with morality. Morality in *Dhamma* arises from the necessity for man to love man. It does not involve the sanction of God.

The Final Chapter deals with Ambedkar's conception of morality. Ambedkar's conception of morality is mainly developed on the basis of Buddhist principles. His attempts end up in the reinterpretation of Buddhism, which is depicted in Buddha and *Dhamma*. *Dhamma* is the main conception of Buddhism. Ambedkar qualifies it as *Saddhamma.* Thus, Morality in Buddhism converges in the social and individual aspects in coherent manner. Ambedkar makes clear that Belief in *Ishwara* (God) is not essentially part of *Dhamma*, and the *Dharma* based on Union with Brahma is a false *Dhamma*. According to Ambedkar, the Hindu social order lacks the spirit of solidarity. For Ambedkar, the social order of Hinduism does not contain any principle of social change.

Chapter – I

Philosophy, Religion and Morality: An Overview

This chapter deals with philosophy, its relation with faith and morality, and the way these ideas area unit entangled with each other in human life. Although we tend to area unit victimisation three totally different words, namely, philosophy, faith and morality, and talking regarding disentangling them and presumptuous them to own relations among themselves (implying their separateness), they need not continuously been therefore, as any perfunctory survey of the history of those subjects on an individual basis or a part of human thinking, would create it clear. Not that the joint family of those disciplines, at one moment or bit by bit, gained separation and independence from one another and stay clearly distinct from one another while not intersections, over-lapping, mutual influences, borrowings and confrontations. If they're connected, by an equivalent token, in fact, for that terribly reason, conjointly stand as totally different entities. They are distinct not solely owing to correspondingly varied subject-matters however conjointly owing to other ways during which these disciplines approach them. In this precise sense, their divergence is the maximum amount a matter of the objects of study as strategies of enquiry and nature of the target.

Plato says that the 'Philosophy could be a method of living and dying.' Aristotle states that 'Philosophy is that the science that considers truth.' Cicero aforementioned 'Philosophy is that the director of our lives, friend of virtue and enemy' Spencer says that 'Philosophy is bothered with everything as a universal science.' Ludwing Wittgenstein says that 'Philosophy could be a battle against to be meant of our intelligence by means that of language.' For Windelhand 'Philosophy is that the essential science of universal worth."[4] Educator says, "Whenever philosophy is taken seriously it's forever been assumed that it signification achieving knowledge that might influence the conduct of life."[5]

'Philosophy' could be a Greek signified "the love of wisdom". It's a group of two totally different words, 'Philos' and 'Sophia' that mean love and knowledge severally. Knowledge isn't merely information of the many things; rather it's the attention of the upper values of life. Philosophy begins with marvel, doubt and curiosity as philosopher explicit. It grows out of our awareness regarding the issues of human existence and seeing the human existence as one thing in would like of rationalisation. Philosophy doesn't shirk facing the troublesome and unsolved issues, fascinated by man, and those philosophers' sought-after answers. Philosophy is primarily involved with the soul, God, immortality, world, data and similar different issues that once more owe their solutions to the correct estimation of life. Several queries, however, are answered tentatively and plenty of issues still stay unresolved. As writer has aforementioned, "To be a thinker isn't simply to own refined thoughts, nor even to found a college, however to like knowledge on live, in step with dictates, a lifetime of simplicity, independence, liberality and trust."[6] Thus, to think isn't simply to browse and to grasp philosophy, it's additionally to suppose and feel philosophically.

The thinker is that the man who tries to ascertain the total, the whole reality. He tries to grasp facts within the lightweight of universal principles. There square measure alternative ways of analysing the fact of the whole truth. Philosophy ought to conceive to provide a coherent read of the character of the factor by the correlation of the various views into a unified read of the total. This seems to be no additional intelligent than crude metaphysical thinking or non-secular dogma that sees the planet, created by God with a purpose in mind or the primitive belief within the mystical forces behind each side of phenomena. Philosophy not solely works with some assumptions however conjointly queries them. The philosopher's task isn't simply finding the universals among the apparently absolute or as Mao-Tse-Tung same "proceeding from the actual to the overall however asking the question of what's universal within the initial place."[7] Therefore, the philosopher's job isn't solely to seek out the totality hidden at a lower place the absolute, totality binding the fragments however conjointly to question the terribly plan of a totality of that everything and each facet could be a half.

However, Philosophy in Republic of India isn't viewed because it is completed within the west. Darshanam is that the translated Sanskrit word used for philosophy, and is usually accepted in Republic of India. 'Darshanam' virtually suggests that "seeing". 'The word 'Darshanam', to visualise Dasgupta says, "True philosophical information has its earliest use within the Vaisesika-sutra of Kanarese that I take into account as pre-Buddhistic."[8] As Tarkalamkara points out, the particular founding father of the systems ne'er used the word to their philosophy; the older treatises just like the Artha-sastra were quite unaware of the word, the word of philosophy in that being *anviksiki*, that later came to square for logic. In any case, there have been philosophies during this country before the word *darshana* came to square for them.

There are uncertainties on the particular that means itself. Derived from the foundation *darshanas*, virtually means that 'the act of perception' however our fashionable students are usually reluctant to ascertain any implication of physical perception or the sense of the fashionable European logic in it. The ultimate aim of Indian thought is that the perception, the direct realisation of the atman. All the *darshanas* aim at verity information of the atman consistent with their own angles of vision. This intuition of atman, means that cycle of rebirth or liberation. So *darshana* or philosophy, as formed by the Indians, means that merely the discipline that's causative to liberation, i.e., the *Moksa-Sastra* in Indian nomenclature.

In modern world Philosophy is related to quality, normatively, rationality, coherence, naturality, nature of reality and scientific thought. Philosophy within the East is meant to be Associate in Nursing art of life and even how of living. The correct aim of expounding, in line with fashionable Indian tradition, "is to not acquire information for its own sake except for the sake of constructing life higher."[9] However, what constitutes the concept of constructing life higher is somewhat slippery. Associate in nursing in sensible terms it'd yet be an evasive characterisation. Betterment of life was notoriously formed in a very unambiguously narrower and hierarchic terms at intervals Hindu society. So the betterment of life is in question; the vishwakalyanam wasn't solely exclusive of the classes deemed therefore marked inferior however conjointly insists that those classes are condemned to a permanent state of subjugation.

Therefore, the Hindu tradition of philosophy isn't within the least or in any manner precursor to abundant later and fashionable philosophies of observe. In alternative words, the Hindu tradition of philosophy was performing artist instead of sensible or utilitarian. Philosophy in Republic of India may be a personal angle towards life and universe. However, these defenses, even the glorifications of bound trends, practices and personalities in Indian tradition might higher be characterised as sorts of mysticism instead of any full-fledged philosophy with typical procedures of inquiry and therefore the inherent scope for verification and difference.

Philosophy of Religion

The word 'Religion' comes from a Latin word which suggests to bind. In an exceedingly reversal of Jamesian paradigm, faith isn't simply a belief however behaviour. Faith is one that binds America all at once in an exceedingly whole approach. It involves the total of an individual's beings personality. The study of faith is unfolded across a superfluity of disciplines as well as that of philosophy. The phrase "philosophy of Religion" could be a name for scientific study of faith, it's continuously rational and intellectual.[10] It may be translated into spiritual expertise. God, faith, worship, prayer, tradition, revelation and immortality are the issues that verify the factors of the spiritual expertise. Spiritual expertise can't be explained by intellect while not the employment of figures, symbols and analogies.

Reason and rationality are the most considerations of philosophy of {faith} and it's restricted to data and understanding and doesn't increase faith and feeling. Philosophy of faith in its broader scope ought to embody major religions like Hinduism, Islam, Christianity, and Buddhism etc., and a couple of primitive religions like philosophical system, animatisms and materialism etc. Philosophy of faith observes the character of the spiritual data and explores the character of final reality. Here, the character of man is that the object of the philosophical enquiry.

The nature of philosophy of faith is perceived otherwise at completely different times and area. Its concern is especially with the primary order queries just like the existence of God. Initial order ideas means that, that directly study the character of reality. For instance, world, space, time, life and mind whereas second order ideas means that, that isn't directly talking regarding the character of reality. Initially, the philosophy of faith was understood to be Associate in Nursing organ of spiritual teachings however within the gift times it's understood as a philosophical puzzling over religion, even as philosophy of science is philosophical puzzling over science and philosophy of art could be a philosophical puzzling over art. Thus, puzzling over philosophy could be a second order plan in its philosophy of faith.

From the higher than argument, it's obvious that philosophy of faith needs a freedom to invest regarding religion. The philosophy of faith suggests that to review the idea proposition and reasoning that's used in theology.[11] It's a theoretical study and thus a thinker of faith makes associate degree analysis of the idea of faith. The Philosophy of faith may be a second order concept that suggests that it's considering philosophy. Theologian's square measure involved chiefly with the primary order question like whether or not God exists or not, whether or not the God is benevolent or not etc. But, many non-secular themes square measure mentioned within the system scriptures. Because the philosophical science is principally involved with the theoretical queries regarding any specific science, the philosophy of faith deals with specific religions. The existential thinkers articulate the human dispensation and suffering however a philosophy of faith has solely to ensure the idea of faith.

The theme of faith is therefore immense, and complete systematic comprehensive study of it's not possible. For example, Buddhism accepts faith while not God however in Christianity it's not possible while not God. Hinduism accepts faith. Hence, faith is feasible while not God. Faith has been multifariously understood and interpreted; faith is one issue to the social scientist, another to the social scientist and even another issue to the man of science. The Marxist read of faith is totally different from that of a mystic read. Thus, every universal interpretation of faith either of a Buddhist or that of soul or Christian is totally different from each other. There is such a definition, which can be accepted and honoured by all.

If the scope and nature of the philosophy of faith is to comprehend the whole horizon of the non-secular expertise and claims and counter-claims to that, it still remains to be seen what tools it's at its disposal to hold out that tasks and capabilities. Induction, deduction, analysis and synthesis are the strategies, (or) analytical ways, that are used extensively in some cogent of empiricism brands of philosophy of faith.

Induction implies a procedure of observation of empirical development and cataloguing them then sorting out patterns in them. During this means, it income to classify the items and entities supported noticeable and through empirical observation verifiable strategies of replicability.[12]

Deduction is that the method to gain a selected proposition from a general proposition, as an example, all men are non-secular. Gandhi may be a man, so Gandhi is non-secular. Here we will take any theory or law and apply it to any explicit case so as to unravel the non-secular and philosophical issues.

Analysis means that calling it quits a posh truth into its constituent factors or parts. It's a method of distinction between completely different parts concerned in a very specific state of expertise so they may be clearer. This in fact encounters several method issues significantly in its confrontation with a number of the foremost pervasive claims of the spiritual or claims created on behalf of it. A perceived or a minimum of, claimed unity with the God or just with a notion (such as that supposedly happens in some Platonic versions of love-experience) is predicated on a claim on the emergence of one thing that happens only such union or unity of various selves or parts takes place.

Deconstruction may be a advanced operation that proven to be terribly troublesome to gestate. Though, philosophical theory feeds on the development of newer aperies than resolution them, if it's reduced to its lifeless barebones, philosophical theory is yet one more strategy of unpacking. With some heuristic distortion, we have a tendency to think about the philosophical theory because the new avatar of the recent technique of analysis-breaking-up things. However, philosophical theory has a lucid edge over the recent technique of research. If the strategy of research cuts up the totalities into its constituent and sliceable elements, the philosophical theory debunks the terribly plan of totality and unity. However, it's best-known for its capability to contractibleness of the unities and totalities however not however quite with success established reasonableness of the elements.

Synthesis is that the method involves connecting along the scattered parts during a specific expertise that brings into light-weight new patterns and facts. The idealistic philosophers have ordered stress on synthesis, although its materialist icons too among its votaries, like revolutionary. Synthesis isn't simply delivery along of distinct things and weaving them into an entire. It's not simply imposing a harmony and order on the chaotic parts. It's additionally delivery one thing in every of the weather and one thing new into the life. This terribly arrangement of unity self-introduces one thing new within the terribly institution. Synthesis isn't solely a thought restricted to the weather seen as separate and scattered, it may also be in terms of influences on things alien or bridging between unrelated items and conducting a barrowing between reciprocally unknown spheres. They begin regarding one another only this external operation is settled, i.e., once a synthesis is achieved. No matter be the implications and impossibilities of the synthesising, it's a reality of life and thought, most significantly of faith. This can be what makes this operation necessary for a philosophical study of faith, morality and philosophy.

Nevertheless, within the Nineteen Thirties radically a brand new theology cut off the scene by overcoming the hurdles of empiricism. at first theologist presents it in 1918, in his 'commentary on the letter to the roomers'. Among the various enticing options of liberation theology, was a sensible and demanding perspective towards religious thought and criticism against this observe of faith by progressive social outlook. The new philosophical study of faith makes its own freelance contact with the philosophical movements of the past and gift and seeks philosophical appraisal and understanding of man's non-secular expertise. Theologist Emil Brunner had wanted to interrupt utterly an ancient philosophy of faith.

Another necessary purpose of read on faith is philosophic naturalism. It provides a hostile criticism of supernaturalism. In Whitehead's thought one discerns a replacement role for God in reference to the method. On the opposite hand, system reflection has continuing to control from a posture that persists in vocation itself 'religion'. One additional development of the recent past has been a dynamic interest within the non-western religions. The older approach to the comparative study of religions seems quite dead. The new interest is within the oriental religion that seems to get on the rise. The new approach is principally involved with the human non-secular thoughts and philosophical ideas applying to the developed society (or) developing society.

Otto Pfleiderer defines philosophy faith (of faith) as "systematic investigation and comprehension of the totality of phenomena that within the lifetime of man compose religion. Study of philosophy of faith is loosely divided into two main divisions one is "science of faith" (Empirical study of religion) and therefore the alternative is "philosophy of religion." Science of faith is merely involved with the investigation and rationalisation of empirical facts."[13] The question of truth and values carry US over into the realm of the philosophy of faith. Philosophy of faith, its thought and in vital examination of the empirical truth of faith arrives at a constructive read of what ultimately and comprehensively religion is. Thus, it's each vital and constructive aspects.

The philosophy of faith starts from the popularity that within the lifetime of humanity there's one thing referred to as religion. Faith mustn't be analysed and understood exclusively on the content of the faith. Primarily faith ought to be analysed as a sort of expression. Meaning primary concern of the philosophy of faith isn't the ideas and beliefs of religions. The sensible and empirical aspects of faith and its objective implications square measure the first concern of philosophy of faith.

Religion is typically thought of as a priority regarding 'ultimate's, however, philosophy of faith cannot be strained to review of the ideas of 'ultimate's. Philosophy considers faith as an expression of the notion of ultimates. That is, analysing 'ultimate' in relation with empirical reality of faith. Therefore, it looks that the sole method for hope of any advance towards a contemporary philosophy of faith is, to turn, as freely as doable, from initial metaphysical prejudice to faith as really found.

William James' work of art forms of non-secular expertise is one in all the foremost basic fashionable texts of philosophy on the question of faith. In Charles Taylor's words, this text lost none of its attraction, relevancy or ability to supply insights even these days, well once quite a century. His engagement with James's nice work, disclosed as varieties of religion lately, originally delivered as Gifford lectures at capital in 1991. This tiny book, consisting of four lectures, provides an honest entry purpose for US to enter this huge space with necessary humility and indispensable clarity. In these lectures, Charles Taylor, arguably provides a wonderful outline of William James' argument.

Taylor may be a communitarian whereas James's well-known reflection on faith locates it firmly within the experiential self formed in Individualistic terms. Taylor's well-known integrity of presenting his opponent's purpose of read with impeccable accuracy is at add this small book. By drawing indirectly from philosopher however from Taylor we have a tendency to may really get a more robust image than alternative wise would are the case as a result of Charles Taylor not solely offers a concise outline however conjointly implicitly juxtaposes it to other accumulated data on the faith, from theology, philosophy and historical studies of faith since philosopher.

William James, having placed faith at the extent of expertise initial and foremost, makes an important distinction: between what he calls first-hand and used non-secular expertise. It's therefore not simply at the extent of expertise alone however additionally within the history of faith itself. Specifically, first-hand expertise is what a private undergoes and juxtaposes it to the boring habit of the ritual sponsored by the establishments or custom. "First-hand" is for James each individual and experiential, thus "lived" expertise. Second-hand selection could be a by-product expertise. It's bimanual right down to him by external mechanisms and influences, community or non-secular life or establishments like Church.

This constitutes, for James, what he calls a "second-hand non-secular life." It is the "religious genius"[14] of people who ad lib expertise bound not thus simply expressible moments of revelation, enlightenment or no matter one might like better to decision them supported the distinct traditions of religions or sects or instructive biases. As an example, Savior was one such non-secular genius who skilled one thing and practiced and preached what he believed he was to mention that set the pattern for the following second-hand construction of whole organised and institutionalised Christianity. Though' first hand used non-secular experiences are completely different it absolutely was the primary that sets the pattern for the second however it absolutely was additionally a deviation, degeneration and departure from the legitimacy of the initial genius.

The first hand non-secular expertise that is authentic forms the "dull habit" of the 'masses' through establishments. So the non-secular experience's journey from the individual genius to "massification" isn't simply associate degree enlargement however additionally a dilution. Authentic non-secular expertise is one during which, "the feelings, acts and experiences of the people in their solitude" is that the shaping characteristic. Once the instant of degeneration of the organised faith arrives it's already corrupt and constitutes a veritable fall. Now, the times of "inwardness" square measure over, the "spring" and "purer" day's square measure gone. Then it's no marvel that original or first-hand non-secular experiences of the geniuses "always appeared as a unorthodox type of innovation."[15] It absolutely was not however with the support of lots, at least, majority and "authentication" by the powers either of spiritual or temporal kind. This doesn't mean that James works with straightforward or oversimplified classification of pure and impure forms of non-secular expertise.

Second hand experiences aren't merely false. They are what they are- second-hand. Rationalisations, symbols area unit perfections and enhancements of the first spiritual expertise of the genius. During this manner, James places the second-hand spiritual expertise squarely at the bound or a minimum of, outside the correct realm of the authentic. it's not that the second-hand is just one thing sort of a burial of the spiritual spontaneousness. Even at the stage of a "massified" or "generalised" spiritual life, real spiritual expertise remains and exists.

However, it will thus solely within the "experience" of the "individuals" in their "solitude". Here, Taylor sees in James what may be known as a double individualisation of the religions. Thus, each the origin and therefore the continuation of real spiritual expertise area unit completely individualistic for William James.

In fact, the terribly mode of first-hand spiritual expertise is sure to be individualistic and therefore the web site of such happening is that the "inner" realm of the individual. Charles Taylor calls this; "take on faith," and it's specifically fashionable. He explores the links with such a conception that has one thing to try and do with numerous traditions of religion traditions together with the protestant tradition of god and faith. During this variant of the spiritual history, "religion is personal". In these western traditions and spiritual imaginations over a amount of your time, with their complicated interaction with numerous non-religious processes of the up-to-datedness, stressed the devotion, at the price of denigration of the ritual. This denigration is a component of a bigger method of disentangling the religions from the communal and social aspects. Predominance of the stress constitutes some notion of "controlling the God" and thus strengthens faith at the price of weakening God Himself.

It is here, Charles Taylor introduces the foremost beautiful however forthwith convincing original thesis of his own drawing from each the history of correctness and faith. Normal accounts of the secularisation method, from the Enlightenment thinkers to today's Richard Dworkin, see secularisation because the "progressive retreat of the faith from its previous iniquitousness to a secluded and debilitated institutional area as a results of the struggles against non-secular beliefs and power of its establishments."[16]

Taylor locates secularisation drive from inside faith itself and not simply in anti-religious or non-religious concepts and forces. He even argues that the separation of church and state was conjointly galvanised by the thought to safeguard the "personal faith." In fact, the strain on the commitment and devotion conjointly cause purging the unconvincing parts in faith. According to Charles Taylor, what's missing in William James' account is what he calls, "religious association," his "certain individualism" doesn't accommodate the "phenomenon of collective spiritual life." This development, for Charles Taylor, "is not simply the results of (individual) spiritual associations however that in a way constitutes or is that the connection."[17]

For Hoffoding faith is the conservation of values,[18] 'Alexander sees it as religion in ability. Patrick says, "Religion is that the consciousness of our sensible relevance an invisible non secular order."[19] Whitehead states "Religion is that the vision of one thing that stands on the far side, behind and at intervals, the passing flux of immediate things."[20] W.T. Stace defines faith "as the hunger of the soul for the not possible, the unrealisable, and also the unthinkable."[21] In step with Kant "Religion could be a matter of the desire, it being understood and known with sensible reason, that's to mention bound acts need to be done or that bound attitudes need to be adopted."[22] Will Durant Drake describes faith as follows: "This disposition of the center and can, through that man involves take care of the very best things and to measure in gentleness and inward calm higher than the surface aspects and accidents of life, we call, in its inner nature, spirituality; once it's embodied in outward forms and establishment, and spreads among the full communities, we have a tendency to decision it a faith."[23]

Coming to a number of the foremost illustrious definitions offered within the strands of recent Indian philosophy, Hindu Vivekananda believes that "Religion isn't in doctrines, in dogmas nor in intellectual argumentation; its being and changing into, and its realisation."[24] It implies that the faith is that the art of living, through right action, a way to live our lifestyle harmonised, inside ourselves and with others and live a lifetime of peace and happiness. Ramakrishna Paramahamsa says, "Religion is associate degree expertise. Faith makes no sense unless its truths area unit full-fledged. Is your thirst happy before you drink water once you area unit thirsty? Religions area unit like so-many methods resulting in an equivalent goal, i.e., God."[25]

Radhakrishnan's interpretation of faith is his affirmation of the identity of the self and supreme reality. "The essence of faith could be an artificial realisation of life. The non-secular man has the information that everything is important, the sensation that there's harmony beneath the conflicts and therefore the power to comprehend the importance and therefore the harmony."[26] As well, "Religion isn't a variety of knowledge... whereas faith implies a metaphysical read of the universe."[27] Aurobindo states that, "Religion is an endeavour to form the reality dynamic within the soul of man."[28]

Philosophy, Religion and Theology

The relation between philosophy, theology and faith is sort of a vital one within the recent thought. It's principally owing to the respectable distinction of opinion on the character of relation. Positivism considers philosophy as a sophisticated discipline on the far side each faith and theology. The proponents of empiricist philosophy think about subjective propositions as no meaningful that embody each faith and theology. On the opposite hand Barthian theology claims to be quite freelance of philosophy. During this argument faith, theology, philosophy and philosophy of faith square measure intimately and dialectically connected. The intimate relation between these fields lies principally on the concept that these square measure human activities and human ways that of acting existing. The analysis of however human activities square measure connected is essentially involved with the structure of those disciplines, not with the inner content of any field.

Religion is primarily "an act of worship, of commitment; associate act of the full man at work and at play, during which he confesses his religion, his trust, his hope in some reality. Faith is that the method man acts towards or responds to reality and power of reality."[29] Thus, primarily faith isn't a theoretical matter. The commitment or trust is that the heart of faith. A close analysis of human existence reveals that commitment could be a necessary condition for human existence. "To be human is to be committed."[30] The commitment towards one thing is an indisputable fact within the human existence. The thing of commitment could vary in keeping with everyone. However, there should be a commitment. It should be towards faith, some first principles, basic assumptions, and initial hypothesis. Since the commitment is important, to exist is to measure upon the premise of some final concern and commitment. The commitment is that the basis of, or supposition for, man's cultural and inventive activities as well as all interpretations of the which means of reality. Any analysis of the means of reality is grounded on and offered at intervals the restrictions of an existential commitment. And faith forms this commitment, i.e., the required basis of all human activities.

Since all interpretation of the means of reality as a personality's activity is predicated on bound commitment, theology is also firmly non-moving during this religions commitment. But theology can't be thought of as a mere non-secular commitment; rather it's a mode of reflection of commitment. "Theology is associate interpretation of the means of the facility of reality."[31] It's a theoretical analysis of the facility of reality to that we've given our religions response. The phrase 'power of reality' suggests that the facility or energy, that makes America, accepts that these square measure one thing real. Why did we tend to believe that there's one thing known as real, instead of nothing? So, it are often seen that theology is associate analysis of the existential relationship between the facility of reality and therefore the self. And these analyses on reality are often done solely on the idea of a selected commitment. That's the dialectical relation between faith and theology.

Apart from the issues of those fields, philosophy is a trial to research the structure of the given, the important being. It's associate in nursing interpretation of the fact. The event of rational analysis on the fact may be done solely by commitment as existing individual. This commitment is owing to the facility of reality. In theology we have a tendency to be analysing the character of the facility of reality. In philosophy we have a tendency to analysing the structure and nature of the important, that has been brought forth by the facility of reality. It's quite obvious that philosophy, like theology, is carried on upon the premise of religions commitment. At this juncture the dialectical relation between faith, philosophy and theology is obvious. One's philosophical analysis might influence one's commitment which can have an effect on one's philosophy. Moreover, there's a school of thought presupposed by each philosophical analysis and a philosophical analysis and position implicit in each system position.

Theology and philosophy by themselves square measure however fragmentations of a complete worldview. This worldview is going to be completed once the connection between these two fields developed. And this is often the task of the philosophy of faith. Specifically the task of philosophy of faith is to elaborate the connection of philosophical analysis of the important to system of rules analysis of the ability of the important and also the relationship of each to the non-secular commitment that is their foundation.

Aurobindo says that "Philosophy is that the intellectual seek for the basic truth of things; faith is that decide to create the reality dynamic within the soul of man. They're essential to every other; a faith that's not the expression of philosophical truth degenerates into superstitious notion and obscurantism, and a philosophy that doesn't dynamise itself with the non-secular spirit could be a barren light-weight, for it cannot get itself practiced."[32] Equally, "Religion imparts a dynamic, active, and sensible orientation to philosophy."[33] Radhakrishnan says, "the downside religion can't be solved by non-secular faith alone. The religion needs to be sustained by metaphysical knowledge.... solely reasoned religion will provide coherence to life and thought."[34] And conjointly "Religion isn't a sort of data... whereas faith implies a metaphysical read of the universe, it's to not be confused with philosophy."[35]

S. K. Saksena expresses that faith is solely the sensible application of the reality achieved by philosophy.[36] Whereas, the faith is that the necessary completion or application of the reality, it's not identical with philosophy. Hindoo Nikhilananda says, that 'In the Hindu tradition there has been no sharp division between faith and philosophy,' "the former is that the emotional and sensible approach to reality, the latter is that the intellectual."[37] Both is faith indivisible from philosophy, as a result of the two attitudes of thought and follow are clearly distinguishable. In fact, they're intimately related; it will nearly be same that philosophy while not faith is "empty" which faith without philosophy is "blind".

Morality and Religion in Greek Philosophical Thought

Moral philosophy thinks about with what folks suppose and have to be compelled to suppose in deciding what's the proper course of action, or is what to be done, or is one that may cause one thing that's sensible. The character of ethical philosophy is itself philosophically debatable. Philosophy of alternative branches, like philosophy of science, thinks about with a definition and evolution of assumptions created by specialist professional. Scientists manufacture and check scientific theories, whereas philosophy of science asks, 'what may be a scientific theory?' and 'Can the reality of scientific theories be established? The substantive theories of science square measure typically known as by philosophers 'first-order theories',[38] wherever the philosophical theories regarding the character of science square measure known as a second-order.' Unlike, say, physics, there's no established science of morality with its own community of specialists. We tend to all face ethical issues directly, and can't simply leave their resolution to the specialists. So there's no in agreement methodology for finding ethical issues. Thus, it's fallen to philosophers to handle substantive ethical questions about what would represent a decent life, what square measure our ethical obligations, and the way we must always resolve ethical dilemmas.

Moral philosophy is split into two components, meta-ethics and normative ethics.[39] Whereas the latter is primarily involved with however folks got to conduct their lives, the previous addresses queries like 'Are there any objective truths of ethicality?' and what's it that distinguishes moral reasons for action from different justifications or rationalisations?' for many of the philosopher's read that philosophy is, like philosophy of science, very simply a second-order activity. initial order ethics, that was spoken slightingly by these purists as 'moralising', ought to be left to moralisers, United Nations agency would come with among their ranks priesthood, doctors, teachers, and politicians, however not at all philosophers in their skilled capability.

Meta - moral theories may be divided into two main teams, in line with the solution that they provide to the queries that are ethical judgments in objective. To mention that an ethical judgment is objective is to mention that its rightness or wrongness is freelance of the private preferences and inclinations of a person or cluster of people. Some philosophers argue that "moral philosophy is meta-ethics, and no additional."[40] However there square measure people who suppose that there's additional to ethical philosophy- specifically, some suppose that is named 'normative ethics', what this will be understood by method of a future thought of psychological feature theories of ethics. Since psychological feature theories say that ethical judgments square measure the work of reason and since reason is by its nature systematic, it's not shocking that they must additionally say that their philosophy provides a system which gives steering on what's virtuously right or smart. Such philosophies are aforesaid to enter the realm of 'normative ethics'.

Its value noting that philosophers UN agency belongs to the present college of thought don't deny the legitimacy, or the importance, of meta-ethics. Their objection is merely to the read that meta-ethics is all that's to ethics, which the philosophers in and of itself are thus virtuously neutral. This brings United States to the question of morality and also the have to be compelled to enquire if such neutrality is feasible or conceivable, if so, what problems are at stake in our concern with the ethical.

Morality contains beliefs regarding the character of man, beliefs regarding ideals, regarding what's sensible or fascinating or deserve pursuit for its own sake, rules giving birth down what got to be done and what ought to not be done and motives that incline America to decide on the proper or wrong course. "Morality is sort of totally involved with relation between with however they got to behave towards one another. With what general rules governing relation between man and man, a society got to adopt."[41] The realm of morality is proscribed to those qualities of humanity that concern there being along to peace and unity.

Ethics as philosophy cares with ethicality and its issues and judgments or with moral issues and judgments. However, the word ethics isn't forever used for this branch of philosophy; generally it's used as simply another word for "morality", and generally to talk over with the ethical code of a private or cluster. Morality doesn't operate in anybody clearly outlined sphere of human action. Morality is all pervasive; regulation relations among folks all told spheres- production, standard of living and leisure. Morality is objectively multifunctional. It reveals the worth and which means of men's existence, or transports him to the realm of futile dreams or superstitious notion, arouses a sense of pleasure and satisfaction, or torture him with pangs of conscience and guilty feeling. It regulates man's behaviour from the purpose of read of the opposition between sensible and evil. The liberty of the need, immortality of the soul and also the existence of God area unit the postulates of morality. Morality could be a quite prescription. Morality performs the operate of providing normative goals in standard of living, permitting man to vindicate his behaviour with the assistance of ethical motivation. Morality could be a variety of communication incorporating Associate in nursing angle to the social atmosphere, society and also the world.

There square measure several definitions of the word 'morality.' the things below square measure those wherever authors specifically used the term "moral" or "morality". Socrates outlined morality as "how we tend to have to be compelled to live"[42] and why. David Hume views that the "morality is attribute during a approach which could turn out a lot of a similar result as if ethical action were shown to be rational."[43] Socrates in his early dialogues mentioned the character of the 'holy' with Euthyphro, World Health Organisation may be a non-secular skilled. Euthyphro is taking his own father to court for murder, and although standard Greek morality would condemn such an action as impiousness, Euthyphro defends it on the premise that the gods behave within the same kind of approach, in keeping with the standard stories. Socrates makes it clear that he doesn't believe these stories; as a result of they attribute immorality to the gods. This doesn't mean, however, that he doesn't believe the gods. He was observant in his non secular practices, and he objects to the charge of not basic cognitive process within the city's gods that was one among the bases of the prosecution at his own trial.

Socrates' drawback with the standard stories regarding the gods provides rise to what's typically known as 'the Euthyphro dilemma'. If we have a tendency to try and outline the 'holy' as what's treasured by the gods (and goddesses), we'll be moon-faced with the question, 'Is the holy therefore as a result of it's treasured by the gods, or do they adore it as a result of its holy?' Socrates makes it clear that his read is that the second (though his argument for this conclusion is obscure).[44] However, his read isn't associate degree objection to ligature morality and faith along. He hints at the tip of the dialogue that the proper thanks to link them is to envision that when we have a tendency to move we square measure serving the gods in addition. However it's vital that within the *Theaetetus*, Socrates' read once more that our goal is to be as like god as attainable, and since god is in no approach and in no manner unjust (in the sense of 'unrighteous'), however, as even as it's attainable to be, nothing is a lot of like god than the one in all North American nation World Health Organisation becomes correspondingly as even as attainable. In many dialogues this thought is connected with a belief within the immortality of the soul; we have a tendency to become like god by being attentive to the immortal and better part of ourselves.

This train of thought sees the god or gods as sort of a magnet, drawing America to be like them by the ability of their goodness or excellence. In Plato's particle, the divine is compared to a magnet to that is hooked up a series of rings, through that the attraction is passed. This conception is additionally pervasive in philosopher, Plato's student for twenty years. Within the Nicomachean Ethics, as an example, the words 'god' and 'divine' occur roughly doubly as typically because the words 'happiness' and 'happy'. This is often vital, providing Aristotle's moral theory is (like Plato's) 'eudaemonist' (meaning that our morality aims at our happiness). Mention of the divine isn't simply standard, for philosopher, however will necessary philosophical work. Within the Eudemian Ethics, "he tells America that the goal of our lives is service and contemplation of god. He thinks that we tend to become like what we tend to ponder, and then we tend to become most just like the god by considering the god. Incidentally, this is often why the god doesn't ponder us; for this is able to mean changing into but the god that is not possible."[45]

Sometimes philosopher uses the phrase 'God or understanding' (in Greek, nous). The activity of the god, he says within the philosophy, is nous thinking itself. The best human action is that the most god-like, specifically concerning about over the god and about things that don't modification. Aristotle's virtue ethics, then, has to be understood against the background of those system premises. He's thinking of the divine, to use Plato's trope, as magnetic, drawing us, by its engaging power, to measure the most effective quite life potential for America. Philosopher provides a traditional account of the virtues such an individual displays (such as spirit, virtually virility, which needs the proper quantity of concern, between cowardliness and rashness). However, the virtuous person in every case acts 'for the sake of the noble (or beautiful)', and philosopher regularly associates the noble with the divine.

There square measure tensions in Aristotle's account of virtue and happiness. It's not clear what his final read is of the relation between the activity of contemplation and therefore the alternative activities of a virtuous life. However, the association of the very best human state with the divine is pervasive within the text. Within the same manner, the very best and most god-like human doesn't care regarding alternative people at large except to the degree they contribute to his own best state. Philosopher doesn't say that we've got obligations to alternative people at large simply because they're people at large. Finally, he ties our happiness to our finish (in Greek, telos); for humans, as for all living things, the most effective state is activity in accordance with the natural perform that's distinctive to every species. For humans the most effective state is happiness, and therefore the best activity among this state is contemplation.

The Epicureans and Stoics UN agency followed philosopher differed with one another and with him in many ways, however, they united in fastening morality and faith along. For the Epicureans (as for philosopher within the Metaphysics), the gods don't care concerning US, although they're amused by observing our tragicomic lives (rather as we glance at soap operas on television).[46] We will be discharged from an honest deal of tension, the Epicureans thought, by realising that the gods aren't attending to penalise US. Our goal ought to be to just like the gods as we will, enjoying ourselves while not interruption, except for US this implies limiting our needs to what we will acquire while not frustration. The Stoics likewise tied the simplest quite human life, for them the lifetime of the sage, to being like god. The sage follows nature altogether his needs and actions, and is so the nearest to the divine. One among the virtues he can have is 'apathy' (in Greek apatheia), that doesn't mean listlessness, however detachment from wanting something apart from what nature, or the god, is already providing.

The second line of thought derived during this entry starts with the Hebrew Bible and continues with the Greek scriptures known as by Christians 'The New Testament'. Morality and faith are connected within the Hebrew Bible primarily by the class of God's command. Such commands return already within the first chapter of Genesis, and that they are available in two sorts. First, God creates by command, as an example '*Let there be light*'.[47] Then, once the creation of animals, God provides a second quite command, 'Be fruitful and multiply', and repeats the command to the humans, he creates within the divine image.[48] Within the second chapter there's a third quite command. God tells Adam that he's liberal to eat from any tree within the garden; however he should not eat from the tree of the data of fine and evil.

Once Eve and Adam refuse, and eat that fruit, they're expelled from the garden.

There is a family of ideas here that's totally different from what we have a tendency to meet in Greek philosophy. God is putting in a sort of covenant by that humans are going to be blessed if they adjust the commands God provides them. Human disobedience isn't explained within the text, except that the serpent says to Eve that they'll not die if they eat the fruit, however are going to be like God, knowing smart and evil, and Eve sees the fruit pretty much as good for food and pleasing to the attention and fascinating for gaining knowledge. Once they eat, Adam and Eve apprehend that they're naked, and area unit shamed, and conceal from God. There's a avoidance from God and from obedience to God that characterises this as a 'fall into sin' and is Genesis describes this basic state as a corruption of the guts.

In the Torah, the story continues with Ibrahim, and God's command to depart his ancestral land and head to the land God secures to offer him and his offspring.[49] Then there's the command to Ibrahim to kill his son, a deed prevented at the eleventh hour by the availability of a ram instead.[50] Abraham's nice grandchildren find you in Egypt, thanks to famine, and also the individuals of Israel suffer for generations beneath Pharaoh's yoke. Beneath Moses the individual's square measure finally liberated, and through their wanderings within the desert, Moses receives from God the Ten Commandments, in two tables or tablets.[51] The primary table issues our obligations to God directly, to worship God alone and keep God's name holy, and keep day of rest. The second table issues our obligations to different citizenry, and every one of the commands square measure negative (do not kill, commit free love, steal, lie, or covet) apart from the primary, that tells US to honour our fathers and mothers. God's commands, taken along, offer US the law. an extra term belongs here, specifically 'kingdom'. The Greeks had the notion of a kingdom, beneath a person's king (though the Athenians were within the classical amount suspicious of such associate degree arrangement). However they didn't have the concept of a kingdom of God. This concept is explicable in terms of law, and is introduced in and of itself in Exodus in reference to the covenant on Mt. Sinai. The dominion is that the realm during which the laws get.

In the writings that Christians decision 'The New Testament' the theme of God's commands is recapitulated. Jesus Christ sums up the commandments into two, the command to like God with all one's heart and soul and mind,[52] and also the command to like the neighbour as thy self.[53] The primary of those in all probability sums up the primary 'table' of the Ten Commandments to Moses, and also the second sums up the second. The will is in contrast to the Hebrew Bible, however, in presenting a narrative a few man who is that the good exemplification of obedience and who incorporates a life while not sin, will students disagree regarding the extent to that Jesus Christ really claimed to be God, however the standard interpretation is that he did build this claim; in order that we are able to see in his life the clearest attainable revelation in human terms of what God is like and at a similar time a revelation of what our lives have to be compelled to be like. Within the 'Sermon on the Mount' Jesus Christ problems variety of radical injunctions.[54] He takes the commandments within the heart; as an example, we tend neither to square measure needed not simply nor to murder, however to not be angry, not simply nor to commit criminal conversation, however to not lust. We tend to square measure told, if somebody strikes America on the proper cheek, to show to him conjointly the left.

Jesus tells North American nation to like our enemies and people United Nations agency hate and dun North American nation, and during this approach he makes it clear that the love commandment isn't supported reciprocity.[55] Finally, once he's asked 'Who is my neighbour?', he tells the story of a Samaritan (traditional enemies of the someone's) United Nations agency met a wounded Jew he failed to apprehend by the aspect of the road, was stirred compassionately, and went out of his thanks to meet his needs; the Samaritan was 'neighbour' to the wounded human. There's a distinction between the two traditions delineate up to now, particularly the Greek and also the monotheism. Plan the concept of God that's central within the on top of account of the Greeks is that the idea of God attracting North American nation, sort of a reasonably magnet, in order that we have a tendency to want to become additional like God.

In the on top of account of the somebody and Christian scriptures, the central notion was that of God commanding USA. It's tempting to alter this distinction by expression that the Greeks favour the great, in their account of the relation of morality and faith, and therefore the faith account favours the correct or obligation. The notion of obligation appears to form most sense against the background of command. However, the image is over-simple as a result of the Greeks had area in their account for the constraint of desire; therefore the temperate or brave person in Aristotle's picture has wishes for food or sex or safety that need to be disciplined by the love of the noble. On the opposite facet, the faith account adds God's like to the notion of God's command, in order that the covenant that within which the commands area unit embedded could be a covenant by which God blesses USA, and that we area unit given a route towards our highest sensible that is union with God.

In the theologiser amount, or the amount of the first Fathers, it had been preponderantly Plato and therefore the Stoics amongst the Greek philosophers whose influence was felt. The Japanese and Western components of the Christian church split throughout the amount, and therefore the Japanese church remained softer than the Western with language regarding humans being deified (in Greek theiosis). Within the West, Doctor of the Church emphasised the gap between the globe we tend to are in as resident aliens and our citizenship within the heavenly national capital, and even in our next life the space between ourselves and God. "He describes within the Confessions the route by that his heart or can, alongside his understanding, affected from religious belief through Neo-Platonism to Christianity."[56]

The Neo-Platonists (such as Plotinus) schooled a world-system of emanation, whereby the one (like Plato's variety of the Good) flowed into Intellect (the realm of the Forms) and from there into the World-Soul and individual souls, and eventually into bodies, from wherever it came back to itself. Theologizer accepted that the Platonists aforementioned, just like the starting of the introduction of John, that the Word (in Greek, logos) is with God and is God, since the Intellect is that the mediating principle between the 'One' and also the 'Many.'[57] Theologiser command that Plato had declared that the supreme sensible, possession of that alone provides US beautification is God, 'and so (Plato) thought that to be a thinker is to be a fan of God'. However the Platonists failed to say, just like the finish of John's introduction, that the Word is formed flesh in Redeemer, and then they failed to have access to the thanks to salvation discovered in Christ or God's grace to US through Christ's death.

Augustine provides grandness to the virtue of dotty what got to be wanted, particularly God. John says, that 'Love and do what you may.' However, this is often not a denial of the ethical law. He command that humans United Nations agency really love God also will act in unison with the opposite precepts of divine and ethical law; although love doesn't just fulfill the cardinal virtues (e.g., temperance, courage, justice) however transforms them by supernatural grace.[58]

The influence of theologizer within the resulting history of ethics resulted from the actual fact that it had been his synthesis of Christianity and Greek philosophy that survived the destruction of the Western Roman Empire. Particularly noteworthy is philosopher, from whom we have a tendency to get the definition of the thought of 'person' that has been elementary to moral theory. To grasp this, we'd like to travel back to the history of the event of the philosophical system of the Trinity. The church had to clarify however the daddy, the Son and therefore the Holy Ghost might be distinct and nonetheless not three totally different gods.

The ism of the Trinity involves be understood in terms of three persons, one God, with the persons standing in numerous relations to every alternative. Then again this term 'person' is additionally accustomed perceive the relation of the second person's divinity to his humanity. The church came to speak concerning one person with two natures, the person standing beneath the natures. The Greek philosophers didn't have any term that we will translate 'person' within the fashionable sense, as somebody (as opposition something) that stands beneath all his or her attributes. Boethius, however, defines 'person' as 'individual substance of rational nature,' a key step within the introduction of our gift construct.

Religion and Morality in Christian-European Philosophy

In the West, information of most of Aristotle's texts was lost, however, not within the East. They were translated into Syrian, and Arabic, and eventually into Latin, and re-entered Christian Europe within the twelfth century in the middle of translations of the nice

Arabic commentaries. This new rebirth (a 'renaissance') of learning gave rise to a crisis, as a result of it vulnerable to undermine the harmony established from the time of Augustine between the authority of reason, as painted by Greek philosophy, and therefore the authority of religion, as painted by the doctrines of the Christian church. The problems ('the world, the soul, God') become in one kind or another focus of philosophical thought for ensuing six centuries.

Thomas Aquinas undertook the project of synthesis between philosopher and Christianity, though' his version of Christianity was already deeply influenced by Saint Augustine, then by Neo-Platonism. Aquinas, like philosopher, stressed the ends (vegetative, animal and generally human) given to humans within the cosmos. He delineate each the cardinal virtues and also the system virtues of religion, hope and love. Aquinas's theory is eudaemonist within the sense antecedently defined; 'And that the can naturally tends towards its own last finish, for each man naturally wills beatitude. And from this natural willing square measure caused all different willing, since no matter a person wills, he wills on account of the end'. The principles of natural ethical law square measure the universal judgments created by right reasoning concerning the varieties of actions that square measure virtuously applicable and inappropriate for human agents. Saint holds that reason, in knowing these principles, is collaborating within the eternal law. However, within the long-term, the synthesis that saint achieved became authoritative in Roman Catholic education.[59]

There was a recent tradition of thought from the opposite major order of friars, the Franciscan, beginning with Bonaventure, who command that whereas we are able to learn from each philosopher and philosopher, and each also are in error; the larger error is Aristotle's. One different figure from this tradition ought to be mentioned, John theologizer (literally John from Duns). There are a unit three notable variations between him and Doctor. First, Scotus isn't a Eudaemonist. He takes a double account of motivation from Anselm, who created the excellence between two affections of the desire, the love for advantage (an inclination towards one's own happiness and perfection) and also the affection for justice (an inclination towards what's sensible in itself freelance of advantage). Scotus says that we have a tendency to area unit born with a ranking of advantage over justice that must be reversed by God's help before we are able to be pleasing to God. We must always be willing, he says, to sacrifice our own happiness for God if that were to be necessary, that it's not (by God's grace). Second, he doesn't assume that the ethical law is obvious or necessary. He takes the primary table to be necessary, since it derives (except for the 'every seventh day' provision of the command concerning the Sabbath) from the mandatory principle that God is to be wanted. However, the second table is contingent, tho' fitting our nature, and God may order completely different commands even for kinsfolk.

There is a elementary similarity within the approach the relation between morality and faith is formed between Scotus and also the two Reformers theologian and theologiser, although neither of them create the distinctions concerning concept that Scotus (the 'subtle doctor') will. Luther says, 'what God wills isn't right as a result of he ought or was sure thus to will; on the contrary, what takes place should be right, as a result of he thus wills'. Calvin says 'God's can is such a lot the very best rule of morality that no matter he wills, by the actual fact that he will sit, should be thought of righteous'. The Counter-Reformation in Roman Catholic Europe was powerfully influenced by St. Thomas Aquinas. Francisco Diamond State Suarez claimed that the precepts of concept are often distinguished into those (like 'Do sensible and avoid evil') that square measure famed now and intuitively by all traditional folks, those (like 'Do no injury to anyone') that need expertise and thought to grasp them, however that square measure then taken for granted, and people (like 'Lying is usually immoral') that don't seem to be taken for granted however are often derived from the additional basic precepts. However, Suarez accepted Scotus's double account of motivation.[60]

Religion and Morality in Modern European Philosophy

The history of rationalism from René mathematician to Gottfried Wilhelm Leibniz could be a history of re-establishing human information on the muse of rational principles that might not be doubted, once fashionable science began to shake the normal foundations supported by the authority of Aristotle and also the church. Mathematician wasn't primarily 'an ethician, however he set the supply of ethical law (surprisingly for a rationalist) in God's Will.'[61] "One's can isn't right in willing some specific smart unless he refers it to the good on associate degree finish, since the natural appetence of any half is ordered to the good of whole."[62] The foremost vital rationalist in ethics was Benedict philosopher. He was a person, however, was condemned by his contemporaries as unorthodox. Like mathematician, he tried to duplicate the strategies of pure mathematics in philosophy.

Substance, in step with Baruch de Spinoza, exists in itself and is formed through itself,[63] it's consequently one, infinite, and identical with God[64] there's no such issue as concept, since all events in nature ('God or Nature') square measure equally natural. Every human mind may be a restricted side of the divine intellect. On this read (which is Stoic) the human task is to maneuver towards the best potential rational management of human life. Leibniz was, like Descartes, not primarily associate degree ethician. He said, however, that 'the highest perfection of any thinking being lies in careful and constant pursuit of true happiness.'[65] The rationalists weren't denying the spatial relation of God in human ethical life, however their stress was on the access we've got through the sunshine of reason instead of through piece of writing or ecclesiastic authority.

After Gottfried Wilhelm Leibnitz there was in Deutschland a long-running battle between the rationalists and therefore the Pietists, United Nations agency tried to stay faithful the goals of the Lutheran Reformation. Smart samples of the two faculties' square measure Christian Kaspar Friedrich Wolff and Christian August Crusius. Kaspar Friedrich Wolff was terribly productive in popularising of the thought of Gottfried Wilhelm Leibnitz. He took from Gottfried Wilhelm Leibnitz the predestinationist principle that we are going to forever choose what pleases North American nation most, and therefore the principle that pleasure is that the apprehension of perfection, in order that the quantity of enjoyment we tend to feel is proportional to the quantity of perfection. He saw no downside concerning the affiliation between virtue and happiness, since each of them result directly from our perfection, and no downside concerning the affiliation between virtue and duty, since a requirement is just an act in accordance with law, that prescribes the pursuit of perfection. His views were offensive to the Pietists, as a result of he claimed that Kung Futzu already knew (by reason) all that mattered concerning morality, although he failed to recognise something concerning Christ.

August Cruises accepted Scotus's double theory of motivation, and command that there square measure actions that we have a tendency to have to be compelled to do no matter any ends we've, even the top of our own perfection and happiness. It's plausible to check here the origin of Kant's moral principle. However, he conjointly another a third motivation, what he known as 'the drive of conscience' that is 'the natural drive to acknowledge a divine ethical law.'[66] His plan was that we've among North American country this separate capability to acknowledge divine command and to be drawn towards it out of a way of dependence on the God United Nations agency prescribes the command to North American country, and can penalise North American country if we have a tendency to refuse (though our motive shouldn't be to avoid punishment).[67]

The history of empiricism in Britain from Thomas Hobbes to David Hume is additionally the history of the commit to re-establish human information. Hobbes aforementioned that each one reality is bodily (including God), and every one events square measure motions in house.[68] The longest portion of Leviathan is dedicated to faith, wherever Thomas Hobbes argues for the authority of Scripture that he thinks is required for the authority of law. He argues for the authority within the interpretation of Scripture to lean thereto same sovereign, and to not competitor religion authorities (whose competition had been seen to exacerbate the miseries of war each in Britain and on the Continent).

John Locke followed Thomas Hobbes in etymologising morality from our have to be compelled to live along in peace given our natural discord; however, he denied that we have a tendency to area unit automatically enraptured by our needs. He united with Thomas Hobbes in language that ethical laws area unit God's imposition, however, disagreed by creating God's power and benevolence each necessary conditions for God's authority during this respect.[69] He conjointly command that our reason will calculate counsels or recommendation regarding ethical matters; however, solely God's imposition makes law (and thence obligation), and that we solely comprehend God's imposition from revelation. He so devoted sizable attention to justifying our belief within the dependability of revelation.

The deists like William Hyde Wollaston, believed that humans will reason from their expertise of nature to the existence and a few of the attributes of God, that special revelation is consequently excess, that God doesn't intervene in human affairs (after creation) which the nice life for humans finds adequate steering in philosophical ethics. Frances Hutcheson wasn't a nonreligious person, however will offer associate example of the type of steering concerned. He distinguished between objects that square measure naturally smart, that excite personal or self-serving pleasure, and people that square measure virtuously smart, that square measure advantageous to all or any persons affected. He took himself to be giving a reading of ethical goodness as *agape*, the Greek word for the love of our neighbour that Jew prescribes. This love is benevolence, Hutcheson same, and it's developed within the principle 'That Action is best, that procures the best Happiness for the best Numbers'. As a result of the definitions of natural and ethical smart manufacture a doable gap between the two, we want a way to believe that morality and happiness square measure coincident.

Hutcheson thought that God has given North American nation an ethical sense for this purpose. This psyche responds to samples of benevolence with approbation and a novel quite pleasure, and benevolence is that the solely factor it responds to, because it were the sole signal it picks up. It is, like Scotus's warm-heartedness for justice, not confined to our perception of advantage. The results of our having psyche is that once intending the nice of others, we tend to 'un-designedly' find you promoting our own greatest smart as a result of divine sense we find yourself gratifying ourselves at the side of others. God shows benevolence by initial creating North American nation benevolent then giving North American nation this psyche that gets joy from the approbation of benevolence.

David Hume is that the initial figure during this narrative which will properly be connected to the Enlightenment. For Hume "an action, or sentiment, or character, is virtuous or vicious as a result of its read causes a pleasure or uneasiness of a selected kind."[70] The denial of locomotion to reason is a component of his general skepticism. Since the thought of morality implies one thing universal, there should be some sentiment of sympathy or (he later says) humanity, that is common to any or all people in general, and that "recommends identical object of general approbation."[71] Hume thought we tend to may get typical ethical conclusions from these ethical sentiments, that nature has as luck would have it given America. He was additionally skeptical regarding any arrange to derive conclusions containing 'ought' from premises containing solely 'is', though' students discussion regarding the scope of the premises he's talking regarding here. Most likely he enclosed premises regarding omnipotence or nature or action. This doesn't mean he was controversy against the existence of God. He thought (like Calvin) that we tend to cannot admit rational proofs of God's existence, even if humans have what Calvin calls a way of the divine.

The Enlightenment in France had a additional anti-clerical flavour (in half as a result of the history of religious doctrine, distinctive to France), and for the primary time during this narrative we have a tendency to meet real atheists, like Barond' Holbach who command not solely that morality didn't would like faith, however that faith, and particularly, Christianity, was its major impediment. Francois-Marie Arouet was, particularly towards the tip of his life, opposition Christianity, however to not faith generally. He accepted from a people deists the thought that what's true in Christian teachings is that the core of human values that are universally true altogether religions, and (like the German rationalists) he loved philosopher. Jean-Jacques Rousseau aforementioned, famously, that man is born free, however all over he's enchained.[72]

This supposes a disjunction between nature and modern society, and Rousseau control that the lifetime of primitive kinsfolk was happy inasmuch as they knew a way to board accordance with their own innate needs; currently we'd like some reasonably accord to safeguard United States of America from the corrupting effects of society upon the right love of self. Nature is known because the whole realm of being created by God, United Nations agency guarantees its goodness, unity, and order. Rousseau control that we tend to don't want any treater between United States of America and God, and that we will attain salvation by returning to nature during this high sense and by developing all our schools harmoniously. Our final happiness is to feel ourselves together with the system that God created.

Kant outlined that "morality isn't instrumental to our rational sensible; our rational good consists in acting ethical."[73] Philosopher is that the most significant figure of the Enlightenment in European country, however his project is totally different in some ways from those of his French contemporaries. Kant's mature project was to limit human data "in order to create area for faith."[74] He accepted from philosopher that our data is confined inside the bounds of doable perception; however he failed to settle for skeptical conclusions concerning deed or the soul. Reason isn't confined, in his read, to an equivalent limits as data, and that we are rationally needed to carry beliefs concerning things as they're in themselves, not simply things as they seem to US especially, we tend to are needed to believe God, the soul and immortality. Philosopher thought that "humans got to be able to believe that morality during this difficult type is consistent within the long-term gaily, if they're aiming to be able to uphold within the ethical life while not rational instability."[75] He failed to settle for the three ancient theoretical arguments for the existence of God (though he was sympathetic to a modest version of the philosophical doctrine argument). However, the sensible argument was decisive for him, although he commands that it had been doable to be virtuously sensible while not being a theist, even supposing such a footing was rationally unstable. "According to philosopher, the rational being utters the commands of morality to himself."[76]

A whole succession of Kant's followers tried to 'go on the far side' Kant by showing that there was finally no have to be compelled to create the separation between our data and also the noumenon beyond our data. Martyr Wilhelm Friedrich Hegel accomplished this finish by proposing that we should always create the reality of concepts relative to their original historical context against the background of a history that's progressing towards a ending of 'absolute knowledge', within which Spirit (in German Geist, which implies additionally 'mind') understands that reality is its own creation and there's no 'beyond' for it to understand. Hegel is giving a philosophical account of the Biblical notion of all things returning to God, 'so that God is also beat all'. During this world-history, Hegel settled the Reformation as 'the all-enlightening sun' of the brilliant day that's our fashionable time.[77] He thought that the varied stages of information are stages of freedom, every stage manufacturing first its own internal contradiction, so a radical transition into a brand new stage. The stage of absolute freedom are going to be one within which all members freely by reason endorse the organic community and concrete establishments within which they really live.

Hegel's followers split into 'Right Hegelians' and 'Left Hegelians' (or 'Young Hegelians'). Right Georg Wilhelm Friedrich Hegelians promoted the widely positive read of the Prussian state that Hegel expressed within the Philosophy of Right. Left Hegelians rejected it, and with it the Protestant Christianity that they saw as its vehicle. During this manner "Hegel's peculiar manner of promoting Christianity concluded up inflicting its vehement rejection by thinkers who shared several of his social ideals."[78] David Friedrich Strauss wrote the lifetime of Jesus Critically Examined, launching the historical-critical technique of Biblical scholarship with the suggestion that a lot of the Biblical account is story or 'unconscious invention' that has to be separated out from the historical account. Ludwig Andreas Feuerbach wrote The Essence of Christianity in that he pictured all faith because the means that by which "man comes his being into sound judgment, and so once more makes himself an object to the present projected image of himself.[79]

Feuerbach thought faith resulted from humanity's alienation from itself, associated philosophy required to destroy the spiritual illusion in order that we tend to might learn to like world and not divert this love onto a notional object. Subversive followed Feuerbach during this diagnosing of faith, however he was interested primarily in social and political relations instead of science. He became suspicious of theory (for example, Hegel's), on the grounds that theory is itself a symbol of the facility structures within the societies that turn out it. 'Theory,' Marx writes, "is realised in an exceedingly individuals solely in up to now because it could be a realisation of the people's needs."[80] And 'ideologies' and 'religion,' he believes, arise from 'conditions that need [these] illusions'. Marx came back to Hegel's thoughts concerning work revealing to the employee his price through what the employee produces, however Marx argued that beneath laissez-faire economy the employee was alienated from this product as a result of others owned each the merchandise and therefore the means that of manufacturing it. Marx urged that the sole thanks to forestall this was to destroy the establishment of personal property.[81] So he believed, like Hegel, current through history towards freedom, however he thought it might take Communist revolution to bring this concerning.

A very completely different response to Georg Wilhelm Friedrich Hegel (and Kant) is found within the work of philosopher a spiritual thinker World Health Organisation started, like Georg Wilhelm Friedrich Hegel and Immanuel Kant, from Protestantism. Kierkegaard mocked Georg Wilhelm Friedrich Hegel perpetually for presuming to grasp the complete system within which human history is embedded, whereas still being situated during a specific little a part of it. On the opposite hand, he used philosopher classes of thought himself, particularly in his plan of the aesthetic life, the moral life and therefore the non-secular life as stages through that folks develop by means that of first internal contradiction and so radical transition. Kierkegaard's relation with Immanuel Kant was problematic similarly. In either /or he caricatured Kant's moral thought (as well as Hegel's) within the person of decide William, World Health Organisation is stuck inside the moral life and has not been ready to reach the lifetime of religion. On the opposite hand, "his own description of the non-secular life is filled with echoes of Kant's *faith inside the Boundaries of Mere Reason.*"[82] Kierkegaard thought we've got to comprehend that God's help is important even for the sort of penitence that's the transition into the non-secular life. He additionally recommended that inside the non-secular life, there's a 'repetition' of the aesthetic life and therefore the moral life, though' during a remodeled version.

Nietzsche was deeply influenced by philosopher, particularly his read of the need (which Nietzsche known as '*the will of Power*'), and was first attracted and so repelled by Wagner, World Health Organisation was additionally one amongst Schopenhauer's disciples. Nietzsche saw clearly the intimate link between Christianity and also the moral theories of his predecessors in Europe, particularly Immanuel Kant. In *On the kindred of Morals*, he says, "The advent of the Christian God, because the most god earned up to now, was so in the course of the utmost feeling of guilty liability on earth. Presuming we've bit by bit entered upon the reverse course, there's no tiny likelihood that with the irresistible decline of religion within the Christian God, there's currently additionally a substantial decline in mankind's feeling of guilt"[83] this can be the 'death of God' that Nietzsche declared, and that he foretold would even be the tip of philosopher ethics. It's more durable to grasp what Nietzsche was for, than what he was against. This can be partially an inheritance from philosopher, World Health Organisation thought any system of constructive moral thought a delusion. However, Nietzsche clearly loved the traditional Greeks, and thought we'd be comfortable with a 'master' morality like theirs, instead of a 'slave' morality like Christianity. "Mastery over himself additionally essentially offers him mastery over circumstances, over nature, and over all a lot of short-willed and unreliable creatures."[84] By this last clause, he meant mastery over others, and also the model of this mastery is that the '*overman*' World Health Organisation is freed from the hostility by the weak of the robust that Nietzsche thought lay at the idea of Christian ethics.

Hume had range of successors in GB United Nations agency accepted the read (which David Hume took from Hutcheson) that our basic obligation is to figure for the best happiness of the best number. William Paley thought he may demonstrate that morality derived from the desire of God and needed promoting the happiness of all, that happiness was the adding of pleasures, which we'd like to believe that God is that the final mortal of happiness if we tend to square measure to sustain motivation to try and do what we all know we tend to out to do.[85] Jurist rejected this system of rules context. His grounds were radically philosopher, that the sole 'real' entities square measure publicly evident, and then don't embrace God (or, for that matter, right or time or relations or qualities). He thought he may give a scientific calculus of pleasures, wherever the unit that stays constant is that the minimum state of sensibility that may be distinguished from indifference. He thought we have a tendency to may then separate totally different 'dimensions' during which these units vary, like intensity, duration, certainty, nearness (how presently the pleasures can come), fecundity (how several different pleasures this pleasure can produce) and purity. Discarding the system of rules context created ethical motivation problematic, for why ought to we have a tendency to expect (without God) a lot of units of delight for ourselves by contributive to the bigger pleasure of others? Bentham's answer was to hope that law and social custom may give people with adequate motives through the threat of social sanctions, which what he known as 'deontology' (which is personal or personal morality) may mobilise hidden or long-range interests that were already gift however obscure.

John Stuart Mill was raised on strict utilitarian principles by his father, an acquaintance of legal expert. In contrast to legal expert, however, Mill accepted that there are qualitative variations in pleasures merely as pleasures, and he thought that the upper pleasures were those of the intellect, the sentiments and imagination, and also the ethical sentiments. He determined that people who have tough each these and also the lower pleasures tend to like the previous. At the age of twenty, he had a collapse, and a protracted amount of 'melancholy'. He complete that his education had neglected the culture or cultivation of feeling, of that hope could be a primary instance. In his 3 Essays on faith, he came back to the thought of hope, voice communication that 'the indulgence of hope with relevancy the government of the universe and also the destiny of man when death, whereas we tend to acknowledge as a transparent truth that we've no ground for quite a hope, is legitimate and philosophically defensible'; while not such hope, we tend to are unbroken down by 'the fateful feeling of "not price while."[86] Mill failed to believe, however, that God was almighty, given all the evil within the world, and he insisted, like Kant, that we've to be God's co-workers, not simply passive recipients of God's help.

Henry Sidgwick in strategies of Ethics distinguished three methods: philosophical theory, egocentric Hedonism and school of thought or Universalistic Hedonism. Of those three, he rejected the primary, on the grounds that no concrete moral principles square measure axiomatic, which after they conflict (as they do) we've got to require consequences under consideration so as to choose the way to act. However, Sidgwick found the relation between the opposite two strategies far more problematic. Every principle severally gave the impression to him axiomatic, however once taken along they gave the impression to be reciprocally inconsistent. He thought about two solutions, psychological and metaphysical. The psychological resolution was to usher in the pleasures and pains of sympathy, in order that if we tend to aid to any or all we tend to find yourself (because of those pleasures) creating ourselves happiest. Sidgwick rejected this on the idea that sympathy is inevitably restricted in its vary, and that we feel it most towards those highest to USA, in order that though we tend to embody sympathetic pleasures and pains beneath self-centeredness, it'll tend to extend the divergence between egocentric and utilitarian conduct, instead of bring them nearer along.

The metaphysical resolution was to usher in a god UN agency wishes the best total smart of all living things, and UN agency can reward and penalise in accordance with this need.[87] 'Shaftsbury says morality to be natural and freelance of supernatural sanctions. Fichte says ethical acutely aware gave the importance that it's set philosophy in term of it. Anarchist claims that morality derives from Associate in nursing evolved issue of international logistic support. Friedrich Wilhelm Nietzsche says "moral system a division of two sorts, that of master or slave morality."[88] Santayana derives 'morality as break away ethics. He distinguished pre-rational and post-rational styles of morality.'[89]

Philosophy, Religion and Morality in Contemporary Thought

In the twentieth century, skilled philosophy distributed into two streams, generally known as 'Analytic' and 'Continental', and there have been periods throughout that the two colleges lost contact with one another. Towards the top of the century, however, there have been a lot of philosophers who might speak the languages of each traditions. Martin Heidegger was at first trained as a scholar, and wrote his thesis on what he took to be a piece of Duns Scotus. He took a meeting beneath Edmund Husserl at Freiburg, and was appointed to succeed him in his chair. Husserl's programme of 'phenomenology' was to recover a way of certainty regarding the planet by finding out in thorough detail of the psychological feature structure of look. Philosopher departed from philosopher in approaching being through a spotlight on 'Human Being' (in German Dasein) as involved especially for its fate in associate alien world, or as 'anxiety' (Angst) towards death.[90] During this sense he's the primary existentialist, although he didn't use the term. Philosopher emphasised that we have a tendency to square measure 'thrown' into a world that's not 'home', and that we have a radical alternative regarding what potentialities for ourselves we are going to build actual.

Heidegger John Drew here from Soren Aabye Kierkegaard, and he's additionally similar in describing the danger of falling back to mere conventionality, what philosopher calls 'they' (das Man). On the opposite hand he's not like Soren Aabye Kierkegaard in thinking of ancient Christianity as only one a lot of convention that authentic existence needs US to urge on the far side. In philosopher, as in philosopher, it's onerous to seek out a positive or constructive ethics. Heidegger's position is somewhat compromised, moreover, by his initial embrace of the party. In his later work he emotional more and more towards a sort of sacred mysticism. His romantic emotion of the fashionable world and his distrust of system-building led to the espousal of either silence or poetry because the best thanks to be receptive the 'something' (sometimes he says 'the earth') that reveals itself solely as 'self-secluding' or concealment itself off from our numerous conceptualisations.[91]

Jean-Paul Sartre did use the label 'existentialist', and aforementioned that 'Existentialism is nothing else than an endeavour to draw all the results of a coherent atheist position.'[92] He denied (like Scotus) that the ethical law may be deduced from attribute, however this was as a result of (unlike Scotus) he thought that we tend to provide ourselves our own essences by the alternatives we tend to build. His locution was, 'Existence precedes essence'. 'Essence' is here the process property of an issue, and Sartre gave the instance of a cutting implement, that is given its definition by the skilled worker World Health Organisation makes it. The essence first of all, "man exists, turns up, seems on the scene, and, solely later on, defines himself."[93] On this read there aren't any outside commands to attractiveness to for legitimating, and that we area unit condemned to our own freedom. Sartre thought of mortals as attempting to be God (on a philosopher account of what God is), even if there's no God. This is often associate inevitably bootless enterprise, that he known as 'anguish'.

Moreover, we tend to inevitably want to decide on not only for ourselves, except for the planet. We want, like God, to form group in our own image, 'If we would like to marry, to own kids, notwithstanding this wedding depends alone on my very own circumstances or passion or want, we involving all humanity in matrimony and not just myself. Therefore, we to blame for myself and for everybody else. We making a definite image of many of my very own selecting. In selecting myself, we select man to acknowledge that this project doesn't be is needed by honesty, and to cover this from ourselves is 'bad faith'. One kind of unhealthy religion is to fake that there's a God United Nations agency is giving North American country our tasks. Another is to fake that there's a 'human nature' that's doing a similar issue. To measure genuinely is to understand each that we tend to produce these tasks for ourselves, which they're futile.

The twentieth century additionally saw, among Catholicism, varieties of Christian philosophical theory and new variations of the system of theologist.

Jacques Martian developed a style of religious doctrine that maintained the conception, however regarded moral judgment as not strictly psychological feature however target-hunting by pre-conceptual emotive inclinations. He took a lot of philosopher read of history than ancient religious doctrine, granting development within the human information of conception, and he defended democracy because the applicable method for human persons to realise freedom and dignity. The notion of the worth of the person and therefore the capacities given to persons by their creator was at the middle of the 'Personalism' of Pope John Paul II's.[94]

The Acting Person influenced by liquid ecstasy Scheler construct theory has been obsessed and changed a lot of recently by two philosophers. World Health Organisation write in an exceedingly vogue nearer to the analytic tradition, John Finnis and, in an exceedingly completely different and incompatible manner, Alastair Macintyre Finnis holds that our information of the elemental ethical truths is axiomatic, then isn't deduced from attribute. His construct and Natural Rights was a landmark in group action the fashionable vocabulary and synchronic linguistics of rights into the tradition of construct. Macintyre, World Health Organisation has been on an extended journey back from communism to Thomism, holds that we are able to apprehend what quite life we tend to have to be compelled to go on the premise of knowing our natural finish that he currently identifies in system of rules terms. He's still influenced by a philosopher historicism, and holds that the sole thanks to settle rival information claims is to examine however with success every will account for the form taken by its rivals.[95]

Michel Foucault followed philosopher in aiming to uncover the 'genealogy' of varied uptodate styles of thought and apply (he was involved, as an example, with physiological property and mental illness), and the way relations of power and domination have made 'discourses of truth'[96] In his later work he delineated four totally different aspects of the 'practice of the self' during which we've got been engaged. We have a tendency to choose the wishes, acts, and thoughts that we have a tendency to attend to virtuously. We have a tendency to acknowledge ourselves as virtuously sure by some explicit ground, e.g., divine commands, or rationality, or attribute. We have a tendency to remodel ourselves into moral subjects by some set of techniques, e.g., meditation or mortification or consciousness-raising.

Finally, we have a tendency to propose a 'telos' or goal, the approach of life or mode of being that the topic is aiming at, e.g., self-mastery, tranquility or purification. Foucault criticised Christian conventions that tend to require morality as a legal and infrequently universal code of laws, and to ignore the inventive apply of self-making. Although Christian and post-Christian moralists flip their attention to style, he thought they have an inclination to specialise in the confession of truth concerning oneself, a mode of expression that is traditionally joined to the church and also the trendy psycho-sciences. Foucault most popular stressing our freedom to make ourselves as moral subjects, and develop 'a new style of right' and a 'non-disciplinary style of power.' He didn't, however, tell United States way more concerning what these new forms would be like.

Jurgen Habermas planned a 'communicative ethics' that develops the Kantian part in Marxism. By analysing the structure of communication (using speech-act theory developed in analytic philosophy) he lays out a procedure which will rationally justify norms, although he doesn't claim to grasp what norms a society can adopt by victimisation this procedure. The two concepts behind this procedure area unit that norms area unit valid if they receive the consent of all the affected parties in free sensible communication, and if the results of the overall observance of the norms (in terms of however every person's interests area unit affected) area unit acceptable to any or all.[97] Habermas thinks he fulfills during this approach Hegel's aim of accommodative the individual and society, as a result of the communication method extends people on the far side their personal views within the method of reaching agreement. Spiritual convictions have to be compelled to be left behind, on this theme, as a result of they're not universalisable within the approach the procedure needs.

The post-modernism may be a call to try to away with any notion of a unified and continuous self. Therefore, it looks the terribly question of a post-modern engagement with faith is out of place. However, inside no time, post-modernism has come back to be one amongst the foremost productive grounds of re-imagining the faith. If the post-modernism is basically associate degree intellectual skepticism of all foundations, "the faith is that the most foundational of human thought enterprises."[98] Then one may suspect however they might be anyway connected. Even the foremost dynamic conceptions of spiritual expertise, with their notion of a Self that isn't simply "be" however during a state of changing into assume bound continuity to thus notional self.

Not solely this, it marked a proliferation of latest analytical tools to create sense of faith and therefore the non-secular. However, a way deeper thought would create it clear that such a development isn't that stunning in the least. If the intellectual outcomes or counter-parts of what came to be known as contemporaneousness discredited all non-secular rituals, symbols as well as the terribly notion of religion, the post-modernism did a similar to all or any the post-Enlightenment thought. It questioned the viability and truthfulness of the self-descriptions of Rationality, Reason and Secularity. During this sense what discredited and defeated the faith is exactly what has been shown to be another narrative and deeply imperfect intellectual project by post-modernism. Thus, indirectly, each faith and post-modernism has a standard enemy. Of course, within the philosophical realm, the unremarkable logic of "the enemy of the enemy is our friend"[99] doesn't work. There should be a standard ground for faith and post-modernism to come back to dialogue.

Interestingly enough, it had been one in every of the explanations for our gift day larger awareness that most of the major concepts of post-enlightenment thought- catholicity, secularism, Humanism- are shown by post-modernist sensibilities that were a minimum of partly spiritual in origin. One in every of the vital consequences of post-modern confrontations with the terribly plan of sound judgment is that the system of rules or perhaps the thought created by the trustworthy itself has begun to be seen as no a lot of inferior to outsider, scientific accounts. During this dramatic amendment, post-modernism was greatly motor-assisted by phenomenological and philosophical precedents. With the entry of post-modernism, even the accounts provided by believers received the standing of being authentic material for enquiry and came out of the cabalistic world of system of rules and ecclesiastic reach. All of it's been the case not just because of an enclosed history of concepts, of course. The dramatic changes within the course of twentieth century conjointly provided the impetus and explanation for such remodelling and re-opening a number of the previous certainties and fixities. However, we have a tendency to be here completely considering their impact on the sector of concepts and a lot of specifically, philosophical concepts.

Thus, the entry of post-modernism marked the re-entry of the spiritual. In keeping with a number one intellectual of Post-Modernity, David Lyon, one among the options of this modified intellectual mood consists of, "One…that social theory ought to be a lot of accommodative to non-secular assumptions once excluded by definition from social rationalisation."[100] As we have a tendency to note earlier, this shift isn't thanks to changes within the intellectual history alone. The revival of non-secular movements, avowal of non-secular Right and Terrorism's invocation of faith forged a heavy doubt on the social theory's simple prediction and assumption that because the history and societies progress, the faith would any interact and lose its hold. Post-modern sensitivity pointed to the current reality in its attack on the foundational assumptions of modernity's thought.

Another conducive think about this can be the challenges exhibit by post-colonial theory that problematical the narrow-mindedness of euro-centrism with its Christian underpinnings and showed the partisanship of the project of modernness and its Universal claims. If such is that the case with the catholicity of the Western values, allow us to see what's the case with one among the foremost immediate and vital issues for our study, the standing of faith, morality and philosophy in and for Hindu System.

In the top of discussion we tend to treat the philosophical analysis of morality and faith. This discussion chiefly goes through the tracing of the philosophical conceptions of each faith and morality. Here we tend to analyse the philosophical conceptions of Greek philosophers to post trendy philosophers. Through this chapter we tend to pave the bottom for different Chapters. And that we discuss the problems of relation between morality and faith that area unit with issue.

References

1. Edward Craig, (1998), *Encyclopedia of Philosophy*, Routledge, New York, p. 275.
2. John E. Smith, (1949). *Religion and Morality,The Journal of Religion,* No. 2, Vol. 29.
3. Richard, Dworkin, (1972), *Religion and Morality*, Macmillan Publishing Co., Inc. Canada, p. 163.
4. Wittgenstein, L, *Philosophical Investigations*, Translated by G.E. M. Anscombe Basil, Blackwell Publisher, Oxford, 1976,Section 109.
5. John Dewey, ed, David Sidorsky, *The Essential Writings*, Harper & Row Publications, New York,1977, p. 2.
6. Bhattacharya, Hari Mohan, *The Principles of Philosophy*, Oxford University Press, Calcutta, 1975, p. 12.
7. Roger Scruton, *A Short History of Modern Philosophy; from Descartes to Writtgenstain*, Routledge, and Kegan Paul, London, 1981, p. 5.
8. Chatopadyaya, D. P., *Indian Philosophy, A Popular Introduction,* People Publishing House, New Delhi, 1975, p. 28.
9. Alexander Lyon Macfie, *Eastern, Influence on Western Philosophy*, Edinburgh University Press, George Square, Edinburgh, 1988, p. 29.
10. Mohapatra, A.R., *Philosophy of Religion*, Sterling Publishers Private Limited, New Delhi, 1985, p. 5.
11. John Hick, *Philosophy of Religion Part – II,* Prentice-Hall of India Private Limited, New Delhi, 1978, p. 1.
12. Chalmers, *What is this thing called Science?* Oxford University Press, London, 1986, p. 219.
13. Alban G. Widgery, *The Philosophical Review, in Towards a Modern Philosophy of Religion*, Vol. 38, No. 5, Cornell University, London, (Sep. 1929), pp. 422-423.
14. Taylor Charles, *Religion Today,* Harward University Press, Cambridge Mass, London, 1995, p. 18.
15. Taylor Charles, *Religion Today,* Harward University Press, Cambridge Mass, London, 1995, p. 29.
16. Richard, Dworkin, *Religion and Morality*, Macmillan Publishing Co., Inc., Canada, 1972, p. 151.
17. Taylor Charles, *Religion Today,* Harward University Press, Cambridge Mass, London, 1995, p. 34
18 Alexander, *Space, Time and Deity*. Vol. II, The Gifford Lectures at Glasgow, 1916-1918, MacMillan & Co., London, 1920, p. 408.
19. Patrick, G. T. W., *Introduction to Philosophy*, George Allen & Unwin, London, 1925, p. 367.

20. Whitehead, A. N., *Science and the Modern World*, Cambridge University Press, Cambridge, 1933, p. 12.
21. Stace, W. T., *Time and Eternity*, IGNCA, New Delhi, 1990, p. 3.
22. Charles Worth, M. J., *Philosophy of Religion*, Cambridge University Press, London, 1998, p. 106.
23. Durant Drake, *Problems of Religion*, Washington Square, New York, 1967, p. 244.
24. Mahadevan T.M.P., *Contemporary Indian Philosophy*, Sterling Publishers Private Limited,1981, p. 108.
25. Donald H. Bishop, *Indian Thought An Introduction*, Wiley Eastern Private Limited, New Delhi,1975, p. 352.
26. Charles Worth, M. J., *Philosophy of Religion*, p. 106, Mahadevan T.M.P, *Contemporary Indian Philosophy*, Sterling Publishers Private Limited, 1981, p. 248.
27. Shankar Srivastava Rama, *Contemporary Indian Philosophy*, Sarda Publications, Ranchi, 1984, p. 290.
28. Radhakrishnan Sarvepally and Charles A. Moore, *A Source book in Indian Philosophy*, Princeton University Press, New Jersey, 1977, p. 578.
29. Harold A Durfee, *The Journal of Religion*, Vol. 32, No. 3, University of Chicago Press, Chicago, Jul, 1952, p. 189.
30. *Ibid*, p. 190.
31. *Ibid*, p. 192.
32. Adhar Das, *Sri Aurobindo and the Future of Mankind*, University of Calcutta, Calcutta, 1934, p. 53.
33. Aurobindo Sri, *Heraclites*, Arya Public House, Calcutta, 1947, pp. 46-47.
44. Moore, C.A. ed., Philosophy *and Culture –East and West*. London: George Allen & Unwin Ltd., 1951, p. 34.
35. Radhakrishanan and Moore, eds., *A Source Book of Indian Philosophy*, George Allen & Unwin Ltd., London,1951, p. 614.
36. "*Relation of Philosophical Theories to the practical Affairs of Men*," in C.A. Moore, ed., *Philosophy and Culture –East and West*. London: George Allen & Unwin Ltd, 1951, p. 36.
37. *Ibid*, p. 42
38. Parkinson G.H.R, *An Encyclopedia of Philosophy* (Ed), *The Nature of Moral Philosophy*, Richards Lindley, Routledge, UK. March 1988, p. 517.
39. William K. Frankena, *Ethics*, Prentice - Hall of India Private Limited, New Delhi, 1988, pp. 4-9.
40. *Ibid*, p.10.
41. Paul Edwards, *The Encyclopedia of Philosophy*, (ed), Vol. VII, Macmillan Publishers, London, 1978, p. 151.

42. James Rachel's, *The Element of Moral Philosophy,* 2nd ed, Mc Grawhill Inc, New Delhi, 1993, p. 1.
43. Geoffrey Thomas, *The Moral Philosophy of T. H. Green*, Clarendon Press, Oxford, 1987, p. 82.
44. John E. Hare, ed, Bryn Mawr, *Plato Euthyphro*, Commentaries by Plato, Bryn Mawr Commentaries Publishers, PA, 1985, p. 436.
45. Michael Woods, Aristotle: *Eudemian Ethics,* (Ed), Oxford University Press, New Delhi, 1986, p. 236.
46. Aristotle, *Metaphysics* / translated by Richard Hope, Columbia University Press, New York, 1960, p. 345.
47. John A. Hutchison, *Biblical Foundations of Democracy*, Published by the National Association of Biblical Instructors to Foster Religion, UK, 1957, Sections, 1. 3.
48. *Ibid*. Section, 1. 22.
49. The Bible, *Old Testament*, Genesis, Chapter -17, Verses 7-8.
50. *Ibid*, Chapter - 22, Verses 1-14.
51. *Ibid*, Exodus, Chapter - 20, Verses, 1-17 and Chapter -31, Verse 18.
52. *Ibid, Deuteronomy*, Chapter -6, Verse 5.
53. The Bible, *Old Testament, Leviticus,* Chapter -19, Verse 18.
54. The Bible, *New Testament, Matthew,* Chapter -5, Verse 7.
55. The Bible, *New Testament, Matthew,* Chapter -5, Verses 43-48, and *Luke* Chapter – 6 Verses 27-36.
56. Augustine, *The City of God Against the Pagans*, University Press, Harvard, 1963, p. 126.
57. The Bible, *New Testament*, John Chapter-1, Verses 1-5.
58. The Bible, *New Testament*, John 1st Chapter-4, Verses 8.
59. Thomas St. Aquinas, *The Summa Theologica I,* Benziger Bros. Edition Publishers, London, 1947, p. 91.
60. Martin Luther, *The Bondage of Will*, Fleming H Revell & Co, New York, 1990, pp. 95-96.
61. Descartes René, *New Essays on Human understanding*, University Press, Cambridge, 1981, p. 239.
62. Wagner, Michael. F. *An Historical Introduction to Moral Philosophy*, Prentice Hall, New Jersy, 1991, p. 122.
63. Spinoza, *Spinoza's Ethics and on the Correction of the Understanding* translated by Andrew Boyle, Everyman's Library Publishers, New York, 1977, def. 3
64. *Ibid*, I, prop. 15.
65. Leibniz, *New Essays on Human Understanding*, Cambridge University Press, Cambridge, 1981, Section XXI, p. 51.

66. August Cruises, *A Guide to Rational Living; Moral Philosophy from Montaigne to Kant*, Cambridge University Press, Cambridge, 1990, pp. 132 and 574.
67. *Ibid*, p. 135.
68. Hobbes, Thomas, *Leviathan*, edited by Thomas Hobbes and C.B. Macpherson, Penguin Books, Baltimore, 1968, Ch. 13.
69. Locke, John, *Two Treatises, of government* / Edited by Peter Laslett, The Cambridge University Press Publishers, USA,1988, IV. XIII 3.
70. Hume, David, *Treatise of Human Nature*/ edited by L.A. Biggie Shelby and P.H. Nidditch Clarendon Press Publication, Oxford, 1978, Section, III.1& III. 2.
71. Hume, David, *Enquiry Concerning the Principles of Morals*, Oxford University Press, London, 1976, Chapter-IX. Section, I. 221.
72. Rousseau, Jean-Jacques, *The Social Contract*, Chapter- I, Oxford University Press, Oxford, 1994, Section 1. 1.
73. Geoffrey Thomas, *The Moral Philosophy of T. H. Green*, Clarendon Press, Oxford, 1987, p. 107.
74. Kant, Immanuel, *Critique of Practical Reason*, Hackett Publishing, London, 2002, Section, B xxx.
75. Kant Immanuel, *Prolegomena to Any Future Metaphysics*, Cambridge University Press, Cambridge, April 2004, p. 41.
76. Mac Intyre Alasdair, *Short History of Ethics : A History of Moral Philosophy from the Homeric age to the Twentieth Century*, Routledge and Kegan Paul Publisher, London, 1998, p. 194.
77. Georg Wilhelm Friedri Hegel, *The Philosophy of History*, Barnes & Noble Publishing House, New York, 2004, p. 412.
78. Schopenhauer Arthur, *The World as Will and Representation* / Translated by E.F.J. Payne, Dover Publications, New York, 1958, pp. 56-57.
79. Ludwig Andreas Feuerbach, *The Essence of Christianity*, Harper Collins Publishers, New York,1957, p. 30.
80. Marx, Karl, "*Critique of Hegel's Philosophy of Right*," *Early Writings*, translated by Annette Jolin and edited by Joseph O'Malley, Cambridge University Press, Cambridge, 1970, p. 252.
81. Marx, Karl, "*Economic and Philosophic Manuscripts*," *Early Writings*, Moscow Progress Publishers, New York, 1982, p. 348.
82. Kant Immanuel, *Religion within the Boundaries*, Cambridge University Press, Cambridge, 1998, p. 283.
83. Nietzsche, F., *On the Genealogy of Morals*, Doubleday Publications, New York, 1956, pp. 59-60.
84. *Ibid*, pp. 90-91.

85. Paley William, *The Principles of Moral and Political Philosophy*, R. Faulder Publishers, New York, 1799, Chapter- II, Section 4.
86. Mill, J.S. *Three Essays on Religion: Nature, the Utility of Religion, and Theism,* Libri. Amherst, New York, May 1998, pp. 249-50.
87. Sidgwick Henry, *The Methods of Ethics: Indianapolis*, Hackett Publishing Company, London, 1981, p. 321.
88. Nietzsche Friedrich, *Birth of Tragedy and the Genealogy of Morals*, New York, Doubleday Publication, 1956, p. 236.
89. William L. Reese, *Dictionary of Philosophy and Religion*, New Jersey: Humanities Press, 1975, p. 369.
90. Heidegger Martin, *Being and Time,* tranlated by John Macquarrie and Edward Robinson, Basil Blackwell Publication, Oxford, 1978, Vol. I, p. 6.
91. Heidegger, Martin, *Poetry, Language, Thought*, translated by Albert Hofstadter, Harper & Row. Co Publications, New York, 1975, p. 222.
92. Sartre, Jean-Paul, *Existentialism and Human Emotions*, Citadel Place: Secaucus, New Jersy, June 1984, p. 51.
93. Heidegger, Martin, *Poetry, Language, Thought*, translated by Albert Hofstadter, Harper & Row. Co Publications, New York, 1975, p. 15 and 222.
94. John Paul II's, *The Acting Person,* D Reidel Publishers Complex, Germany, April 1979, Chapter- I and II.
95. Alasdair Macintyre, *The Short History of Ethics*, Routledge &Kegan Paul, London; at the Alden Press, Oxford, 1976, p. 37.
96. Foucault Michel, "*Truth and Power*, Prentice Hall Publishers, New Jeresy, 1991, p. 242.
97. Habermas, Jürgen, *Reason and the Rationalisation of Society: The Theory of Communicative Action,* Volume I, English translation by Thomas McCarthy, Beacon Press, Boston, 1984 (originally published in German in 1981), p. 236.
98. Flanagan, Kieran and Jupp, Peter. C (ed), *Post Modernity, Sociology and Religion*, McMillan, 1996, p. 102.
99. *Ibid*, p. 105.
110. Flanagan, Kieran and Jupp, Peter. C (ed), *Post Modernity, Sociology and Religion*, McMillan, 1996, p. 110.

Chapter – II

Religion and Morality in the Semitic Tradition

This chapter deals with the conception of religion and morality in the Semitic tradition comprised of three main religions namely; Judaism, Christianity and Islam. In Semitic tradition, there is a clear distinction between God and human and other creatures. However, still it maintains the supremacy and absoluteness of the God. It emphasises mainly that the human and all other creatures are the creations of God. In a nutshell, the supremacy of one absolute God over all creation is emphasised in the Semitic religions. And the creations are governed by the power of God. And after the short span of life in this world, there is an after life. Nature of that after life is being determined by God by judging the actions as good or bad. In this context the aim of this chapter is to analyse the concept of god and how the Semitic traditions historically maintain supremacy of God, the conception of man, the notion of morality and the relationship between God and man. And how all these concepts are shared in all the Semitic traditions like Judaism, Christianity and Islam.

The remarkable position regarding Semitic religions is that all are giving incredible importance to the ethical principles and norms. The ethics has been given quite tremendous emphasis by Semitic religions. But it is essential to understand the nature of the Semitic ethical principles. In all Semitic religions the concept of ethical principles are quite interlinked with the notion of God. The nature that is attributed to the concept of god is clearly transmitted to the ethical notions also.

Ethical principles are defined in the basis of man-god relations of the religions. In Christianity and Judaism, man is defined as the image of God. Even though the God governs the entire world, free will is given to all human beings. That is, actions are being decided by themselves only. Therefore, human has the will to retain his/her original nature (i.e. Image of God) by doing the actions, which are in accordance with the God's will. Since man is the image of God, Man is identical to the will of God.[1] These are the basic motive behind the construal of the ethical principles. Here the goal or purpose of the ethical formulation is the description of the divine nature of God in accordance with the conditions of God. That is an ethical ideal in Christianity is exhibiting the God's divine nature in the world. That is why the notion of Jesus Christ, Son of God, is quite important, in the ethical formulation of Christianity. Son of God, is actually exhibiting the divine nature of god in the context of world. Through Jesus Christ, the mainly exhibited ethical characteristics are love towards the world and sacrifice for the world.

In the analysis of Judaism and Christianity, we can see that ethics is defined and conceived as divine. That is, ethical principles are the descriptions of the divine nature or the ethical ideal is the imitation or reproduction of divine nature. Ethics is understood as the relation between human and human's relation to nature and other beings. And ethics is a kind of standardising of this relation by putting forward certain norms and standards. Love, sacrifice, all these ethical principles are trying to give some kind of description or insistence to the human relation only. Even though ethics is a part of human relation, Christianity and Judaism are giving a divine account to these ethical principles. That is, their ethical account, in a certain sense, can be described as divine account to the human question.

Ethical principles of the Semitic religions are highly reasonable and appraisable. However, the primacy of the divine nature in the construal of ethics is actually questionable.[2] That is the translation of these highly appraisable ethical doctrines into the praxis cannot be seen a successful one. The failure of the application of these doctrines into the world cannot be analysed as mere practical problem, rather than that I consider it as a theoretical difficulty. Theoretical difficulty in the sense, that ethical principles are not sensitive or specific to the human context. It is because it is formulated in the divine framework. Ethical principles, which are defined in the divine framework, would be entirely different from the principles, which are evolved as response to human situations; even then, both talk about same principles. Specificity to the human situations is exactly the thing, which is lacking in the ethical formulations of the Semitic religions. Amidst this imperfection, one can see that it still opens up the possibility for better interpretation of ethical doctrines in specific relation to the human situations.

Thought of God Existence

Today people are doubtful about traditional and orthodox religious beliefs unless established in a scientific manner. But some religious thinkers say that religion and science can't be viewed as competing concepts. The readings in this section show that a great diversity of opinions exists among philosophers regarding truth and value of religion. The people's job is to assess carefully, the various arguments to determine which are sound. There are two arguments that are presented in favour of the existence of God. One is argument from agreement, which says that, as the majority of human kind believe in God and so it can be taken as proof and other is the argument from scripture, which says that existing religious scriptures are the proof of God. "These two may not be absolute in nature because if majority believe is truth, it may not be true and so is the scriptures."[3]

Some major arguments for God's existence in Semitic tradition are based on the modern theological way. This led to two specific problems that theology, inspired by Greek philosophy, set for itself: (1) the attempt to prove the existence of God, and (2) the attempt to justify God in view of both the apparent shortcomings of the creation and the existence of evil in history (*i.e.,* the problem of theodicy). Efforts to explain the ways of God to humans, particularly in respect to the problem of the existence of evil, are called theodicy. This form of justification of God has addressed profound human impulses and has relied upon strenuous exercises of human reason, but it has also led to no finally satisfying conclusions. The problem, which was already posed by Augustine and treated in detail by Thomas Aquinas, became of pressing importance in the European Thirty Years' War (1618–48) and its aftermath. At that time Gottfried Wilhelm Leibniz, who did more than anyone to develop the concept of theodicy, endeavoured to defend the Christian notion of God against the obvious atheistic consequences that were evoked by the critical thinkers of his time. This was because of the behaviour of the Christian churches, which were engaged in a war of mutual extermination.

The result of such theological efforts, however, was either to declare God himself as the originator of evil, to excuse evil as a consequence of divine "permission," or instead as with Hegel to understand world history as the justification of God (the true theodicy, the justification of God in history). These answers satisfied neither the Christian experience of faith nor thoughtful reflection. The German philosopher Immanuel Kant set the terms for much modern reflection on God's existence when he challenged the grounds of most previous efforts to prove it. Kant contended that it was finally impossible for the human intellect to achieve insights into the realm of the transcendent. Even as he was arguing this, modern science was shifting from grounds that presumed the nature of God and God's universe to autonomous views of nature that were grounded only in experiment, skepticism, and research. During the nineteenth century, philosophers in Kantian and scientific traditions despaired of the attempt to prove the existence of God.

During the same period, some Western intellectuals turned against the very idea of God. One strand of Hegelian thinkers, typified by the German philosopher Ludwig Feuerbach, attempted to unmask the idea of religion as illusion. To Feuerbach, faith was an ideology designed to help humans to delude themselves. The idea of dialectical materialism, in which the concept of "spirit" was dropped by thinkers such as Karl Marx, developed in this tradition. It also characterised religion as "bad faith" or "the opiate of the people,"[4] designed to seduce them from efforts to build a good society through the hope of rewards in a life to come.

At the same time, at first chiefly in Britain, scientific thinkers in the tradition of Charles Darwin hypothesised that evolutionary processes denied all biblical concepts of divine creation. Some dialectical materialists incorporated Darwinian theories in a frontal attack on the Christian worldview. Some Christians contended that this was a perversion of evolution, since certain Christian teachings on divine creation, such as *creatio continua* ("continuing creation"), were both biblical and compatible with evolutionary theory. At the turn of the twentieth century, some thinkers in both Britain and the United States optimistically reworked their doctrine of God by congruence with evolutionary thought.

Conception of God in Judaism

The idea of God has been subject to a continuous development in Jewish thought. But since the time of the prophets, the one constant element in that concept has been ethical monotheism. In Judaism God is the living and creative essence of the Universe. God is a transcendent and immanent, creator, and also father and personal God. The biblical text and rabbinic text both though reveal an awareness of philosophical issues like the nature of God or the question of creation they do not present a coherent and systematic analysis of these questions. Judaism is not and cannot be viewed as an abstract intellectual system, although some of its affirmations may be couched in such terms. It affirms divine sovereignty that was disclosed in creation (nature) and in history, without necessarily insisting upon-but at the same time not rejecting metaphysical speculation about the divine.[5]

Judaism insists that the community has been confronted by the divine not as abstraction but as person, with whom the community and its members enter into relationship. It is-as the concept *Torah* indicates a programme of human action, rooted in this personal confrontation. Divine personhood, most particularly disclosed in the use of the pronoun "*thou*" in direct address to God. The community and the individual, confronted by the Creator, teacher, redeemer, addresses the divine as living person, not as theological abstraction. Thirteen Articles constitute the creed of Judaism. They are: 1. The belief in the existence of a Creator. 2. The belief in his Unity. 3. The belief in his In-corporeality. 4. The belief in his Eternity. 5. The belief that all worship and adoration are due to him alone. 6. The belief in Prophecy. 7. The belief that Moses was the greatest of all Prophets, both before and after him. 8. The belief that the Law was revealed to Moses on Mount Sinai. 9. The belief in the Immutability of this revealed Torah. 10. The belief that God knows the acts of men. 11. The belief in Reward and Punishment.

12. The belief in the coming of the Messiah. 13. The belief in the Resurrection of the dead.

The first five beliefs concern about the God, the next four beliefs concerns the revelation. The next two concern to God's knowledge of the deeds of humankind and his concern about them. The last two concern the coming of the Messiah and the resurrection of the dead. First five fundamentals have generated considerable debates about the nature of God. In the Shema-often regarded as the Jewish confession of faith, or creed-the biblical material and accompanying benedictions are arranged to provide a unified statement about God and his relationship to the world and Israel, as well as Israel's obligations toward and response to God. In this statement, God, who is the Creator of the universe and who has chosen Israel in love ("Blessed art thou, O Lord, who has chosen thy people Israel in love"),[6] expressed by the giving of Torah, is declared to be "one"; his love is to be reciprocated by men who lovingly obey *Torah* and whose obedience is rewarded and rebellion punished. The goal of this obedience is God's "redemption" of Israel, a role foreshadowed by his action in bringing Israel out of Egypt.

One of the most intractable problems in Jewish thought is that of the divine omniscience. It holds the doctrine of ethical monotheism and emphasises the teachings of the oneness and uniqueness of God. "Medieval philosophers concerned with safeguarding the freedom of human action, worried whether God's foreknowledge of future contingent entailed the necessary occurrence of these events. That the force of God's knowledge need not be causal....the problem of divine omniscience has been resolved in favour of indeterminism. With respect to future contingents, God knows their ordered nature or essence and he knows that they are contingent, but he does not know which alternative will become actualised."[7]

Mysticism, an approach to the transcendent through the medium of experience, has been a part of Judaism from its origin in the biblical period. Kunin notes that "the biblical mystical experiences, particularly those found in the prophetic texts, are usually considered to be prophecy rather than mysticism. The distinction, however, is more to do with establishing the nature of authority-prophecy is authoritative."[8] Further, "the distinction between prophecy and authority become most relevant by the rabbinic period, at which the rabbis were developing new models of authority. Authority was no longer seen to be derived from literal communication or experience of God but rather through the process of engagement with God's word."[9]

At the centre of the liturgical formulation '*belief*' is the concept of the '*divine unity*'. In its original setting, it may have served as the theological statement of the reform under Josiah, king of Judah, in the seventh century BCE when worship was centered exclusively in Jerusalem, and all other cultic centers were rejected, so that the existence of one shrine only was understood as affirming one deity. The idea, however, acquired further meaning and it was understood towards the end of the pre-Christian era to proclaim against dualistic religious formulations in the Greco-Roman world-the unity of divine love and divine justice, as expressed in the divine names YAHWEH and Elohim, respectively.

Further expansion of this affirmation is found in the first two benedictions of the liturgical section, which together proclaim that the God who is the Creator of the universe and the God who is Israel's ruler and lawgiver are one and the same-as against religious positions that insisted that the Creator God and the lawgiver God were separate and even inimical. Subsequently, this affirmation was developed in philosophical and mystical terms by both medieval and modern thinkers. "The first Jewish philosopher was 'Philo' a cultured Alexandrian whose commitments to his people were evident...Adopting the Stoic techniques of allegory, Philo presented the Torah as a paradigm of rational legislation. Plato has called for a law that grounds its commands in reason, not sheer sanctions or obscure mystery. Underlying the Law authority was God's role as creator, not as arbitrary lord but as source of wisdom manifest in the nature."[10]

The Judaic affirmations about God have not always been given the same emphasis nor have they been understood in the same way. This was true in the Middle Ages, among both philosophers and mystics, as well as in modern times. In the nineteenth century, western European Jewish thinkers attempted to express and transform these affirmations in terms of German Idealist philosophy: more recently, philosophical naturalism was offered as the suitable content of Judaism, while retaining the traditional God language. The meaningfulness of the whole body of such affirmations, moreover, has been called into question by the philosophical schools of Logical Positivism and Linguistic Analysis. Most recently, the destruction of 6,000,000 Jews during the Nazi period has raised the issue of the validity of such concepts as God's presence in history, divine redemption, the covenant, and the chosen people. In every case, however, there challenges must deal with the structure of ideas noted here.

The concept of "creed," or "confession of faith," underscores in the first benediction the relation of God to the world as that of Creator to creation. The assertion is that his activity is not in the past but is ongoing and continuous. He "makes new continually, each day, the work of creation". This "creed" is concerned as well to come to terms with the ever-present problem of evil. Judaism, however, did not flinch from confronting the problem of pain and suffering in the world and affirming the paradox of suffering and divine sovereignty, of pain and divine providence, refusing to accept the concept of a partial God—a God that is Lord over only the harmonious and pleasant aspects of reality.

The second and the third benedictions deal with divine activity within the realm of history and human life. God is the teacher of men. Through the giving of instruction he acts in the life of mankind in historical events; he has chosen a particular people-Israel-in love to witness to his presence and his desire for a perfected society; he wills, as redeemer, enable man to experience that perfection. These activities, together with creation itself, are understood to express divine compassion and kindness as well as justice (judgment). Within this complex of ideas, other themes are interwoven. In the concept of the divine Creator there is a somewhat impersonal or remote quality—of a power above and apart from the world—which is underscored by such expressions as the threefold declaration of God's holiness, or divine otherness.

Thus, Judaism has strong belief in God, the God of Israel, will be the God of the whole world. In Israel, Judaism is considered as a privileged religion where finally the messiah is supposed to appear. This privilege marks Judaism as slightly anti- altruistic. The concluding phrase of the second benediction of the liturgical section referred to above reads: "who has chosen thy people Israel in love."[11] Here the basis of the relationship between God and Israel set forth in the biblical narrative is clearly and succinctly stated: the choice of this people was determined by no other factor than divine love. The patriarchal narratives, beginning with Genesis, presuppose the choice. "For you are a people consecrated to the Lord your God: of all the peoples on earth the Lord your God chose you to be His treasured people. It is not because you are the most numerous of peoples that the Lord set His heart on you and chose you-indeed you are the smallest of peoples; but it was because the Lord loved you and kept the oath He made with your fathers that the Lord freed you with a mighty hand and rescued you from the house of bondage, from the power of Pharaoh king of Egypt."[12]

Christian Doctrine of God

The central Christian affirmations about God are condensed and focused in the classic doctrine of the Trinity, which has its ultimate foundation in the special religious experience of the Christians in the first communities. This basis of experience is older than the doctrine of the Trinity. "This doctrine asserted that God is three in one and one in three. The Jewish origins of Christianity were reflected in the idea of god as one, while the Jewish Christian experience of Jesus and of the power of the spirit that had been felt as the new community took shape yielded the notion that Jesus was also divine and so was the spirit."[13] It consisted of the fact that the God came to meet Christians in a three-fold figure: firstly, as Creator, Lord of the history of salvation, Father, and Judge, as revealed in the Old Testament; secondly, as the Lord who, in the figure of Jesus Christ, lived among human beings and was present in their midst as the "Resurrected One"; and lastly as the Holy Spirit, whom they experienced as the power of the new life, the miraculous potency of the Kingdom of God. Thus, the Christian doctrine has the internal coherence of God as a trinity of persons. God is not a solitary, undifferentiated God; God is exemplified in the life of reciprocal love of the divine tri-personal life.

The problem is that how to reconcile the encounter with God in this threefold figure with faith in the oneness of God which was the Jews' and Christians' problem of many centuries. In the first two centuries of the Christian era, however, a series of different answers to this question stood in juxtaposition and none of the Christian theologians had considered them speculatively. Within the Christian perception about the experience of God, definite characteristic features stand out: Firstly, God as person, says that "I am who I am" designated in Exodus. According to this it is the personal consciousness of human beings that awakens? in the encounter with God understood as a person: "The Lord used to speak to Moses face to face, as a man speaks to his friend."[14]

Secondly, God is also viewed as the Creator of Heaven and Earth. The believer, acknowledges the divine omnipotence as the creative power of God, which also operates in the preservation of the world, and also trusts in the world, which—despite all its contradictions—is understood as one world created by God according to definite laws and principles and according to an inner plan. The decisive aspect of creation, however, is that God fashioned humans according to the divine image and made the creation subject to them. This special position of humans in the creation, which makes them coworkers of God in the preservation and consummation of the creation, brings a decisively new characteristic into the understanding of God.

Thirdly, this new characteristic that the God as the Lord of history, constitutes the main feature of the understanding of God in Old Testament. According to this understanding, the God selected a special people, made a special covenant with them and through the Law the divine agent binds this "people of God" in a special way. God set before them a definite goal of salvation that is the establishment of a divine dominion. However, whenever these special people are unfaithful to the covenant, God reveals through the prophets and admonish the people by proclamations of salvation. Fourthly, This God of history also is the God of judgment. Israelite genuinely believes that the God of history is also the God of Judgment and comes through the history of divinely-led people, with this inner logic, leads with proclamation of God as the Lord of world history and as the Judge of the world.

Lastly, in contrast with the Old Testament conception of God, New Testament illustrates the specific conception of God as Father, through the teachings of Jesus Christ. The faith in God lies in fact according to New Testament that this faith is so closely bound up with the person, teaching, and work of Jesus Christ that it is difficult to draw boundaries between theology (doctrines of God) and Christology (doctrines of Christ). The religious experience that forms the basis of the messianic self-understanding of Jesus is the recognition that the Messiah-Son of man is the Son of God. The special relationship of Jesus to God is expressed through his designation of God as Father. Jesus in his prayers used the Aramaic word *abba* ("father") for God, which is otherwise unusual in religious discourse in Judaism. This father–son relationship became a prototype for the relationship of Christians to God. Appeal to the son-ship of God played a crucial role in the development of Jesus' messianic self-understanding.

The early church experienced and recognised the incarnate and resurrected Son of God in the person of Jesus. The disciples' testimony served as confirmation for them that Jesus really is the exalted Lord and Son of God, who sits at the right hand of the Father and will return in glory to consummate the Kingdom. From the beginning of the church, different interpretations of the person of Jesus have existed alongside one another. The Gospel, According to Mark, for example, understands Jesus as the man upon whom the Holy Spirit descends at the baptism in Jordan and who is declared the Son of God through the voice of God from the clouds. Two schools of thought developed - one associated with Antioch in Syria and the other with Alexandria in Egypt. The theological school of Antioch followed the humanity of Jesus and viewed his divinity in his consciousness of God, founded in the divine mission that was imposed upon him by God through the infusion of the Holy Spirit. "The incarnation was the doctrine that God had become human in Jesus. And this should not be interpreted as some kind of spirit coming to dwell in a body? Jesus of Nazareth was human and really was divine in his very identity as one person."[15]

Another view was the Catechetical school of Alexandrian theology. This view is expressed by the Gospel, According to John, which regards the figure of Jesus Christ, as the divine Logos become flesh. Here, the divinity of the person of Jesus is understood not as the endowment of the man, Jesus with a divine power, but rather as the result of the descent of the divine Logos—a preexistent heavenly being—into the world: the Logos taking on a human body of flesh to be realised in history. Thus, the struggle to understand the figures of Jesus Christ created a rivalry between the theologies of Antioch and Alexandria.

In Christian theology, two tendencies stand in constant tension with each other. On the one hand, there is the tendency to systematize the idea of God as far as possible. On the other, there is the tendency to eliminate the accumulated collection of current conceptions of God and to return to the understanding of the utter transcendence of God. Theologians, largely, have had to acknowledge the limits of human reason and language to address the "character" of God, who is beyond normal human experience but who impinges on it. However, because of the divine–human contact, it became necessary and possible for them to make some assertions about the experience, the disclosure, and the character of God. Mystics of the Christian religion argue that God cannot be understood by the categories of human thought. Because of their religious experiences, the mystics of Christianity of all eras have concurred in the belief that one can make no assertions about God, because God is beyond all concepts and images.

In Christian theology, the Holy Spirit of God becomes one of the most elusive and difficult themes, because it refers to one of the three Persons in the God, but does not evoke concrete images the way "Father" or "Creator" and "Son" or "Redeemer" do. Reference to the Holy Spirit includes the true creative element in the life of the church. It works in an apparently contradictory sense: by virtue of its authority, the Holy Spirit establishes law and breaks the same law, it institutes order and breaks the order, and it founds tradition and breaks that tradition. It is the conservative as well as the revolutionary principle in church history. It guarantees the continuity of the church and yet it interrupts this continuity through new creations. Both sides of this activity stand in a characteristic relationship of tension to one another.

The essence of the expression of the Holy Spirit is free spontaneity. The Spirit blows like the wind, "where it wills," but where it blows it establishes a firm norm by virtue of its divine authority. The spirit of prophecy and the spirit of knowledge (*gnôsis*) are not subject to the will of the prophet and the enlightened one; revelation of the Spirit in the prophetic word or in the word of knowledge becomes Holy Scripture, which as "divinely breathed" "cannot be broken" and lays claim to a lasting validity for the church[16]. All the expressions of church life—doctrine, office, polity, sacraments, power to loosen and to bind, and prayer—are understood as endowed by the Spirit. The same Holy

Spirit, however, also comes forth as the revolutionising, freshly creating principle in church history.

Concept of God in Islam

The most concise definition of God in Islam is given in the four verses of *Surah Ikhlas* which is Chapter 112 of the *Qur'an*. God is described in the *Qur'an* as both the Creator, the originator of all that exists, and the Judge, the end point that exists. The *Qur'an* says 'He is Allah, The One and only the one. 'Allah', the Eternal, Absolute. "He begets not, nor is He begotten. And there is none like unto Him."[17] The word '*Assamad*' is difficult to translate. It means 'absolute existence', which can be attributed only to Allah (*swt*), all other existence being temporal or conditional. It also means that Allah (*swt*) is not dependant on any person or thing, but all persons and things are dependant on Him. "God alone... is understood to be one whose very nature is to exist: everything else must have existence bestowed upon it by the One to whom everything that is traces its origination."[18]

Surah Ikhlas of the Glorious *Qur'an* is the touchstone of theology. '*Theo*' in Greek means God and '*logy*' means study. Thus, Theology means study of God and to Muslims this four line definition of Almighty God serves as the touchstone of the study of God. Any candidate to divinity must be subjected to this 'acid test'. Since the attributes of Allah given in this chapter are unique, false gods and pretenders to divinity can be easily dismissed using these verses. The Muslims prefer calling the Supreme Creator, Allah. If God only takes a human form but does not become a human being, He should not possess any human qualities. We know that all the 'God-men', have human qualities and failings. They have all the human needs such as the need to eat, sleep, etc.

According to this the worship of God in human form is therefore a logical fallacy and should be abhorred in all its forms and manifestations. That is the reason why the *Qur'an* speaks against all forms of anthropomorphism. The Glorious *Qur'an* says in the following verse: "There is nothing whatever like unto Him."[19] The attributes of Almighty God preclude any evil since God is the source of justice, mercy and truth. God can never be thought of as doing an ungodly act. Hence, we cannot imagine God telling a lie, being unjust, making a mistake, forgetting things, or having any such human failings. Similarly, God can do injustice if He chooses to, but He will never do it because being unjust is an ungodly act.

The *Qur'an* the sacred book of Islam says that the "Allah is never unjust in the least degree."[20] God can be unjust if He chooses to be so, but the moment God does injustice, He ceases to be God. God can make mistakes if He wants to, but He does not make mistakes because making a mistake is an ungodly act. The *Qur'an* says: "...my Lord never errs."[21] The moment God makes a mistake, he ceases to be God. Many religions at some point believe, directly or indirectly, in the philosophy of anthropomorphism i.e. God becoming a human. Their contention is that Almighty God is so pure and holy that He is unaware of the hardships, shortcomings and feelings of human beings. In order to set the rules for human beings, He came down to earth as a human. Not only does god possess unique attributes, but also each attribute of Almighty God is sufficient to identify him.

Similarly the attribute of Almighty God should be unique. If we say God is the constructor of buildings, it is possible and true, but it is not unique. Thousands of people can construct a building, but each attribute of God is unique and points to none but Allah. For example, God is the creator of the universe. If someone asks who the creator of the universe is, the answer is only one, i.e. Almighty God is the Ultimate Creator. Islamic thought held the view tenaciously to the premise that the universe is freely created and continuously sustained by a sovereign God."[22] Similarly, following are some of the many unique attributes possessed by none other than the Creator of the universe, Almighty Allah: "*Ar-Raheem*", the Most Merciful "*Ar-Rahman*", the Gracious "*Al-Hakeem*", the Most Wise So when one asks, "Who is '*Ar-Raheem*', (the Most Merciful)?", there can only be one answer: "Almighty Allah".[23]

Besides the attribute being unique, it should not contradict other attributes. Similarly, if someone says that God is the Creator of the Universe and has one head, two hands, two feet, etc., the attribute (Creator of the Universe) is correct but the associated quality (in the form of human being) is wrong and false. Since there is only one God, all the attributes should point to one and the same God. Both these unique qualities belong to one and the same person. Similarly, to say that "the Creator of the universe is one God and the Cherisher is another God is absurd because God possesses all these attributes combined together."[24]

Polytheists argue that the existence of more than one God is not illogical. According to them, if there were more than one God, they would dispute with one another, each god trying to fulfill his will against the will of the other gods. This can be seen in the mythology of the polytheistic and pantheistic religions. If a 'God' is defeated or unable to defeat the others, he is surely not the one true God. Also popular among polytheistic religions is the idea of many Gods, each having different responsibilities. Each one would be responsible for a part of man's existence e.g. a Sun-God, a Rain-God, etc. This indicates that one 'God' is incompetent of certain acts and moreover he is also ignorant of the other Gods' powers, duties, functions and responsibilities. There cannot be an ignorant and incapable God. If there were more than one God it would surely lead to confusion, disorder, chaos and destruction in the universe. But the universe is in complete harmony. "Muslims are thus called upon to be monotheists to believe in and worship only one God…with Muhammad as the final messenger."[25]

The important category called '*Tawheed ar-Ruboobeeyah'*. '*Ruboobeeyah'* is derived from the root verb "*Rabb*" meaning Lord, Sustainer and Cherisher. Therefore, '*Tawheed-ar-Ruboobeeyah*' means maintaining the unity of Lordship. This category is based on the fundamental concept that Allah (*swt*) alone caused all things to exist when there was nothing. He created or originated of all that exists out of nothing. He alone is the sole Creator, Cherisher, and Sustainer of the complete universe and all between it, without any need from it or for it. The second category is '*Tawheed al Asmaa* was *Sifaat'* which means maintaining the unity of Allah's name and attributes. This category is divided into five aspects: Allah must be referred to according to the manner in which He and His prophet have described Him without explaining His names and attributes by giving them meanings other than their obvious meanings. Secondly, Allah must be referred to without giving Him any new names or attributes. For example, Allah may not be given the name *Al-Ghaadib* (the Angry One), despite the fact that He has said that He gets angry, because neither Allah nor His messenger have used this name. According to this, while referring to God; we should strictly abstain from giving Him the attributes of those whom He has created.

God is portrayed in the Bible as repented for His bad thoughts in the same way as humans do when they realise their errors. This is completely against the principle of Tawheed. God does not commit any mistakes or errors and therefore never needs to repent. The key principle that deals with Allah's attributes is given in the *Qur'an* in Surah Ash-Shura: "There is nothing whatever likes unto Him, And He is the One That hears and sees (all things)."[26] Thus, to refer to a human with the attribute of God is referring to a person as one who has no beginning or end (eternal) is against the principle of *Tawheed*. Some Divine names in the indefinite form, like '*Raoof*' or '*Raheem*' are permissible names for men, as Allah has used them for Prophets; but '*Ar-Raoof*' (the Most Pious) and *Ar-Raheem* (the most Merciful) can only be used if prefixed by '*Abd*' meaning 'slave of' or 'servant of' i.e. '*Abdur-Raoof*' or '*Abdur-Raheem*'. Similarly '*Abdur-Rasool*' (slave of the Messenger) or '*Abdun-Nabee*' (slave of the Prophet) is forbidden.[27] The central theme of Islamic teaching and practice has consistently been that of the submission to Allah, the Creator and the Judge of the Universe. Submission to God is understood not passively, but rather actively in the sense of making to submit.

According to Iqbal, the famous Indian philosopher, God is immanent since God comprehends the whole universe, but also transcendent since God is not identical with the created world. Nature, however, does not confront God in the same way as it confronts humanity, since it is a phase of God's consciousness. All life is individual. There is a gradually rising scale of selfness running from the almost inert to God who is the Ultimate Ego. God is not immobile nor is the universe a fixed product; God is constantly creative and dynamic and the process of Creation still goes on. The *Qur'anic* saying, 'Toward God is your limit' gives Iqbal an infinite worldview and he applies it to every aspect of the life of humanity and the universe.

The Nature and Objective of Soul in Islamic Philosophy

The discussion of the human soul, its existence, nature, ultimate objective and eternity, occupies a highly important position in Islamic philosophy and forms its focus. For the Muslim philosophers, like their Greek predecessors, the soul consists of non-rational and rational parts. The non-rational part, they divided into the plant and animal souls, the rational part into the practical and the theoretical intellects. They believe that the non-rational part is linked essentially to the body, but some considered the rational part as separate from the body by nature and others that all the parts of the soul are by nature material. These philosophers agree that "the soul is in the body, its non-rational part is to manage the body, its practical intellect is to manage worldly affairs, including those of the body, and its theoretical intellect is to know the eternal aspects of the universe."[28] They thought that the ultimate end or happiness of the soul depends on its ability to separate itself from the demands of the body and to focus on grasping the eternal aspects of the universe. Most of them believed that the non-rational soul comes into being and unavoidably perishes. Some, like *al-Farabi*, believed that the rational soul may or may not survive eternally; others like Ibn Sina believed that it has no beginning and no end; still others, such as Ibn Rushd, believed that the soul with its entire individual parts comes into the existence and is eventually destroyed.

Many Muslim philosophers concerned themselves with the subject of the soul. However, the most detailed and most important works on this subject are those of *al-Kindi*, *al-Farabi*, Ibn Sina and Ibn Rushd. Muslim philosophers recognised the first issue that confronts the human mind with regard to the soul is its existence. Ibn Sina or Avicenna as he is known in the West, at the very beginning of his inquiry about the soul in *al-Shifa*' (Healing), asserts that the existence of the soul from the fact that we observe bodies that perform certain acts with some degree of will. These acts are exemplified in taking nourishment, growing, reproducing, moving and perceiving. Since these acts do not belong to the nature of bodies, for this nature is devoid of will, they must belong to a principle they have other than bodies. This principle is what is called 'soul'.

This argument is intended to prove the existence of the animal soul, which includes the plant soul. The soul is the source of acts performed by the will, not inasmuch as it is 'a substance' (an independent entity), but inasmuch as it is 'the principle of such acts'. The rational soul, on the other hand, need not look outside itself to infer its existence. It is aware of its existence with immediacy, that is, without any instruments. Ibn Sina's example of the suspended "man is intended to prove that the rational soul is aware of itself apart from any body."[29] His argument boils down to the view that, even if the adult rational soul is not aware of anything material, not even its body, it remains aware of its own existence.

While Islam made it incumbent on Muslim philosophers to occupy themselves extensively with the study of the soul and to make certain statements that in some cases appear consistent with Islamic beliefs, Greek philosophy had the upper hand in forming the real convictions of Muslim philosophers with regard to the nature of the soul. Unless otherwise specified, reference to the soul here is limited to the terrestrial soul to the exclusion of the celestial one, since Muslim philosophers concerned themselves primarily with the former. It must be pointed out at the outset that '*soul*' (nafs) was used in more than one sense in Islamic philosophy; the term was used to refer to the plant or vegetative part of a living being, the animal or sensitive part, the rational part and finally the totality of all three parts. The first two are the non-rational soul and the totality is the human soul, and 'human soul' is used only in the sense of this fourth type of soul. The plant, animal and rational souls are also called powers or parts of the soul. Only from the context can one understand whether a Muslim philosopher was using 'soul' in the broad sense to mean the human soul (the totality of the parts of the soul), or in the narrow sense to mean a specific part of the human soul.

Inasmuch as it has a certain relation to a body, the soul is a form for that body, that is, the perfection of that body. It is a form because a natural body is composed of matter and form, which in the case of animals are body and soul. Since it has been shown that the soul is the source of will and therefore is not matter, it remains a form. Perfection is of two types, primary and secondary. A primary perfection is what makes a thing actually a species, as shape does for the sword, or a genus, as sensation and movement do for animals. A secondary perfection is an act necessitated by the nature of the species or genus, such as cutting for the sword and touching for animal. The soul is a primary perfection of a natural body capable of performing the secondary perfections necessitated by this primary perfection. Together with its body, the soul constitutes a material substance. This substance can be the subject of plant, animal or human life.[30]

Al-Farabi asserts that even though the soul is of different parts, it is a unity with all its parts working for one end, happiness. While the plant soul, for example, serves a specific function, it also serves the powers that are higher than the animal powers it in rank. Without nourishment, growth and reproduction, the animal powers cannot perform their necessary functions. Similarly, while the function of the animal powers is to have sensation and movement, by performing this function they also promote the functions of the powers above them, the rational ones. The operations of the animal powers, especially those of the senses, are particularly important for the attainment of the final end. The external senses strip the forms from material objects and convey them to the internal senses. The more they are transferred internally, the less mixed with matter do they become. Since the innermost sense they reach is the imagination, they are there in their purest material existence.

The role of the objects of the imagination is not always clearly defined in Islamic philosophy. Occasionally it is said by somebody like Ibn Sina to be one of preparation for the theoretical intellect to receive the universals from the agent intellect. At other times, Ibn Sina, like other Aristotelians such as Ibn Rushd, takes these objects to be the ingredients out of which the universals are made after the last process of purification. It seems, however, that in either case the light of the agent intellect is needed to complete the process. In the former case, this light gives the intelligible forms to the theoretical intellect when this intellect is prepared. In the latter case, it sheds itself on the objects of the imagination, which are then reflected on the theoretical intellect without their matter. Since the theoretical intellect is in its first stages in potentiality, it cannot act on the objects of the imagination directly; hence the need for the agent intellect, which is pure actuality. The role of the practical intellect in all this is to put order into the body. This set free the theoretical intellect from preoccupation with the body and helps the powers whose function is necessary for theoretical knowledge to function unhampered.

Muslim philosophers assert that the soul comes into existence simultaneously with the coming into existence of the body, however,

Ibn Sina believe that the rational soul is in essence of non-material thinking only the non-rational soul. Others, such as Ibn Rushd, who believe that the rational soul is originally not separate from matter, contend that the whole human soul comes into existence. The latter believe that since the rational soul grasps the universals from particular sensible, and since such sensible are material and have a temporal beginning, this soul must also be material and must have a temporal beginning. Those who attribute non-materiality to the essence of the rational soul, such as al-Kindi and Ibn Sina, assert that this soul pre-exists the body. While all of them agree that "the non-rational soul is destroyed after the destruction of the body, they differ with regard to the end of the rational soul."[31] Al-Kindi and Ibn Sina, for example, strongly adhere to the view that all rational souls are indestructible because by nature they are simple. Al-Farabi reminds us that the reason for eternal existence is the rational soul's knowledge of the eternal aspects of the universe.

Iqbal's philosophy is often described as the philosophy of *khudi*, or the Self. For him, the fundamental fact of human life is the absolute and irrefutable consciousness of one's own being. For Iqbal, the advent of humanity on earth is a great and glorious event, not an event signifying human sinfulness and degradation. He points out that according to the *Qur'an*, the earth is humanity's 'dwelling-place' and 'a source of profit' to it. Iqbal does not think that having been created by God, human beings were placed in a super sensual paradise from which they were expelled on account of an act of disobedience to God. Pointing out that the term 'Adam' functions as the symbol of self-conscious humanity rather than as the name of an individual in the Quraan, Iqbal describes the 'Fall' as a transition from 'a primitive state of instinctive appetite to the conscious possession of a free self, capable of doubt and disobedience'.[32]

For Iqbal, Adam's story is not the story of the 'First Man' but the ethical experience, in symbolic form, of every human being. Following the *Qur'anic* teaching that though human beings come from the earth, God's spirit has been breathed into them, Iqbal holds on the one hand that human beings are divinely created, and on the other hand that they have evolved from matter. Unlike dualists, Iqbal sees no impassable gulf between matter and spirit, nor does he see human beings as a mere episode or accident in the huge evolutionary process. On the contrary, the whole cosmos is there to serve as the basis and ground for the emergence and perfection of the Ego. Humanity's evolution has not ended, for the destiny of human beings lies 'beyond the stars'.

The purpose of life is the development of the Self. In order that they may achieve the fullest possible development, it is essential for human beings to possess knowledge. Iqbal distinguishes between two aspects of the Self, the efficient and the appreciative. The efficient self is that which is concerned with, and is itself partially formed by, the physical world. It apprehends the succession of impressions and discloses itself as a series of specific, and consequently numerable, states. The appreciative self is the deeper self, of which one becomes aware only in moments of profound meditation when the efficient self is in abeyance. The unity of the appreciative self is that in it, each experience permeates the whole. The multiplicity of its elements is unlike that of the efficient self. There is change and movement, but this change and movement are indivisible; their elements interpenetrate and are non-serial in character.

Iqbal believes ardently that human beings are the makers of their own destiny and that the key to destiny lies in one's character. He constantly refers to the *Qur'anic* verse, 'Verily God will not change the condition of a people till they change what is in themselves'[33] Humanity's mission on earth is not only to win greater freedom but also to gain immortality. According to Iqbal 'it is not ours by right; it is to be achieved by personal effort, man is only a candidate for it.'[34]

Concept of Man in Judaism

In Genesis there are two terms 'image' and 'likeness' which indicates clearly the biblical understanding of man's essential nature: he is created in the image and likeness of God. Thus, the man is image of God in Judaism.[35] The Jewish community that was deeply influenced by Greek philosophical ideas offers a dualistic interpretation of man. For some thinkers the divine likeness is immortal, intellectual soul as contrasted to the body. Still other thinkers, both ancient and modern, have understood that likeness to be ethical, with particular emphasis placed on freedom of the will. The biblical view of man as an inseparable psychosomatic unit meant that the death was understood to be his dissolution. Yet, although man ceased to be, this dissolution was not utter extinction. Some of the power that functioned in the unit may have continued to exist, but it was not to be understood any longer as life. The existence of the dead in *Sheol,* the neither world, was not living but the shadow or echo of living.

Thus, for most of the biblical writers this existence was without experience, either of God or of anything else; it was unrelated to events. To call it immortality is to empty that term of any vital significance. However, this concept of *Sheol,* along with belief in the possibility of occasional miraculous restorations of dead individuals to life, and perhaps even the idea of the revival of the people of Israel from the "death" of exile, provided a foothold for the development of belief in the resurrection of the dead body at some time in the future.

In subsequent apocalyptic literature, a sharper distinction between body and soul was entertained, and the latter was conceived of as existing separately in a disembodied state after death. Although at this point the doctrine of the resurrection of the body was not put aside, nonetheless, the direction of thinking changed. The shades of *Sheol* were now thought of as souls, and real personal survival - with continuity between life on earth and in *Sheol* was posited. True life after death was now seen as release from the bondage of the body, so that in place of, or alongside of, the afterlife of physical resurrection was set the afterlife of the immortal soul.

Christian Doctrine of Man

Christian theologians used the general term man to cover both sexes when referring to human beings. The literature on the subject consistently refers to anthropology in theology as "the doctrine of man," but it must be understood as that of "human" or "*human being.*" The starting point for the Christian understanding of what it is to be human is the recognition that humans are created after the image of God. This idea views God and humans joined with one another through a mysterious connection. God is thought of as incomprehensible and beyond substance; yet God desired to reflect the divine image in one set of creatures and chose humans for this. Man as the image of God belongs, therefore, to the self-revelation of God in quite a decisive way. God, being reflected in the human creature, makes this being a partner in the realisation of the divine self; there is constant interaction between man and God.[36]

The idea of the human being as the creature created according to the image of God was already being interpreted in a twofold direction in the early church. Man like all other creatures of the universe is a creation of God. This creature is thus not divine but at the same time is not created out of nothingness; as creatures human beings stand in a relationship of utter dependency on God. The divide between God and humanity had been bridged forever. This bonding between God's nature and human nature had become inseparably eternal in the person of Jesus.

Thus, humanity has nothing from themselves but owe everything, even their being, exclusively to the will of the divine Creator; they are joined with all other fellow creatures through a relationship of solidarity. This idea of the solidarity of the creatures among one another almost completely receded behind the idea of the special position of humans and their special commission of dominion. The idea of solidarity with all creatures has been expressed and practiced by but few charismatic personalities in the history of Western devoutness, such as by Francis of Assisi in his "Canticle of the Sun", "Praised be Thou, my Lord, with all Thy creatures, especially with our sister sun."[37] The second aspect of the idea of the human being as a creature operated very much more emphatically: the superiority of humans over all other creatures. God placed humans in a special relationship to the divine. God created them in the divine image, thereby assigning to human's a special commission vis-à-vis all other creatures.

The Human as the Image of God

Christian theology attempted to regard the image of God in human beings as restricted simply to their intellectual capability and faculty of perception. In his work *De Trinitate,* Augustine attempted to ascertain traces of divine Trinity in the human intellect. Christian mysticism confronted this dualistic view of humans. It understood humans in their mind–body entirety as being in the image of God. The image of God is stamped all the way into the sphere of human corporeality. The idea of human creation according to the image of God is already based upon the intention of the Incarnation, the self-representation of God in corporeality. Even according to their somatic (bodily) condition, humans are the universal form of being, in whom the powers and creative principles of the whole universe are combined in a personal unity of spirit, soul, and body.

The Christian understanding of evil is also linked with the idea of human creation according to the image of God. Evil cannot, in the Christian view, be derived from the dualistic assumption of the contrasts of spirit and body, reason and matter. According to the Christian understanding, the triumph of evil is not identical with the victory of matter, the "flesh," over the spirit. The only genuine departure point for the Christian view of evil is the idea of freedom, which is based in the concept of the human being as the image of God. The human is person because God is person. It is apparent in Christian claims that the concept of the human as "being-as-person" is the real seal of that human as "being-as-the-image-of-God," and therein lays the true nobility that distinguishes human beings from all other creatures. If the Christian faith is differentiated from other religions through the fact that for the Christian God is person, then this faith takes effect in the thereby resulting consequence that the human being, too, is person. God at the same time entered into a great risk in creating the human as person.

The real sign of God as personal being is freedom. God created humans according to his image; he also gave over to them this mark of nobility-*i.e.,* freedom. Only through this freedom the human beings as partner of God offer free love to God. Only in this freedom God's love is answered through free love in return. This alone constitutes the presupposition of love. Love in its fulfilled form, according to the Christian understanding, is possible only between persons; conversely, the person can be realised only in the complete love to another person. Humans can use this freedom to offer God, their Creator, their freely given love. Yet, in the gift of freedom, there also lay the possibility for humans to decide against God and to raise themselves to the goal of divine love. The event that is portrayed in the Mosaic creation story as the fall of man is essentially the trying out of freedom, the free decision of humans against God. This rebellion consists of the fact that human beings improperly use their God-given freedom to set themselves against God and even to wish to be "like God."[38]

This special interpretation of sin renders the specific Christian understanding of human redemption, the view that Jesus Christ as the historical figure of the Redeemer i.e., the specific Christian view of the incarnation of God in Jesus Christ. Members of Asian high religions have found it difficult to understand the fundamental Christian idea of the incarnation. The religious person of the East is inclined to understand the Christian idea of incarnation as an analogy to the Hindu concept of the *avatâra* (best rendered as incarnation). The starting point of the latter is that the divine descends to Earth ever again and is constantly clothed anew in a human figure, in order to reveal the heavenly truth to every era and all people in a manner comprehensible to them. Thus, it was natural to understand the figure of Jesus Christ also as such an *avatâra*, as a form of descent of the divine to humanity.

The Christian understanding of the incarnation, however, is based upon a fundamentally different idea, which is enclosed in the simple saying of the Gospel According to John, "The Word became flesh."[39] Whereas the *avatâra* concept assumes that the divine appears in the cyclic lapse of time periods-continually occurring, now in this, now in that earthly veil-the incarnation of the divine Logos in Jesus Christ is, according to the Christian view, a definitively unique happening.

"*Rebirth*" has often been identified with a definite, temporally datable form of "conversion." In the history of Christian piety a line of prominent personalities experienced their rebirth in the form of a temporally datable and also locally ascertainable conversion event. Fixation upon a single type of experience, however, is factually not justified. There are numerous other forms of completion of that mysterious event characterised with the expression of rebirth. The mode of experience of rebirth itself is as manifold as the individuality of the person concerned, his special intellectual or emotional endowment, and his special history. The different forms of rebirth experience are distinguished according to not only whether the event sets in suddenly with overwhelming surprise, as when one is "born again" or "sees the light," or as the result of a slow process, a "growing," a "maturing," and an "evolution." They are also distinguished according to the psychic capability predominant at the time that thereby takes charge (will, intellect), the endowment at hand, and the personal type of religious experience.

Rebirth, in voluntary type, is expressed in a new alignment of the will, in the liberation of new capabilities and powers that were hitherto undeveloped in the person concerned. With the intellectual type, it leads to an activation of the capabilities for understanding, to the breakthrough of a "vision." For others, it leads to the discovery of an unexpected beauty in the order of nature or to the discovery of the mysterious meaning of history. Rebirth leads to a new vision of the moral life and its orders, to a selfless realisation of love of neighbours. In the experience of Christian rebirth, the hitherto existing old condition of humanity is not simply eliminated so far as the given personality structure is concerned-a structure dependent upon heredity, education, and earlier life experiences. Instead, each person affected perceives his life in Christ at any given time as "newness of life."

The condition of "fallen" humanity is frequently characterised in the New Testament as "slavery." It is the slavery of human willfulness that wants to have and enjoy all things for itself: the slavery of alienated love, which is no longer turned toward God but toward one's own self and the things of this world and which also, degrades one's own self into the means for egoism and exploitation. The servitude of people fallen away from God is much more oppressive than mere slavery of the senses and of greed for life. It is the enslavement not only of their "flesh" but also of all levels of their being, even the "most spiritual."

Freedom alone also makes a perfect community possible. Such a community embraces God and the neighbour, in whom the image of God confronts human beings in the flesh. Community is fulfilled in the free service of love. Luther probably most pertinently articulated the paradox of Christian freedom, which includes both love and service: "A Christian man is a free lord of all things and subordinate to no one. A Christian man is a submissive servant of all things and subject to everyone."[40] Christian freedom is thus to be understood neither purely individually nor purely collectively. The motives of the personal and the social are indivisibly joined by the idea that each person is indeed an image of God for himself alone, but that in Christ he also recognises the image of God in the neighbour, and with the neighbour is a member in the one body of Christ. Here, too, the evaluative principle of the idea of freedom is not to be mistaken; in it, for example, lay the spiritual impetus to the social and racial emancipation of slaves, as it was demanded by the great Christian champions of human rights in the eighteenth and nineteenth centuries and, through great efforts, pursued and achieved.

The Islam Doctrine of Man

The rationality of God and soul is defined as a primary perfection for an organic natural body in as much as this body can act by rational choice and grasp the universals, is divided into the practical and the theoretical intellectuals. The practical intellectual seeks knowledge in order to act in accordance with the good in its individual body, its family and its state. It must, therefore, know the principles for properly managing the body, the family and the state, that is, ethics and spirituality.

The practical intellectual is the rational soul turning its face downward. The function of the theoretical intellect is to know just for the sake of having the universals (the realities or natures of things). Some of these natures, such as God and the intellect, cannot attach to movement; knowledge of them is metaphysics. Other natures, such as unity, can attach to movement but do not; knowledge of them is mathematics. Still other natures, such as humanity and squareness, can attach to movement in either reality or thought. The theoretical intellect is the rational soul with its face upward.

The practical intellect looks up to the theoretical one and moves its body accordingly. In this, the practical intellect is similar to the celestial soul that looks up to the intellect of its sphere and moves its sphere accordingly. Thus, like the celestial soul, the practical intellect is the link between intellects as such and matter. The perfection of human life is to know God. Since this knowledge is not possible to achieve by philosophy, by faith, or by inspiration from separated intellect, "it is not possible for man to achieve it in this life."[41] Even in the future life, the vision of God cannot be acquired by knowing the angels or other separated souls, but only God himself can give it. That is through the gift of glory, which is an adaptation of the soul to see God. This vision is not comprehensive, but it is available to every soul to the extent of its readiness.

Though humanity is the pivot around which Iqbal's philosophy revolves, Iqbal's 'revaluation of Man is not that of Man qua Man, but of Man in relation to God'. Iqbal's Ideal Person is the Servant of God. The relation between humanity and God is a personal one; hence the great importance of prayer in the thought of Iqbal. The belief in the one living God gives humanity freedom from all false deities and fortifies it against forces of disintegration. Iqbal sees his concept of the Ideal Person realised in the Prophet of Islam, whose life exemplifies all the principles dearest to Iqbal's heart. In his view art, religion and ethics must be judged from the standpoint of the Self. That which strengthens the Self is good and that which weakens it is bad. Iqbal does not admit the absolute existence of evil but regards it as being necessary for the actualisation of moral purpose as vital activity in the world. His bliss (or *al-Shaytan*, Satan) is the counterpart to his Ideal Person.

Morality in Judaism

Judaism teaches that the world is created by a loving all-powerful God who has created human beings as the free agents in his image. God has promulgated certain rules or laws for his children and they have to obey them. Thus, the essence of morality in Judaism is that if we are to live as we should live we must follow God's commandments. Judaism is a religion that oriented towards practical perfection in this world. Practice or the living of a Jewish life is more significant in shaping the Jewish identity. This practical orientation finds its concrete expression in the codified norms of Torah based behaviour called *Halakhah* or Jewish law. While much of *Halakhah* is given over to what we would today call religious or ritual law. Literature on Jewish ethics can be divided into four main categories: biblical, rabbinic, medieval and modern. Perhaps the best-known ethical teachings of the Bible are included in the 'Ten Commandments' that are found in Exodus 20. Of the ten discrete statements in this text, at least six have direct ethical import.....the remaining four relates to the matters of theological and ritual importance.[42]

Man is in a state of tension or equilibrium between the two foci of creation, the "*heavenly*" and the "*earthly*." He necessarily participates in both, and, as such, is the one responsible creature who can truly serve his Creator, for he alone, having both sides of creation in him, may choose between them. It is the ability to make an ethical choice that it is the distinguishing mark of man. This ability is not derived from the "*heavenly*" side but resides in the double basis of man's existence. It is important to recognise this as something other than a body-soul dualism in which the soul is the source of good and the body the basis of evil. Such an attitude, however, did appear in some rabbinic material and it was often affirmed in medieval philosophical and mystical speculations and by some of the later moralists.

The implicit assumption of the pre-patriarchal stories is man's ability to choose between obedience and disobedience. Rabbinic Judaism, taking up the covenant-making episode between God and Noah, developed it as the basis of humankind's ethical obligation. All men, not merely the Jews, were engaged in a covenant relationship with God. Thus, man's nature ethically was explained in rabbinic Judaism not only as a tension between the "*heavenly*" and "*earthly*" components but also as a tension between two "*impulses*." Here again, fragmentary and allusive biblical materials were developed into more comprehensive statements.

It is this ethically free creature who stands within the covenant relationship and who may choose to be obedient or disobedient. Sin, then, is ultimately deliberate disobedience or rebellion against the divine sovereign. This is more easily observed in relation to Israel, for it is here that the central concern of Judaism which is most evident and the subject discussed in detail. It should be noted, however, that according to Judaic tradition, all humankind stands within a covenant relation to God and is commanded to be moral and just, essentially the same choice is made universally.

Morality and Society in Judaism

Jewish affirmations about God and man intersect in the concept of *Torah* as the ordering of human existence in the direction of the divine. Man, however is understood, as an ethically responsible creature responsive to the presence of God in nature and in history. Although that responsiveness is expressed on many levels, it is within the horizontal relationship of man to man that it is most explicitly called for. The Pentateuch legislation sets down, albeit within the limitations of the structures of the ancient Middle East, the patterns of interpersonal relations. The prophetic messages are deeply concerned with these demands and see the disregard of them as the source of social and individual disorder. No segment of society, even the most exalted, is free of ethical obligation. Indeed, the transformation of prophetism from its earlier form as ecstaticism and soothsaying is seen in the ethical confrontation of David by Nathan ("Thou art the man") for seducing Bathsheba and arranging to have her husband killed. What is particularly striking is the affirmation that God is not only the source of ethical obligation but is himself the paradigm of it.

The theme, *imitatio Dei* ("imitation of God"), as developed in rabbinic Judaism, expressed succinctly in a comment on the verse from Deuteronomy quoted above. In response to the question of how it is possible to walk "in all His ways," the reply is made "As He is merciful and gracious, so are you merciful and gracious. As He is righteous so be you righteous. As He is holy, strive to be holy."[43] Indeed even more daringly, God is described as clothing the naked, nursing the sick, comforting the mourners, burying the dead, so that man may recognise his own obligations. Since human beings are created in the image of God it is obvious that one achieves the highest possible level of perfection or self-realisation by becoming similar to the God as humanly possible. This is the basis for what may be the single most important ethical doctrine of the Hebrew Bible, that of *imitation Dei,* the imitation of God. What stands out in the entire development of Jewish ethical formulations is the constant interpenetration of communal and individual obligations and concerns. Although in the Book of Ezekiel emphasis is laid on individual responsibility, "the person who sins shall die," in contrast to the more widespread statement of communal involvement, "visiting the sins of the fathers upon the children".[44] These two aspects of ethical conduct are never entirely distinguished in Judaism. The just society requires the just man, and the just man functions within the just society.

The concrete expression of ethical requirements in legal precepts took place with both ends in view, so that the process of beginning of the holy community and the formation of the *asid* ("pious"), the man of steadfast devotion to God, were concomitant processes. The relationship between the two is of course, often mediated by the historical situation, so that in some periods one or the other moves to the centre of practical interest. In particular, the end of the Judean state truncated the communal aspect of ethical obligations, often limiting discussion to apolitical responsibilities rather than to the full range of social involvements. The reestablishment of the State of Israel in the twentieth century has therefore, reopened for discussion areas that have for millennia been either ignored or relegated to the realm of abstraction. What this implies is that the full ethical responsibility of the Jew cannot be carried out solely within the realm of individual relationships, but must include involvement in the life of a fully articulated community. Righteousness and compassion[45] had been obligations of the state, governing the relationship between political units, as the first two chapters of Amos make evident. At the same time, as Micah 6: 8 shows, doing justly, loving mercy, and walking humbly with God made up the pattern of the individual's obligations as well. However, in the given situation dispersion of Jews could be seen as a revolt against God.

In keeping with the rabbinic understanding of Torah, a passage in the traditional Prayer Book enumerates a series of virtuous acts-honouring parents, deeds of steadfast love, attendance twice daily at worship, hospitality to wayfarers, visiting the sick, dowering brides, accompanying the dead to the grave, devotion in prayer, and peacemaking in the community and in family-life-and concludes by setting study of Torah as the premier virtue. Here it is exhibited as the complex variety of ethical behaviour called for within the Jewish tradition. Parental respect and family tranquility are added, in other contexts, the responsibility of parents for children, the duties of husband and wife in the establishment and maintenance of a family, and ethical obligations that extend from the conjugal rights of each to the protection of the wife if the marriage is dissolved.

The Biblical description of God as upholding the cause of the fatherless and the widow and befriending the stranger, providing him with food and clothing, remained a motivating factor in the structure of the community.[46] Ethical requirements in economic life are expressed concretely in such a passage as Lev.19:35 – 36: "You shall do no wrong in judgment, in measures of length or weight or quantity. You shall have just balances, just weights, a just *ephah,* and a just *hin*"; and in Amos' bitter condemnation of those who "sell the righteous for silver, and the needy for a pair of shoes."[47] Such injunctions, together with many other specific precepts and expressions of moral requirements, established the basis for a wide-ranging programme that sought to govern, both in detail and in general, the economic life of the individual and the community. The object of ethical concern is not only relations within human sharing but also nature.

The animal world, in the Biblical view, requires merciful consideration, so that not only man is commanded to rest on the Sabbath but his domestic animals are to share the rest with him.[48] Mistreatment of beasts of burden is prohibited; and wanton destruction of animal life falls under the ban. In the rabbinic attitude towards brute creation, even inanimate nature is the object of human solicitude. Thus, for example, the food-yielding trees of a city under siege may not be destroyed, according to Deuteronomy legislation.[49] The enlargement of this and other Biblical precepts resulted in the generalised rabbinic prohibition "You shall not destroy" that governs man's use of his environment. The moral implication of humanity's has been created in the image of God underlies both specific laws (such as Thou shalt love thy neighbour as thyself."[50]

Morality in Islam

With regard to the moral teachings of Islam one must discuss in terms of Islamic civilisation rather than in terms of the Islamic creed. This is because the actual conduct of individual Muslim is shaped by a variety of traditions. The teachings of Quran, the ethical-legal doctrine of conduct of *Sharia* and orthodox theology, and the metaphysical-ethical-political speculations of Muslim philosophers and *Sufis*, in each case it is found that each represents a position different from the others within the moral outlook of Islam, probably contributed to the dynamism that exhibited by Islam. The differences among the mentioned strands in the Islamic web of life exhibited themselves to the greatest degree on a metaphysical plane.[51] An appreciation of the social, political, economic, religious, and ethical problems confronting the Muslim nations today requires an understanding of the source and development of Islam, historically and logically.

Islam is among the youngest of the world's major religions. The norms and assumptions that have characterised in the form of beliefs and actions in Islam have their initial inspiration in two fundamental sources. One is scriptural, embodying the message revealed by God through the Prophet Muhammad and recorded in the *Qur'an*, the sacred text. The second is the exemplification of that message in the perceived model pattern of the Prophet's actions, sayings and norms, collectively called *Sunnah*. Muslim regards the *Qur'an* as the ultimate closure in as series of revelations to humankind from God and the *Sunnah* as the historical projection of a divinely inspired and guided human life in the person of the Prophet Muhammad, who is also believed to be the last in the series of messengers from God."[52] The primary source of moral ideas is the *Qur'an* which, while not presenting a single unified code, does have a number of *Surahs* that contain moral injunctions. Wine, gambling, and usury are forbidden, as well as the making of images. Fraud, perjury, and slander are condemned. Penalties are laid down for such crimes as stealing and murder.

The morality of Islam presents a "straight path" of clear-cut duties and commands. Islamic morals are a combination of acts of love and justice on the one hand and legalistic performances on the other. Muhammad, the prophet of Islam is a loving person, helping the poor and slow to take revenge. Nevertheless, Muslims possess the firm belief that one truth has led to much violence on behalf of Allah through the ages. Although the *Qur'an* actually worked to elevate the horribly degraded position of women in Arab society, women continue to be regarded more as possible temptations to sin for men than as human beings with their own responsibilities before God. Many modern Muslims take the *Quran's* approval of multiple wives to be applicable only to ancient times.

The general ethic of the *Qur'an* considers the marital bond to rest on "mutual love and mercy," and the spouses are said to be "each other's garments." The detailed laws of inheritance prescribed by the Qurân also tend to confirm the idea of a central family-husband, wife, and children, along with the husband's parents. Easy access to polygamy (although the normal practice in Islamic society has always been that of monogamy) and easy divorce on the part of the husband led, however, to frequent abuses in the family. In recent times, most Muslim countries have enacted legislation to tighten up marital relationships. *Qur'an* and *Sunnah* elaborated and applied as God's commands and prohibitions, conceived as the *Sharia,* formulated through the respective Muslim Juridical School. Such formulations of commands and prohibitions in Muslim book of law are expressed in ethical terms.

There are number of factors which served to help the unity of the Islamic community. These important five acts of worship commonly known as the five pillars of Islam are common to all Muslims, which have remained basically unchanged in form. The declaration of faith or *Shahada* which is a simple creed consisting of two statements "I declare that there is no god except God, and I declare that Muhammad is the messenger of God."[53] The act of worship through prayer or *salat* or literally bowing down, the act of worship through *zakat* or charity or the giving alms. It is significant that in Islam *zakat* is based not upon income but on the entirety of a person's material possessions, as thus it has considerable effect as regards the redistribution of wealth within the society. The fourth act of worship *sawm* involves in fasting that is abstaining from food and drink. The last act of worship is then the obligation upon all Muslims to make the *hajj* or pilgrimage to Mecca. All these acts of worship are thus indented to facilitate and encourage the submission of the whole of life to God.[54]

Accordingly, five categories are employed for evaluating all acts of the Muslim, firstly, the obligatory acts, such as the duty to perform ritual prayer, paying of *zakat* and the practice of fasting. Recommend acts, which are not considered obligatory, such as supererogatory acts of charity, kindness, prayers etc. Permitted actions, regarding which the laws adopt a neutral stance that is, there is no expectation of reward or punishment for such acts. Acts that are discouraged and regarded as reprehensible but not strictly forbidden: Muslim jurists differ about what actions to include under this category. Lastly, he actions are that categorically forbidden, such as murder, adultery, blasphemy, theft, intoxication etc."[55]

Rights of parents in terms of good treatment are stressed in Islam, and the Qurân extols filial piety, particularly tenderness to the mother, as an important virtue. A murderer of his father is automatically disinherited. The tendency of the Islamic ethic to strengthen the immediate family on the one hand and the community on the other at the expense of the extended family or community did not succeed, however. Muslim society, until the encroachments upon it of modernising influences, has remained basically one which is composed of tribes or quasi-tribes. Despite urbanisation, tribal affiliations offer the greatest resistance to change and development of a modern polity.

So strong, indeed, has been the tribal ethos that, in most Muslim societies, daughters are not given their inheritance share prescribed by the sacred law in order to prevent disintegration of the joint family's patrimony. The virtue of purity is regarded as of prime importance by Islam. The *Qur'an* advanced its universal recommendation of marriage as a means to ensure a state of chastity, which is held to be induced by a single free wife. The *Qur'an* states that those guilty of adultery are to be severely punished with 100 lashes. Tradition has intensified this injunction and has prescribed this punishment for unmarried persons, but married adulterers are to be stoned to death. A false accusation of adultery is punishable by 80 lashes.

Morality in Christianity

Both Judaism and Christianity are at one in maintaining that morality without religion is ultimately impossible. For both, the love of god is the foundation for good life and, the good life was believed to follow as a consistent expression of the personality whose life is turned toward and centered in God. "In Biblical religion man is required to be just and merciful because God is both just and merciful in all relations with his people. Man is required to manifest love in his earthly life because, according to the essence of Christian faith, God is of the nature of love. And in all cases the love of God dwelling within the person of the individual believer is what provides the motive and inspiration for all our human efforts".[56] "Hence the love of God as the basis of morality involves us in no subjugation to an external authority necessitating conduct through fear, but it is rather the understanding attitude and motive of the person who seeks to live the good life and whose life as a member of society then becomes a consistent expression of an individual will and personality rooted in God."[57]

Christianity, in enlarging the world and expanding the soul, made the moral life over anew. The founder of Christianity, Christ, was the creator of spiritual, universal religion with pure morality. His soul was inspired by the idea of creating a view of religious life that it might content the profoundest aspirations of humanity and at the same time assumes a divine character. For the Christian the fellow human is the present Christ himself. In the fellow, Christians see, under the wrapping of misery, degeneration, and suffering, the image of the present Lord, who became human, who suffered, died, and was resurrected in order to lead all humanity back into the Kingdom of God. According to Matthew, the Judge of the world says to the redeemed: "Truly, I say to you, as you did it to one of the least of these my brethren, you did it to me,"[58] and to the damned: "As you did it not to one of the least of these, you did it not to me."[59] Another saying of the Lord is cited by Tertullian: "If you have seen your brother, you have seen your Lord."[60] Here, the relation between religion and morality stressed and well stated in blunt and poignant way. In these sayings morality is determined by the object of religion. If a man possesses love of God and yet fails to manifest this towards his fellow men, it is contrary to the religious morality.

In the self-understanding of the Christian community, two tendencies battle with one another from the beginning of church history. They lead to completely different consequences in the basic orientation of Christians toward fellow Christians and fellow human beings. "We turn to the roots of Christian ethics in the ministry of Jesus, especially the teachings in the so-called synoptic gospels, Mark, Matthew and Luke. The fourth John can be regarded as a selective and mature series of mediations on the main themes of the first three."[61] Thus, in Christianity, the peculiar fact is that when religion becomes spiritual and universal morality finds its own independence and the true source of morality that deals with duty and right, benevolence and value comes from the Christ.

References

1. Seth, A. Pringle Pattison, (1967). *The Idea of God*, Academic Publishers, Oxford University Press, Calcutta, p. 126.
2. Janine Marie Idziak, (1978). *Divine Commands are the Foundation of Morality*, Clarendon Press, Oxford, p. 262.
3. John R. Burr and Milton Goldinger, *Philosophy and Contemporary Issues*, V. K. Batra Pearl Offset Press Private Limited, New Delhi, pp. 104 -107.
4. Ludwig, Andreas Feuerbach, (1957). *The Essence of Christianity*, Harper Collins Publishers, New York, p. 144.
5. Smith, Mark S. (2002). *The early history of God: Yahweh and the other deities in ancient Israel.* Wm. B. Eerdmans Publishing Co.; 2nd ed. Philippines. p. 254.
6. *Ibid.*

7. Phiolip, L Quinn and Charles Taliaferro (ed), and Rudavsky, Tamar, *The Jewish Contribution to Medieval Philosophical Theology; A Companion to Philosophy of Religion*, Blackwell Publishers Inc, USA,1999, p. 44.
8. Helen, K.Bond, Seth. D. Kunin, ed, and Francesa Aran Murphy, *Judaism; A Companion to Religious Studies and Theology*, Edinburgh University Press, New york, 1999, p. 137.
9. *Ibid.*
10. Quinn, Philip. L and Taliaferro, Charles, ed, and Goodman, Lenin E, *Judaism; A Companion to Philosophy of Religion*, Blackwell Publishers Inc, USA 1999, p. 44.
11. Quinn, Philip. L and Taliaferro, Charles, ed, and Goodman, Lenin E, *Judaism; A Companion to Philosophy of Religion*, Blackwell Publishers Inc, USA 1999, p. 45.
12. *Ibid*, p. 46.
13. Helen, K. Bond, Seth. D. Kunin, ed, and Francesa Aran Murphy, Douglas J. Davies, *Christianity; A Companion to Religious Studies and Theology*, Edinburgh University Press, New York, 1999, p. 167.
14. *Ibid*, p. 168.
15. Helen, K. Bond, Seth. D. Kunin, ed, and Francesa Aran Murphy, Douglas J. Davies, *Christianity; A Companion to Religious Studies and Theology*, Edinburgh University Press, New York, 1999, p. 167.
16. Douglas, J. Davies, (1999). (ed), *Christianity: A Companion to Religious Studies and Theology*, Edinburgh University Press, London, p. 234.
17. Arthur, J. Arberry, (Trans), *The Holy Qur'an*, Oxford University, UK, 1983, Chapter - 112, Verse, 1- 4.
18. Quinn, Philip. L and Taliaferro, Charles, ed, and Burrell. David.C *The Islamic Contribution to Medieval Philosophical Theology; A Companion to Philosophy of Religion*, Blackwell Publishers Inc, USA 1999, p. 89.
19. Arthur, J. Arberry, (Trans) *The* Holy *Qur'an*, Oxford University, UK, 1983, Chapter - 4 2, Verse, 11.
20. *Ibid*, Chapter - 4, Verse, 40.
21. *Ibid*, Chapter - 20, Verse, 52.
22. Quinn, Philip. L and Taliaferro, Charles, ed, and Burrell. David. C, *The Islamic Contribution to Medieval Philosophical Theology* in *A Companion to Philosophy of Religion*, Blackwell Publishers Inc, USA, 1999, pp. 89-93.
23. Joseph Kenny, *Philosophy of the Muslim World*, Library of Congress Cataloging-in- Publication, USA, 2003, p. 21.
24. *Ibid*, p. 40.

25. Helen K.Bond, Seth.D. Kunin, ed, and Francesa Aran Murphy, Goddard, Hugh, *Islam; A Companion to Religious Studies and Theology,* Edinburgh University Press, New York 1999, p. 191.
26. *Ibid*, p. 192.
27. Gerhard Böwering, (1998). *God and his Attributes, Islam: The Straight Path*, Oxford University Press, p. 22.
28. Joseph Kenny, *Philosophy of the Muslim World*, Library of Congress Cataloging-in- Publication, USA, 2003, p. 90.
29. *Ibid*, p. 93.
30. Paul Davis. (1983). *God and the New Physics*, Simon & Schuster, London, p. 79.
31. *Ibid*, p. 100.
32. Lal B.K., *Contemporary Indian Philosophy*, Motilal Banarsidass, New Delhi, 1987, p. 313.
33. *Ibid*, pp. 322-324.
34. *Ibid*, p. 329.
35. Abraham Joshua Heschel, (1965). Who is Man, Stanford University Press, California, London, p. 18.
36. Gordon H. Clark, (1992). *Biblical Doctrine of Man,*Trade paperback, Mary land, 2nd ed., p. 48.
37. *Ibid*, p. 64.
38. *Ibid*, p. 75.
39. The Holy Bible, *New Testament*, Chapter - 1, Verse, 14.
40. Helen K. Bond, Seth, D. Kunin, ed, and Francesa Aran Murphy, Douglas J. Davies, *Christianity; A Companion to Religious Studies and Theology*, Edinburgh University Press, New York 1999, p. 173.
41. Harold B. Smith, (1954). *The Muslim World*, Vol.44, American Religious Society, New York, pp. 202- 214.
42. Peter Singer, ed, and Kellner, Menachem, *Jewish Ethics; A Companion to Ethics,* Blackwell Publications, USA, pp. 83-84.
43. Peter Singer, ed, and Kellner, Menachem, *Jewish Ethics; A Companion to Ethic,* Blackwell Publications, USA, p. 84.
44. Richards Swinburne, *The Coherence of Theism,* Clarendon Press, Oxford, 1977, p. 49.
45. Michael Walzer, (2006.) *Law, Politics, and Morality in Judaism,* Princeton University Press, UK, p. 221.
46. The Holy Bible, *Old Testament*, Deuteronomy Chapter-10, Verse, 18.
47. *Ibid*, Amos Chapter-2, Verse, 6.
48. *Ibid*, Exodus Chapter-20, Verse, 10, and Chapter- 23, Verse, 12.
49. *Ibid*, Deuteronomy Chapter-20, Verses, 14 - 20.

50. Singer, Peter, ed, and Kellner, Menachem, *Jewish Ethics,* in *A Companion to Ethics,* Blackwell Publishers, USA,1999, p. 84.
51. Nanji, Azim, (2000). *Islamic Ethics: A Companion to Ethics.* Blackwell Publishers, Massachusetts, UK, p. 107.
52. Singer, Peter, ed, and Nanji, Azim, *Islamic Ethic; A Companion to Ethics,* Blackwell Publishers, USA, 1999, p. 106.
53. Helen, K, Bond, Kunin. Seth D and Murphy, F. Aran, Ed., *A Companion to Religious Studies and Theology*, Edinburgh University Press Ltd. Edinburgh, 2003, Chapter Four: pp. 185-190.
54. *Ibid*, pp. 185-221.
55. Nanji, Azim, '*Islamic Ethics*' in *A Companion to Ethics,* ed., Singer, Peter, Blackwell Publishers, USA, 1999, p. 113.
56. John E. Smith, "*Religion and Morality*"; *The Journal of Religion*, Vol. 29, No. 2, 1949, p. 85-84.
57. *Ibid.*
58. The Holy Bible, *New Testament, Matthew* Chapter-x, and Singer, Peter, and Perston, Ronald, ed, *Christian Ethics; A Companion to Ethics,* Blackwell Publishers, 1999, p. 93.
59. *Ibid.*
60. *Ibid.*
61. Singer, Peter, Ed, and Perston, Ronald, *Christian Ethics; A Companion to Ethics,* Blackwell Publishers, 1999, p. 94.

Chapter – III

Religion and Morality in Indic Tradition

The main concern of this chapter is to have a comparative discussion on the religion and morality in Indic tradition, the philosophical thought of Hinduism, Buddhism and Jainism. An attempt has been made to understand the notions of God, Self, morality in these philosophical traditions. Each of these notions influences one another in its construal and each religion defines these concepts in particular patterns. This pattern would be the deciding factor in the construal of all its major concepts. In certain extent, we can say that the philosophical foundations of Hinduism actually stems from the *Vedic* tradition. Buddhism and Jainism have mainly given importance to the *Dharma* and *ahimsha*. Both Buddhism and Jainism believe that life is full of sufferings. Jainism preaches that liberation is best, while Buddhism preaches that the suffering can only be ended through right actions throughout one's lifetime. In this juncture, the aim of this chapter is to understand that how these traditions substantially differ from Hindu tradition especially in its conception of morality.

Vedic Conception of God

The *Vedas* are the principal source of Hindu philosophy which was composed in Sanskrit over several centuries (2000-1000 BC). According to the *Vedas*, "the supreme reveals himself as Rita, the eternal order."[1] The corpus called *Vedic* literature cannot be accurately classified, it is by convention, considered to be comprised of the four

Vedas (*Rig Veda, Yajur Veda, Sama Veda, Atharva Veda,*) along with the *Brahmanas* (liturgical works), *Aranyakas* ('books composed in the forest') and *Upanisads* (philosophical literature) attached to each of the *Vedas*. The *Vedas*, the chief sacred scriptures of the Hindus, are perennial. They were not composed by mortals, they were revealed, they are more eternal than the universe and, these scriptures were transmitted by oral tradition.

The Rig Veda, the oldest text in India, is a curious document which consists of over a thousand poems or 'hymns'. More or less these vary from epic chants, hymns of praise, and prayers to the gods, to magic spells and fragments of popular songs. Many of the hymns mention the Gods and Goddesses by name; most of them appear to be deifications of natural powers, such as fire, water, rivers, wind, the sun, dusk and dawn. The *Vedic* texts suggest that divinity permeates the whole universe, the fields, the crops, animals, human speech, and so on. This conception involves many Gods and Goddesses, but it is not polytheism, for each God or Goddess is praised as the supreme deity in the verses addressed to them.

Max Muller has coined the term 'henotheism' to denote systems where the position of supreme deity is occupied now by one God or Goddess, then by another, and so on.[2] No more than one God is ever worshipped at a time. There is also an emphasis on monotheism, pantheism and mysticism; the different Gods and Goddesses are said to be different only in name. "Physical images in the Epics and Puranas have psychical and mystical significance and amplify the meaning of *Vedas*. For example, when the Puranas speak of Vishnu reclining on the multi-hooded snake *Ananta*, upon the ocean of milk, it means that the supreme lord rests upon the Infinite coiled upon the waters of eternal existence."[3]

It is often claimed that the Rig Veda represents nature worship, polytheism and a rather crude imagery of Gods and Goddesses. "An important point to be borne in mind in this discussion is that the word "*Deva*' is so very elusive in its nature and is used to indicate many different things. *Deva* is one who gives to man."[4] This claim is certainly unjustified, for all through the Rig Veda there is a sense of all-pervasive divine presence, immanent in humanity and nature, unifying the universe and illuminating it. To the seers of the Rig Veda, nature is a living divine presence with which they can have communion and be existentially united.

The God's of the Rig Veda were invited as guests to feasts, they take food and drink wine, and they were invoked, flattered, propitiated and pleased. Men had direct communion with gods without any mediation. There was a very intimate personal relationship between men and gods, and day-to-day phenomenon was dependent on the gods. The gods were looked upon as intimate friends of their worshippers. The gods were addressed with such phrases as 'father heaven', 'mother earth', 'Brother *Agni*'. The *Vedic* people called 'all the gods' were numbered 'three crores', reflecting the three spheres of the world: the earth, the air and the sky.[5]

Vedic poets sought to penetrate the essence of natural phenomena and sought to explain phenomena by causes analogous to their own experience. Natural phenomena were gradually sharpened, transformed into mythological figures, into gods and goddesses. They worship the sun, the moon, the dawn, the night, the firmament, fire, water, rivers, seasons, herbs, trees, forests, the grass, furrows, agriculture, mountains, stones, wind and so forth not as mere natural forces, not as anthropomorphic Gods and Goddesses, but as the various expressions of one divine foundational reality. 'The real is one; the learned call it by various names: *Agni, Yama*. The only mode of worship is performing sacrifices to Gods and Goddesses. It is not merely that the Gods are one, but that the whole of the universe in its physical, material and natural aspects is permeated by one divine presence. "Two of our philosophical systems arose in strict continuity with the *Vedic* tradition, looked upon the Veda as the most infallible authority and claimed to evolve systematic philosophies on the basis of Veda. These two though sometimes called the Purva-Mimamsa and the *Vedanta*. But the actual affiliation of these two systems to the *Vedic* literature is in need of some clarification."[6]

Concept of God in Jainism

Jainism is said to be one of the oldest religions in the world. It has been pointed out that the "Jainism is a religion-philosophical tradition which is atheistic. It feels that there is no need for admitting a God who creates the universe."[7] References are found in the

Rig Vedic Mantras to Risabha and *Arstanemi*."[8] Jainism does not believe in an entity or being such as God, which is quite distinct from world. For Jainism, God is only embodied souls like men and animals. Gods differ only in the degree, not in kind. "Certain elements of the world when properly developed obtain deification. These are the *arhats,* the supreme lords, the omniscient souls who have overcome all faults. God is only the highest, noblest and fullest manifestation of the powers, which lie latent in the soul of man. Every soul when it reaches its highest perfection becomes a supreme soul."[9] The greater power and perfection belonging to the divine body and organism are the rewards of the good deeds of a former life. The distinction of Jaina conception of God and of other religions would be clear by understanding the fact that Jainism made a distinction between God and liberated souls. According to Jainism, "the liberated souls are above the God. They are never born again. They have no longer any connection with world and exert no influence on world."[10]

The development of the world is rendered possible by the doctrine of indefiniteness of being and interaction of substance. God is not necessary for creation or destruction. "There can be no destruction of things that do exist, nor there creation of things out of nothing. Coming into existence and ceasing to exist, takes place because of their attributes and modes."[11] "God is only the highest, noblest and fullest manifestation of the powers, which lie latent in the soul of man. Every soul when it reaches its highest perfection becomes a supreme soul."[12] "When prayers are addressed to famous *Jinas* who attained liberation, they cannot and do not return answers to the prayers. But there are Gods who watch and control us. They hear prayers and bestow favours. As far as the *Jinas* are concerned, the best mode of worshipping them is to adopt their advice. Mediation or adoration of *Jinas* sanctifies the soul."[13]

Concept of God in Hinduism

Unlike other religions, Hindu idea of God discloses an astonishingly large variety of ideas. Polytheism, henotheism, pantheism and monotheism are all to be found within Hinduism. They are different aspects or expressions of the same Divine Reality. God in His impersonal aspect is called *Nirguna Brahman*, and in His personal aspect, He is called *Saguna Brahman*. *Saguna Brahman*, who is the creator of this world, is omnipresent, all knowing and all-powerful. *Saguna Brahman*, even though sexless, can be addressed and adored by Hindus as both Mother and Father. Creation, preservation and destruction go hand-in-hand in this world. *Saguna Brahman* is not just the creator, but the preserver and destroyer also. The creator aspect of *Saguna Brahman* is called *Brahma*; the preserver aspect, Vishnu; and the destroyer aspect Shiva or Maheshwara. These three form the so-called Hindu Trinity. Different powers or glories of God are personified through imagination and called Deities in Hinduism. Deities are not so many Gods; they are personified expressions of the different powers and glories of the one and only God.[14]

Hinduism believes that out of compassion for His creatures God incarnates on earth in tangible form and becomes part of history. A Divine Incarnation is called an *Avatara*. In Hinduism, there can be many Divine Incarnations. Whenever virtue declines and irreligion prevails, God incarnates on earth to revitalise religion and save the righteous. Hindus believe in an uncreated, eternal, infinite, transcendent and all-embracing principle, which, "comprising in itself being and non-being," is the sole reality, the ultimate cause and foundation, source, and goal of all existence. This ultimate reality is called *Brahman*. As the All, *Brahman* causes the universe and all beings to emanate from it, transforms itself into the universe, or assumes its appearance. *Brahman* is in all things and is the Self (*atman*) of all living beings. *Brahman* is the creator, preserver, or transformer and reabsorber of everything.

Although it is being in itself, without attributes and qualities and hence impersonal, it may also be conceived of as a personal high God, usually as Vishnu (Visnu) or Œiva). Although those Hindus who particularly worship either Vishnu or Eiva generally consider one or the other as their "favourite God" (*ist devatâ*) and as the Lord (*Îúâna*) and *Brahman* in its personal aspect, Vishnu is often regarded as a special manifestation of the preservative aspect of the Supreme and Eiva as that of the destructive function. Another deity, *Brahmâ*, the creator, remains in the background as a demiurge. These three great figures (*Brahmâ*, Vishnu, and Siva) constitute the so-called Hindu Trinity (*Trimûrti*, "the One or Whole with Three Forms"). This conception attempts to synthesise and harmonise the conviction that the Supreme Power is singular with the plurality of Gods in daily religious worship.

Although the concept of the *Trimûrti* assigns a position of special importance to some great Gods, it never has become a living element in the religion of the people.

As stated above in Hindu philosophical systems there are six most prominent schools. The six schools of Hindu thought are Nyaya, Vaisesika, Sankhya, Yoga, Mimamsa and *Vedanta*. While each of these systems had an independent beginning, some came to be designated jointly as twin systems because of certain affinities in their metaphysical theories. Thus, after the grouping, the six systems are referred to as Nyaya-Vaisesika, Sankhya-Yoga and Mimamsa-*Vedanta* in the philosophical treatment of the schools.[15] Each of these developed its own extensive theories regarding both ontological and epistemological categories, but all were in agreement regarding the eternal nature of the individual self and in its ultimate liberation from births and deaths, however they may differ in detail. These schools can also be viewed as representing different philosophical approaches to the understanding of the ultimate categories. They range from the most realistic (Nyaya-Vaisesika) to the most idealistic (*Advaita Vedanta*) in the way they approach the theory of the *atman*.

The *Advaita Vedanta* School of Indian Philosophy, propounded by Sankara believes that God is one; he is the creator, sustainer and destroyer of the world, and is therefore omnipotent and omniscient, and the object of worship.[16] But God is not the ultimate reality. For plurality, and therefore this world, are mere appearances (*maya*), and God, as the creator of the world, is himself related to appearance. Ultimate reality (*Brahman*), on the other hand, is beyond all relations to objects, to humanity, to thought and to language. Ultimate reality is pure, impersonal, universal consciousness, devoid of any internal or external difference. This consciousness is identical with the self of the individual, which is different from other selves and material objects only at the surface level. At the deepest level, every person, as also every material object, is identical with *Brahman*. All reality is *Brahman*. One cannot worship *Brahman*, for worshipping presupposes a distinction between the subject and object of worship. *Brahman* is pure subject and can never become an object of worship or even of Knowledge. One can only be *Brahman*, that is, realise that one is pure, impersonal, universal consciousness.

In the *Vedanta* system, God is conceived under two aspects: God pervades the world, and is beyond it. God is both immanent and transcendent. The world of material objects and living beings contains a plurality of innumerable objects. The question, which arises here is, how can the immanent unity be reconciled with the phenomenal plurality? The two major schools of *Vedanta*, the *Advaita Vedanta* of Sankara and the *Visistadvaita* of Ramanuja, answer this question differently. Ramanuja, argues that "the empirical world of plurality cannot be illusory, for it is reality related to God, who is infinite. The world is, of course not created by an antecedent God; God and the world are necessary for each other."[17] Ramanuja, in his *Visistadvaita* philosophy, conceives the relation between God and the world on the analogy of the self and body of a human being. Just as a human being is an embodied consciousness, so also God is the self and the world is his body. The entire empirical universe is the body of God, who, as the indwelling spirit, is immanent in the universe. But even though both God and the world are real, still God as the soul of the world has supremacy over the world. Thus, unity and plurality are both real; the ultimate reality - God - is unity in difference. The ultimate aim of human life is to see God through self-surrender, not to be identical with him. Going to heaven cannot be the *summum bonum*, for one can stay in heaven only so long as one's merit is not exhausted. So there is necessarily a fall from heaven.

According to Sankara, "manyness or plurality is inconsistent with unity, and as the inner reality is one, the surface reality, that is, the phenomenal world, is only apparent."[18] This apparent world, the world-show, cannot be really related to the inner unity, which is God. The relation between God and the world is like the relation between a piece of rope and the illusory snake for which it is mistaken. The piece of rope is, of course, necessary as the foundation of the illusory snake. So also, God is the foundation of the illusory world. The cause of this illusory appearance is Maya, which has the dual function of covering reality and projecting illusory objects. The world projected by Maya is not real, but it is not wholly real. Thus, the illusory object, the appearance, is neither real nor unreal. It is not real, for when one has spiritual illumination the world-show vanishes, just as, in good light, the illusory snake vanishes and the piece of rope is seen. Nor is it wholly unreal, for a wholly unreal thing (such as a barren woman's son) cannot be perceived. The world is not real, for it is perceived to be real; the world is not real, for it is contradicted by spiritual realisation of the universal unity. The bare identity of consciousness is the only reality; this consciousness is universal, impersonal, and eternal. If the conception of God is necessarily that of a Person, then this universal consciousness cannot be called God; it is *Brahman*.

Sankara says that the *Brahman* is not the creator of the world, for the world is not eternal, and whatever follows from *Brahman* must partake of its eternal reality. *Brahman* is the foundation of the world in the sense in which a real object is the foundation of an illusory object. There cannot be any illusion unless there is a real object, which is mistaken for an illusory object. Thus, illusion differs from hallucination. Identity cannot tolerate any difference; so *Brahman* is pure identity devoid of all internal and external difference. Being aware of identity with *Brahman*, the illumination of the real self is the ultimate aim of life prescribed in the *Upanisads*. However, *Vedanta* was not "in fact based upon an actual comprehensive survey of the entire *Vedic* literature. *Vedanta* took its stand on the *Upanisads* and claimed to be systematising the philosophy contained therein. Not that it expressed any doubt as to the authority of the Samhitas and the *Brahmanas*; but it simply ignored them."[19]

It is said that the "Mimamsa forms the stock-example of how an orthodox system of Indian philosophy is under no obligation to admit the existence of God."[20] God is supposed to be known from the revealed scriptures (*Vedas*). Purva Mimamsa philosophers reject this theory. The revealed texts are only the source of knowing our duty, which is to perform sacrifices. There are names of Gods and Goddesses, but they do not have any reference beyond these names; there is no divinity beyond the names. There is nothing real beyond the texts.

According to Mimamsa, the revealed texts are eternal; they do not have any author. So God is not their author. The universe, too, is eternal and self-sustaining; therefore, God cannot be postulated as the creator, sustainer and destroyer of the world. So Gods and Goddesses are just names that have magical powers to produce merit. When performing sacrifices one has to utter the sentences very carefully; as a result, one goes to heaven after death. Neither God-realisation nor self-realisation is the ultimate aim. In heaven, there are no Gods or

Goddesses, for they are only names. To be in heaven is to enjoy bliss eternally; there can be no fall from heaven. According to Kumarila and Prabhakara, "the individual things of the world have their beginnings and ends; but this does not mean that the world as a whole is ever created or destroyed."[21]

Concept of God in Contemporary Hindu Tradition

Coming to some of the most famous definitions offered in the strands of modern Indian philosophy, Swami Vivekananda believes that "Religion is a path which leads to God, but path is not a house."[22] He says that as of the same gold, various ornaments are made, having different forms and names, so our God is worshipped in different forms and names. Vivekananda's concept of God is quite close to the concept of God in *Advaita Vedanta* and emphasises on all-pervasive nature of God. He says that "the Absolute is that ocean, while you and I and sun and stars, and everything else are various waves of that ocean. And what makes the waves different."[23]

Like *Advaita Vedanta*, Vivekananda also defines *Brahman* as indeterminate. But it can be described as '*Sat-Cit-Ananda*'. The concept of *Sat* (Existence) and *Cit* (Consciousness) are similar to the concepts of *Adavita Vedanta's* concepts. But the concept of '*Ananda*' has been greatly enriched by Vivekananda. He asserts '*Ananda*' is in love. He makes love as the essential core of bliss. By the enrichment of the conception of bliss (*Ananda*) he makes a clear departure from *Advaita Vedanta* from its strict difference with the theistic attitude. By including the notion of love in the concept of bliss, he viewed supreme absolute being as a good and loving being. Thus, along with the impersonal nature of the absolute, a belief in personal God also emerges. In addition, he denies the *Advaita Vedanta* distinction of God and Absolute. He believes that both are not two and God is not the creation of Maya.

Aurobindo says that, "Religion is the attempt to make the truth dynamic in the soul of man."[24] The spirit of reconciliation becomes the guiding principle of Sri Aurobindo's metaphysics. He conceives reality as supremely spiritual and admits that "the claim of the pure spirit to manifest in us its absolute freedom and the claim of Universal matter to be the mould and condition of our manifestation, we have to find a Truth that can entirely reconcile these antagonists and can give to both their due portion in life and their due justification in thought."[25]

For Aurobindo, it is essential to consider the levels or cords of being in order to understand the nature of reality. This does not mean that reality is plural in nature. Reality is essentially one, but creation depends upon the two-fold principle of unity and multiplicity. Creation is the expression of the essential unity. The cords of being are the expressions of reality viewed from the point of view of creation. He talks about such eight principles. They are Existence, Consciousness-force, Bliss, and Super mind, Mind, Psyche, Life and Matter. The first four belongs to the higher hemisphere and the last four belongs to lower hemisphere. The lower hemisphere seeks to represent the stages that evolution has been able to reach and the higher hemisphere seeks to represent the stages into which evolution is going to enter. According to Sri Aurobindo, "the Unity and Multiplicity are in fact, our mental representations of the absolute."[26]

Gandhi's conception of God can be summarised in his famous saying 'Truth is God'. This notion of truth, he formulated in his engagement with the theistic tradition of God (God in a personified form) and the *advaitic* tradition of God (God, without any attributes and indeterminate), Gandhi's philosophy believes in the indeterminate nature of God (*Brahman*). In support of theistic tradition, he firmly affirms that the conception of God is not merely for the satisfaction of reason or intellectual curiosity. He says, "He is no God, who merely satisfies the intellect, if he ever does. God to be God must rule the heart and transform it."[27]

Gandhi's conception of God is not that truth is God, but that God is truth. He says, "In my early youth I was taught to repeat what in Hindu scripture are known as one thousand names of God. But these one thousand names of God were by no means exhaustive. We believe – and I think it is the truth – that God has as many names as there are creatures and therefore, we also say that God is nameless, and since God has many forms we also consider him as formless and since He speaks to us in many tongues, we consider Him to be speechless and so on ...if it is possible for human tongue to give the fullest description, I have come to the conclusion that for myself God is truth."[28]

Radhakrishnan's interpretation of religion is "the insight into the nature of reality (*darshana*) or experience of reality (*anubhava*)."[29] This experience is the response of the whole personality, the integrated self to the central reality. Religion is the self-manifestation of the ultimate reality in Man. It is our real nature in God. A religion represents the soul of the people, its particular spirit, thought, and temperament. Like *Advaitains*, Radhakrishnan also believes in the monistic character of God. He believes that the ultimate explanation of universe has to be monistic. He does not arrive at the conception of monistic character of absolute by carrying the process of abstraction to its maximum limit. On the contrary he has come to realise that the world somehow or other express a unity within its process. The processes of the world reveal that they are not stray or causal process, they reveal a unity. Now this unity cannot be expressed unless the ultimate real is conceived as one.

According to Radhakrishnan, "...Absolute is pure consciousness and pure freedom and infinite possibility. Whereas the first two characters have been explained in the manner of Hegel's Absolute Idealism.[30] According to Radhakrishnan, the absolute has to be spiritual in nature; therefore, we are constrained to think that the absolute is spirit. According to Radhakrishnan, it is a free spirit, it is free in so far as there is nothing to limit it, and there is nothing beyond it and the Absolute is described as Infinite. It is infinite because it cannot be finite. The absolute spirit being the ultimate reality is self-grounded and is the foundation of everything else. Absolute is changeless because it is infinite. Being infinite, it is self-existent and hence completes in it self. It is eternal also.

Radhakrishnan feels that there has to be a principle, a God - a non-temporal and actual being-by that the indeterminateness of creativity can be transmuted into a determinate principle. This shows that the Divine Intelligence—the creative power—has to be conceived as the intermediary between the absolute being and the cosmic process. God is the Absolute in action. The real in relation to itself in Absolute and the real in relation to creation is God.

Concept of God in Buddhism

Buddhists in general are not concerned about the issue of whether God exists or not because they think that, the prime effort is to be taken for relief from bondage for all beings, thus the existence of God and other such issues are not relevant for this task. However, it is to be noted that Buddhism does not challenge the doctrine of theism directly, but it avoids it, considers it as an issue irrelevant and not necessary for the path to nirvana. In one of his sayings to a Brahmin youth named *Sangarawa*, Buddha says that, "one knows on good grounds that there are Gods" and "it is commonly believed taken for granted in the world that there are Gods."[31] In the same way, the Buddhist criticism of revelation is also vastly misunderstood. Buddhism clearly maintains that it is not the care that revelations are impossible. K.N. Jayatilleke makes it clear "they cannot all be true; this does not mean that they are all necessarily false."[32] Buddhist teachings maintain secular and receptive motions, which at the outset would be interpreted as a sympathetic, but obviously, they are not.

Buddhism, since it is not theistic, maintains that the attribute of finiteness or infiniteness could only be held towards the world or universe. One cannot hold these attributes to God, because in Buddhism, anything that is self-existent and not conditioned or affected by causes is not in a position to affect earthly processes. Hence, if it is a finite God, Buddhists might have agreed on the rationale that, then its contingent and thus not really a God of the Judaic Christian traditions. Hence, Buddhism assigns the attribute of infiniteness to the concept of Universe, unlike the monotheistic traditions where it is attributed to God. Buddhism holds the view that it is better not to seek the answer to the question of self-existence of God, because as said earlier, these answers are not relevant to the task they consider as primal, that of relieving from the bondage of the *Samsara*. Buddhist text outrightly denies any role of God in *Samsara*. Self-existence is thus denied in the care of both God and universe.

"The world was without a refuge and without God."[33] Buddhists always are closer to the concept of becoming rather than being. Self-existence assumes the notion of a substratum, or being that is not consistent with the teachings of Buddhism. Anything that persists over time to eternity thus casts doubt among Buddhists and allowed the attribute of infinity to universe under certain conditions such as the possibility of a series of finite events and ultimately leading to infinity. Nevertheless, this concession does not imply the self-existence of universe as well as God.

The acceptance and justification of becoming over 'being' is the crux of Buddhist thought. It is also applied in the concept of self. Almost all other religions hold the notion of a permanent self. This is not accepted in Buddhism and holds that there is no permanent substratum underlying the individual as well as the universe. The orthodox teaching in India holds the view of a permanent self both at the individual and at the absolute, universal level (*Atman*, *Brahman*). Early Buddhism maintained the view called '*Pudgala Sunyata*'[34], which conveys, the message 'emptiness of person'. Nevertheless, the later Buddhist traditions developed this idea into '*Dhamma Sunyata*.'[35] A.L. Basham makes it very clear that "Buddhism knows no being but only becoming."[36] Becoming is hardened through each texts and commentaries that came after the *Dhammpada*. "*Sabbe Dhamma anatta*" which means 'all *Dhammas* are without self' also captures the notion of becoming and its importance in Buddhist teachings.

Buddhism challenges two key monotheistic notions related to God. God is not dependent either for existence or for characteristics upon reality. Secondly, God is eternal without beginning or end. Both these notions are challenged by banking on the idea called '*Pratitya Samutpada*' or mutual dependence or the doctrines of dependent origination. The first of this above notion is challenged by Buddhism by invoking the idea that everything is a process, liable to a causal system. Anything in this world could be conditioned. Everything is related to each other in diverse ways, if such is the case, then how is it possible for a God that is non-dependent on this world can actually affect the happenings in it. This is a serious challenge in the sense that, if we believe in the principle of *Pratitya Samutpada*, then it forbids our belief in an independent God. But the interesting point is that, if we allow the God to be part of the causal system (universe), then the 'God' as understood by the monotheistic religions vanishes. The doctrine of dependent origination is a rational and perfectly sound principle and it resists criticisms because it is both intelligible and rational. It is common for anybody to think that one should be part of the world to come to effect in this world and this is exactly the point raised by Buddhists against the notion of an independent God.

The second notion of the eternality of God is also challenged using the same principle and logic above. Everything is to be understood with sensitivity towards the cause and relation notion and everything causally relational will also be dependent by the very fact that the substratum of a particular entity cannot stay independent of the entities, to which it is causally related. In the same way, something eternal is inconceivable in the Buddhist perspective because it has naturally then lain outside the dynamics of this causal system; which is impossible and hence eternity is negated to all entities. The concession of allowing a non-beginning to universe is actually a series of contingent and finite events / processes. Buddhism does not deny the existence of a creator who is morally perfect but completely denies the existence of a creator who is omniscience, omnipotent and external.

Arguments against the Belief in God

The justification given by theists for the belief and the existence of God are comprised in the ontological argument and the cosmological argument which are countered by Buddhism. Firstly, one cannot say that something exists just because it has a name or it's an idea. Secondly, the ontological argument mistakenly regards existence as an attribute. Buddha says, that "the whole universe, as we know it, is a system of relations, we know nothing that is, or can be unrelated. How can that which depends on nothing and is unrelated to nothing produce things which are related to one another and depend on their existence upon one another?"[37]

The whole issue is related to the notion whether existence is a predicate or not. If it is a predicate or attribute, then the existence of God is to be taken literally as we speak about any other thing which exists. But this violates the Buddhist principle of dependent co-origination. But "the existence is not a predicate. Then the issue is open to inquiry as Hick points out."[38] Existence is to be understood only in terms of causes and conditions.

Buddha does not take God as omniscient or omnipotent. But he agrees on the notion that for the sake of moral grounds, one can believe in the existence of God. Moreover, this does not give the freedom to put everything back to God and lack responsibility and free will. This is one drawback of giving concession to the thought that on moral grounds one can accept the existence of God. The drawback rests in the assumption that if there is such a God then he is responsible for all the happenings in this world. Hence, Buddhist literature can be interpreted as countering the ontological argument.

The cosmological argument stresses the existence of God through five arguments which are interlinked. The first argument says that there exists a prime mover without which the dynamics of this world is impossible. *Dharmakirti* responds to this in an apt way. "God is neither momentary nor he is efficient."[39] Something that exists and is momentary is only capable of engaging in the role of a 'mover.' It should be noted that in the Buddhist teaching, anything that is not conditioned to this world is not in a position to engage causally. The second argument stresses the point that if everything is caused by something, and if this chain is extended back, trucked back; it is inevitable that we end up at a first cause which is the cause of everything existing in this world. Buddhists are comfortable in their position of entertaining an infinite series of finite causes and asks that if there is a God behind all these causes, then what about the cause of that God. The argument (of a first cause) is flawed according to Buddhists because it prevents the moral progress of an individual, because if there is this first cause, then everything depends on it and this assumption leads to inaction and irresponsibility. In such a case, man can have no freedom of his own.

The third argument claims that all things in this world are contingent. That is, they could have existed differently and there could have been a time when nothing existed. In such a state, nothing would have come into existence unless some necessary agency acts. The Buddhist counter argument stresses the idea that the effect presupposes a cause, yet all effects do not presuppose the same cause. It is impossible to give an exclusive explanation about a necessary being which is the cause of everything. The notion of 'exclusivity' is important because, in this world, there do not exist any cause which is exclusive. In other words, there do not exist any cause which is not conditioned and affected by more than one thing. Causes could act in a variety of ways in a variety of mediums. Some of them lose trace and others are determinable. Hence, an exclusive explanation based on a single first cause is unintelligible according to Buddhism.

The fourth argument is basically one about gradation. K.N. Jayathilleke argues that if we go by gradation, then the grade of Buddha is higher than that of God. The trans-theistic nature of nirvana places Buddha above the theistic God. This simply means that the argument of degrees of value to absolute value is one of choice. If all depends on the kind and degree of highest grade one assumes, Buddhists negate this argument and regards it as lesser in its thrust. The fifth argument is more or less similar to the argument posed by William Paley.[40] It brings the analogy of a watch in a desert. And asks the question whether it is caused by any natural resources out of chance or that there is the hand of an intelligent being behind its creation. Buddhists answer this according to the doctrine of *karma*, the process of dependent co-origination according to which the preceding in ceasing to be gives rise to the succeeding.

The analogy of watch is misleading, because in that sense one can argue that the ant-hill is the creation of a potter. The proof that a watch empties a watch maker does not support the argument that a world implies a God. Sharma says, that "we can have production without a thinking cause or a ruling provident."[41] The argument is much closer to that of Himes. We cannot conclude from the fact that the very object in the world is created, the further fact that the world itself is created, for that violates logical consistency. Another attack on the belief of the existence of God stems from the idea that the world looks almost imperfect. And how could a perfect God create this imperfect world. All these are entailed by the Buddhist notion that "nature obeys no laws imposed from without."[42]

Concept of Soul in *Vedic* Tradition

The *Rig Veda* is permeated with a sense of divine unity in all creation; human being has a body and a soul, which is the principle of consciousness which has two levels. At the surface level, the human subject knows objects, performs actions and experiences pleasure and pain. Then there is the deeper level of consciousness, where the subject is simply the witness of the empirical self, unaffected by its pleasures and sufferings, by wants and needs, by motives and intentions. "The word '*atman*' is derived from '*an*' which means to breathe. It is the breath of life."[43] This deeper consciousness is the same as the divinity of the whole universe. This was the identification of the ultimate truth underlying the universe called *Brahman* with the inner self of all beings called the *atman*. It was the same *atman* that was present in all living beings, the differences seen being attributed to the nature of the respective body it occupies.

The inquiry in the *Upanishads* on the notion of soul was mainly speculative. It had the dual purpose of finding the ultimate principle that was the basis of the universe and the true nature of the individual self. It is said that the "*Upanisadic* thought cannot be described either as purely metaphysical or purely ethical—it presents a unified view of reality and life or to be precise, reality in life."[44] The first inquiry led to the postulation of *Brahman* as the source behind the universe. This concept finally settled down with the notion of *Brahman* being described both as immanent in the cosmos and as transcending the same. The other inquiry was directed towards discovering the identity of the self by analysing the inner nature of the human being. Having arrived at the conclusion that the individual self cannot be identified with any one of the senses (both motor and cognitive), through a process of elimination (*Kena Upanisad* 3.4) the mind as being the self was also ruled out as it was obvious that all mental states had something other than the mind as their referent which was also constant. Another feature was the observation that the 'sense-of-me' (personal identity) was invariably associated with consciousness (self-awareness) and knowledge, combined with the persistence of the 'sense of I' in all the three states of waking, dreaming and deep sleep led to the postulation of the *atman* being the inner self, which is the ultimate principle (*Brhadaranyaka Upanisad* 4.3 and 4).

Concept of Soul in Jainism

Jainism brings the whole universe under two everlasting categories. These two classes of things are designated *jiva* ("soul," or "living substance" or "the conscious") and *ajiva* ("*nonsoul*," or "inanimate substance" or "the unconscious"). "In the Jaina writings the word *Jiva* is variously used and denotes life, vitality, soul and consciousness. *Jiva* is living experience."[45] *Ajiva* is further divided into time, space, the principle of motion, stability and matter. The essential characteristics of *jiva* are consciousness (*cetana*), bliss (*sukha*), and energy (*virya*). 'A *jiva* is the combination of two. It is both spiritual and material.'[46] In its pure state, *jiva* possesses these qualities limitlessly. The souls, infinite in number, are divisible in their embodied state into two main classes, immobile and mobile, according to the number of sense organs possessed by the body they inhabit. The first group consists of souls inhabiting immeasurably small particles of earth, water, fire, and air, along with the vegetable kingdom, which possess only the sense of touch. The second group comprises souls that inhabit bodies that have between two and five sense organs. Moreover, the universe is populated with an infinite number of minute beings, *nigodas*, some of which are slowly evolving while the rest have no chance of emerging from their hapless state.

Formless and genderless, *jiva* cannot be directly perceived by the senses. Like the universe, it is without a point of ultimate origin or end. While not all pervasive, it can, by contraction or expansion, occupy various amounts of space. Like the light of a lamp in a small or a large room, *jiva* can fill both the smaller and the larger bodies it occupies. The soul assumes the exact dimensions of the body it occupies, but it is not identical with that body. The soul of an elephant is large, while the soul of an ant is small. Jain reality comprises two components, *jiva* ("soul" or "living substance") and *Ajiva* ("nonsoul" or "inanimate substance"). *Ajiva* is further divided into two categories: nonsentient material entities and non-sentient nonmaterial entities. "In the Jaina writings the word *Jiva* is variously used and denotes Matter (*pudgala*) has the characteristics of touch, taste, smell, and colour; however, its essential characteristic is lack of consciousness."[47] The smallest unit of matter is the atom (*paramanu*). Heat, light, and shade are all forms of fine matter.

The sentient nonmaterial substances are space, time, and the principles of motion and its arrest. They are always pure and are not subject to defilement.

The principles of motion and its arrest permeate the universe; they do not exist independently but rather form a necessary precondition for any object's movement or coming to rest. Jainism believes in concrete identity between the soul and the karmic matter in the state of bondage while the non-Jaina schools are reluctant to admit any real relation between spirit and a number of devices to explain the fact of bondage. The karmic matter, according to the Jainas, mixes with the soul much in the same way as milk mixes with water or fire with iron.[48] In the state of bondage the soul is infected with a kind of susceptibility to establish relation with the non- soul. This susceptibility finds expression in the passion-states of the soul. The karmic matter obscures or obstructs these characteristics of the soul and keeps it away from its supreme state of existence. The soul, under the influence of passions (*kasayas)* and possessed of yoga (that is, the vibrations of body, vocal organ, and mind) attracts karmic matter (*karma pudgala*) which then is inseparably mixed up with the soul. The resultant state is bondage (*bandha)*.[49]

Concept of Self in Hinduism

By the time of the early *Upanisad*s (800-400 BC) the different words used for the self were entrenched in Hindu thought. Some of them are *jiva* (from the root *jiv* - to live, be alive), *atman* (from the root *an* - to breathe), *jivatman* (combining the first two), *purusa* (from the root *puri sete* - lying in the body, embodied), *ksetrajña* (from *ksetram janati* - one who knows the body, embodied self). Thus, it can be seen that the self in all these meanings differs from the usual notion of ego: what a person is, their identity, etc., with which one associates the self in ordinary understanding. While we cannot believe that *Vedic* literature, as it exists today, contains early thought pertaining to the question of personal identity, what we do have is representative of the directions this inquiry took. More importantly, these meanings persisted and were standardised in the course of time, so that in the later schools of philosophy (200-600 AD), as well as in popular Hinduism, these were accepted as words that convey the idea of the self. "The doctrine of unity of the being set forth in these dialogues not only rejects the multiplicity of the world but asserts that the living principle in all beings is the same."[50]

Hinduism believes that the spirit or soul—the true "*self*" of every person, called the *âtman* is eternal. According to the monistic/ pantheistic theologies of Hinduism (such as *Advaita Vedanta* school), this *Atman* is ultimately indistinct from *Brahman*, the supreme spirit. These schools are called non-dualist. The goal of life according to the *Advaita* school is to realise that one's *âtman* is identical to *Brahman*, the supreme soul. The *Upanishads* state that whoever becomes fully aware of the *âtman* as the innermost core of one's own self realises their identity with *Brahman* and thereby reaches *Moksha* (liberation or freedom). Other dualistic schools (*Dvaita* and *Bhakti*) understand *Brahman* as a Supreme Being who possesses personality and, worship

Him or Her thus, as Vishnu, Brahma, Shiva or *Shakti* depending on the sect. The *âtman* is dependent on God while *Moksha* depends on love towards God and on God's grace. When God is viewed as the supreme personal being (rather than as the infinite principle) God is called *Ishvara* ("The Lord"), *Bhagavan* ("The Auspicious One"), or *Parameshwara* ("The Supreme Lord"). However, interpretations of *Ishvara* vary—ranging from non-belief such as followers of Mimamsakas, in *Ishvara* to identifying *Brahman* and *Ishvara* as one as in *Advaita*.

The treatment of *atman* is similar in both Nyaya and Vaisesika, the *atman* is unique, eternal, all-pervading and there are as many selves as there are bodies associated with them. Consciousness is not intrinsic to *atman*, but the self has only one of that, it is many qualities. It is not only an essential quality but also an adventious attribute along with desire, volition, pleasure, pain, love, aversion, virtue and vice.[51]

The system is in agreement with the general theory of the bondage of the *atman* in the round of births and deaths. The reason for this state is lack of true knowledge of the self as distinct from all other things, which is the reason for pain. When correct knowledge dawns through study of the sacred books and by the practice of Yoga, there is the destruction of ignorance and the achievement of the goal of liberation. The fact that the self does not also have the attribute of consciousness in liberation means that the self is not conscious of its own freedom. Although a Supreme self-known as the Lord *(Isvara)* is admitted in the school, it is restricted to being the efficient cause of the world and does not extend to the sphere of liberation of the individual self. Nyaya and Vaisesika do not believe in liberation while still in an embodied state as some of the other systems do (see Nyaya-Vaisesika).

Concept of Self and Non-self (*anatman*) in Buddhism

Contrary to the above theories, Buddhism did not assume the existence of the soul as a metaphysical substance, but admitted the existence of the self as the subject of action in a practical and moral sense. According to Buddhism, self cannot be identified with anything existing in the outside world nor can be grasped as some other concrete physical substance. The self can be realised only when one acts according to universal norms of human existence. Thus, according to

Buddhism, the true self becomes manifest when one acts morally.[52] Practical postulate in early Buddhism makes clear the concept of "one who knows the self" and the stresses the virtue of relying upon oneself. The Buddha taught *Ananda*, his disciple, in his last sermon, "Be you lamps to yourselves. Be you a refuge to yourself. Be taking yourself to no external refuge. Hold fast to the Truth as a lamp. Hold fast as a refuge to the Truth. Don't look for effuse to any one besides yourself."[53]

According to Buddhism, life is a stream of becoming, a series of manifestations and extinctions. The Buddha asks, "every man to enter into deep recesses and examine whether he could ever aware of an unchanging entity called the soul. All one could become aware of one thinks of one's *self* or *soul* is sensation."[54] The concept of the individual ego is a popular delusion; the objects with which people identify themselves—fortune, social position, family, body, and even mind—are not their true selves. There is nothing permanent, and, if only the permanent deserved to be called the self, or *atman*, then nothing is self. There can be no individuality without putting together of components. This is becoming different, and there can be no way of becoming different without dissolution, a passing away. Philosophical corollaries of real importance were also drawn in early Buddhism from the doctrine of *pratityasamutpada*. These were the doctrines of universal impermanence and of the denial of the soul as a substance."[55] It was perhaps thought that "since everything was dependent upon the collocation of certain conditions and since it was perhaps also assumed that nothing born of the collocation of conditions could be permanent."[56]

To make clear the concept of no-self (*anatman*), Buddhists set forth the theory of the five aggregates or constituents (*khandhas*) of human existence: (1) corporeality or physical forms (*rûpa*), (2) feelings or sensations (*vedanâ*), (3) ideations (*saññâ*), (4) mental formations or dispositions (*sankhâra*), and (5) consciousness (*viññâda*). Human existence is only a composite of the five aggregates, none of which is the self or soul. A person is in a process of continuous change, with no fixed underlying entity.

Morality in *Vedic* Tradition

Morality is an integral aspect of philosophical analysis of *Vedas*. The *Brahman- atman* equation and their status as the final truth in an interchangeable manner posed a problem for the philosopher; if something is existent in an absolute sense, it cannot be negated at any time or in any sense. Thus, in order to preserve the immutable nature of *atman* it was conceived as being a permanent entity, existing even after the fall of the body. In *Rg-veda* the conception of *Rta* is of great significance. "*Rta* furnishes us with the standard of morality. It is the universal essence of things. It is *satya* or truth of things."[57]

The concepts of *Dharma* and *karma* had evolved into metaphysical principles that held sway over the lives of individual selves on this earth. It is not possible to trace all the nuances of meaning that *Dharma* went through before it settled down to mean virtue, merit, good conduct and to be raised to the status of the first of the goals of human beings. These goals were four in number, called *Dharma*, *Artha* (pursuit of economic ends within *Dharma*), *kama* (legitimate sensual pleasure within *Dharma*) and *Moksa* (liberation from repeated births to deaths).

Vedas are, in a sense, hymns, but the Gods to which they refer are not persons but manifestations of ultimate truth and reality. In the *Vedic* philosophy, "the basic principle of the universe, the ultimate reality on which the cosmos exists, is the principle of *Ritam,* which is the word from which the Western notion of right is derived. There is thus a belief in a right moral order somehow built into the universe itself. Hence, truth and right are linked; to penetrate through illusion and understand the ultimate truth of human existence is to understand what is right."[58] To be an enlightened one is to know what is real and to live rightly, for these are not two separate things but one and the same. "The *Purusasukta* has the first references to the division of Hindu society into four classes."[59]

The emphasis on duty is represented primarily, if not exclusively, by texts of the *Vedic* tradition. In the Rig Veda, virtue is conformity to cosmic law (*rta*). The "*Rta* denotes the order of the world and everything that is ordered in the universe has *Rta* for its principle. It corresponds to the universals of Plato."[60] That involves not only the performance of various obligatory rites on behalf of the Gods, but also the observance of fidelity and rectitude in human relationships. The *Brahmanas*, devoted to analyse and interpret the rituals, virtue is narrowly conceived as ritual excellence.[61] The sacrifice is understood to yield its result through its own magic; by directly effecting what it symbolizes, not by honouring or ingratiating the Gods to whom it is addressed. Transgression is thus merely a ritual mistake, a blunder or negligence - not an offence against a personal being to which one owes an obligation - either in the context of the sacrifice itself or in human affairs seen as an extension. It produces defilement, materially conceived as a taint or miasma that can only be ritually removed. The *Brahman* declares, for example, that the impurity of the most heinous deeds, even the killing of a *Brahman* (priest), can be wiped away by performing a horse sacrifice.[62]

The ideal of the renunciation (*sannyasa*) of all familial and social obligations for the sake of enlightenment or liberation (*moksa, nirvasa*) from the cycle of rebirth was espoused in various classical Indian traditions and represents a rejection of the *Brahmanical* ideal. Residence in heaven, to be achieved through ritual acts, is declared undesirable because it is impermanent: after the merit of one's good deeds (*karma*) is exhausted, the soul must return to the physical world, where one again experiences suffering. The only possibility of fulfillment is to transcend embodied existence altogether; this is conceived in the *Upanisads* and the *Vedanta* school of philosophy.

The ethics that is thus traced to the very essence of the universe is not without its detailed practical applications. These were based on four ideals, or proper goals, of life: prosperity, the satisfaction of desires, moral duty, and spiritual perfection *i.e.,* liberation from a finite existence. From these ends follow certain virtues: honesty, rectitude, charity, nonviolence, modesty, and purity of heart. To be condemned, on the other hand, are falsehood, egoism, cruelty, adultery, theft, and injury to living things. Because the eternal moral law is part of the universe, to do what is praiseworthy is to act in harmony with the universe and accordingly receive its proper reward; conversely, once the true nature of the self is understood, it becomes apparent that those who do what is wrong are acting self-destructively.

Upanishad's Contribution to *Vedic* Morality

The basic principles underwent considerable modification over the ensuing centuries, especially in the *Upanishads*, a body of philosophical literature dating from 800 BC. The Indian caste system, with its intricate laws about what members of each caste may or may not do, is accepted by the *Upanishads* as part of the proper order of the universe. Morality itself, however, is not regarded as a matter of conformity to laws. Instead, the desire to be ethical is an inner desire. It is part of the quest for spiritual perfection, which in turn is elevated to the highest of the four goals of life. During the following centuries the ethical philosophy of this early period gradually became a rigid and dogmatic system that provoked several reactions.

Jainism and Morality

The Three Jewels constitute the basis of the Jain doctrine of morality: the right knowledge, faith, and practice must be cultivated together because none of them can be achieved in the absence of the others. "The ethics of Jainism are austere, simple and straight forward. The practice of non-violence in thought, word and action is the cardinal virtue."[63] The right faith, according to Jainism, leads to calmness or tranquility, detachment, kindness and the renunciation of pride of birth, beauty of form, wealth, scholarship, prowess, and fame. Right faith leads to perfection only when followed by right practice. Yet, there can be no virtuous conduct without right knowledge, the clear distinction between the self and the non-self. Knowledge without faith and conduct is futile. Without purification of mind, all austerities are mere bodily torture. Right practice is thus spontaneous, not a forced mechanical quality. Attainment of right practice is a gradual process, and a layperson can observe only partial self-control; a renunciation, however is able to observe more comprehensive rules of conduct. The following are the moral codes in Jainism.

The Three Jewels constitute the basis of the Jain doctrinal and ethical stance. Right knowledge, faith, and practice must be cultivated together because none of them can be achieved in the absence of the others.[64] Nonviolence (*Ahimsa*) which consists of not obstructing the life processes of self or of any other living being. This embodies the principle of freedom and equality of all living beings. "The doctrine of *Ahimsa* is central to Jaina ethical thought."[65] Secondly, the truthfulness (*satya*) which means always speaking the truth and supporting what is true according to one's own perception and experience. Thirdly, taking only that which is freely given; i.e. not stealing (*asatya*) which entails not taking anything which does not belong to us, accepting only one's fair share, and, being honest in business dealings. Fourthly, non-possessiveness or *aparigrah* which entails limiting our material possessions and desires. Lastly, chastity or *brahmacharya* entails total celibacy for monks and nuns, and, partial celibacy and no premarital or extramarital sexual activity, for laypersons.

The most fundamental value of Jainism is nonviolence, or *Ahimsa.* "The uniqueness of Jainism lies in the urgency with which it extended the practice of *Ahimsa* to all forms of life."[66] This word is usually found on the Jain symbol of the open palm (which means "stop"). *Ahimsa* is the first of the vows taken by both Jain householders and monks. *Ahimsa* means harming no living being as well as protecting all living beings from harm. While several religions practice nonviolence and peace as a fundamental principle, Jainism is unique in extending this principle to all *jivas* (living beings). For Jains, living beings include not only humans and animals, but also everything one finds on earth. *Ahimsa* must therefore be extended to not only humans and animals, but also to soil, sand, oceans, fires, insects, microbes and plants. "The ethical system of the Jainism is more rigorous than that of the Buddhists. It looks upon patience as the highest good and pleasure as a source of sin."[67]

Two separate courses of conduct are laid down for the ascetics and the laity. In both cases, the code of morals is based on the doctrine of *Ahimsa*, or nonviolence. Because thought gives rise to action, violence in thought merely precedes violent behaviour. Violence in thought, then, is the greater and subtler form of violence because it arises from ideas of attachment and aversion, grounded in passionate states, which result from negligence or lack of care in behaviour. Jainism enjoins avoidance of all forms of injury-whether committed by body, mind, or speech-and subscribes emphatically to the teaching that '*nonviolence is the highest form of religious practice*.' For Jains, this principle, which manifests itself most obviously in the form of vegetarianism, is the single most important component of their tradition's message.

The fundamental tenet of Jain doctrine is that all phenomena are linked in a universal chain of cause and effect. Every event has a definite cause. By nature each soul is pure, possessing infinite knowledge, bliss, and power; however, these faculties are restricted throughout time by the soul's contact with matter. This matter, which produces the chain of cause and effect, of birth and death, is *Karman* (anglicized as *karma*), an atomic substance and not a process, as it is in Hinduism and Buddhism. To be free from the shackles of *Karman*, a person must stop the influx of new *Karmans* and eliminate the acquired ones. Because of *karman* a soul is imprisoned in a succession of bodies and passes through various stages of spiritual development before becoming free from all karmic bondage. These stages of development (*gunasthanas*) involve progressive manifestations of the innate faculties of knowledge and power and are accompanied by decreasing sinfulness and increasing purity.

Karmic particles are acquired as the result of intentional "passionate" action, though the very earliest Jain teachings on this subject claimed that any action, even if unintentional, attracted *Karman*. Acquired *Karmans* can be annihilated through a process called *nirjara* or "wearing away", which includes fasting, restricting diet, controlling taste, retreating to lonely places, along with mortifications of the body, atonement and expiation for sins, modesty, service, study, meditation, and renunciation of the ego. *Nirjara* is, thus, the calculated cessation of passionate action.

Hindu Concept of Morality

The moral doctrines of Hinduism are based upon the teachings of the *Upanishads* and of certain secondary scriptures, which derive their authority from the *Vedas*. "Hindu ethics is mainly subjective or personal, its purpose is to eliminate such mental impurities as greed and egoism, for the ultimate attainment of the highest good."[68] The *Dharmashaatras* defined an elaborate detailed way of life based on the division of society into four 'orders' (*varnas*) priests, warriors, tradesmen and servants or labourers and, for the three highest orders, four 'stages of life' (*ashramas*).[69] Apart from caste, a person's duties, in the Hindu tradition, are determined by the stage of life to which he belongs. Life, which is regarded by Hinduism as a journey to the shrine of truth, is marked by four stages, each of which has its responsibilities and obligations. In that journey a normal person should leave no legitimate aspiration unfulfilled; otherwise physical and mental sickness will follow, putting roadblocks in the way of his further spiritual progress.

The first stage of life covers the period of study, when a student cultivates his mind and prepares himself for future service to society. He lives with his teacher in a forest retreat and regards the latter as his spiritual father. He leads an austere life and conserves his energy, spurning the defilement of the body and mind through evil words, thoughts, or deeds. He shows respect to his elders and teachers, and becomes acquainted with the cultural achievements of the race. Students, rich and poor, live under the same roof and receive the same attention from the teacher and his wife.

With marriage, a person enters the second stage. A normal person requires a mate; his biological and emotional urges in this respect are legitimate. Debarred from marriage are those alone who have a dangerous ailment that may be transmitted to children, or those rare souls who, as students, forsake the world at the call of the spirit. Neither a confession of a sin nor a concession to weakness, marriage is a discipline for participation in the larger life of society. Children endow marriage with social responsibilities; Hinduism does not regard romance as the whole of the married life. Husband and wife are co-partners in their spiritual progress, and the family provides a training ground for the practice of unselfishness. The third period of life is devoted to scriptural study and meditation on God. Healthy householder is the foundation of a good society, discharging his duties as a teacher, a soldier, a statesman, a merchant, a scientist, or a manual worker. He should be ambitious to acquire wealth and enjoy pleasures, but not by deviating from the path of righteousness. The following are the five great duties of a householder; the study and teaching of the *Vedas*; daily worship of the Gods through appropriate rituals; gratification of the departed ancestors by offering their spirits food and drink according to the scriptural injunctions; kindness to domestic animals; and hospitality to guests, the homeless, and the destitute. At this stage, the pleasures and excitements of youth appear decayed and physical needs are reduced to a minimum.

During the fourth stage, a man renounces the world and embraces the monastic life. He is no longer bound by social laws. The call of the infinite becomes irresistible to him; even charity and social service appear inadequate. He rises above worldly attachments, finite obligations, and restricted loyalties; he is a friend of his fellow human beings, of the Gods, and of the animals.[70] No longer tempted by riches, honour, or power, a monk preserves equanimity of spirit under all conditions. He turns away from the vanities of the world, devoting himself to the cultivation of God-consciousness, which is a man's true friend both here and hereafter. During the fourth stage, a disciplined life attains to its full blossoming. Well has it been said: 'When a man is born, he cries and the world laughs; but let him lead a life that when he dies, he laughs and the world cries.'

Thus, it will be seen that every stage of life, as described in the *Vedas*, has its duties and obligations, the right discharge of which requires self-control. Through the disciplines of the four stages of life, a Hindu learns progressive non-attachment to the transitory world. The movement of life has been aptly compared to that of the sun. At dawn, the sun rises from below the horizon, and as the morning progresses it goes on radiating heat and light until it reaches the zenith at midday. During the afternoon, it goes down, gradually withdrawing its heat and light, and at dusk, it sinks below the horizon, a mass of radiance to illumine other regions.

Here, the duties of the householder are replaced by the practice of yoga and asceticism. Nevertheless, specific ethical observances are also recommended as prerequisites for the achievement of higher knowledge through yoga, in particular, nonviolence, truthfulness, not stealing, celibacy and poverty. The liberation traditions criticised the system of the *Dharmashastras* for being overly concerned with ritual and external forms of purity and condoning - indeed, prescribing - the killing of living beings in *Vedic* sacrifices; but it was only in the *Dharmashastras* that the notion of action solely for duty's sake was appreciated. The Hindu scripture "the *Bhagavad Gita* (Song of God) represents an effort of two ideals of the renunciation and the fulfillment of obligation."[71] It teaches that one should integrate yoga and action in the world. Only when acting out of the state of inner peace and detachment that is the culmination of the practice of yoga can one execute one's duty without regard for the consequences of one's actions? On the other hand, without the cultivation of inner yoga, the external forms of renunciation celibacy, mendicancy, asceticism are without significance. It is inner yoga that is the essence of renunciation, yet yoga is quite compatible with carrying out one's obligations in the world.

The key to the individual and social ethics of Hinduism is the conception of *Dharma*. Originally, the word signifies the law of inner growth by which a person is supported in his present state of evolution and is shown the way to future development. A person's *Dharma* is not imposed by society or decreed by an arbitrary God, but is something with which he is born because of his actions in previous lives. "*Dharma* determines a man's proper attitude toward the outer world and governs his mental and physical reactions in a given situation; it is his code of honour."[72] Hinduism emphasises the relative nature of *Dharma*, and does not recognise absolute good or evil; evil may be described as what is less good. One cannot stipulate what is good or evil for all men at all times. The attempts to do so, and to judge all people by a single concept of "*Dharma* or impose upon all a single idea of righteousness, has been the cause of much injustice to humanity."[73] If one wants to give a comprehensive definition of good and evil, one may say that what helps men toward the realisation of God or the unity of existence is good, and its reverse is evil. But one faces difficulties when one tries to work out practical details. By performing his duties in a spirit of worship without seeking any personal result, a man ultimately realises God, in whom alone all duties and values of life find fulfillment.

The affirmative attitude of Hinduism toward life has been emphasised by its recognition of four legitimate and basic desires: *Dharma* or righteousness, *Artha* or wealth, *Kama* or sense pleasure, and *Moksha* or freedom through communion with God or the Infinite. Of these, three belong to the realm of worldly values; the fourth (*Moksha*) is called the supreme value. The fulfillment of the first three paves the way for *Moksha.* Enjoyment, if properly guided, can be transformed into spiritual experience. The suppression of legitimate desires often leads to an unhealthy state of body and mind, and delays the attainment of liberation. *Dharma* or righteousness is to be the basis of both individual progress and social welfare. *Artha* or wealth is legitimate; wealth is indispensable in the present state of society. But money must be earned according to *Dharma*; otherwise it debases a man by making him greedy and cruel. The object of the third legitimate desire is *Kama,* or the enjoyment of sense pleasure. This covers a vast area- from the enjoyment of conjugal love, without which the creation cannot be maintained, to the appreciation of art, music, or poetry.

Life becomes drab and grey unless one cultivates aesthetic sensitivity. But sense pleasures, if not pursued according to *Dharma*, degenerate into sensuality. Wealth and sense pleasure, which are only means to an end, are valuable in so far as their enjoyment creates a genuine yearning for spiritual freedom in the mind of the enjoyer. The fourth legitimate desire, equally irresistible, is related to *Moksha*, or freedom from the love and attachment prompted by the finite view of life. Man, who in essence is spirit, cannot be permanently satisfied with worldly experiences. Nor can man attain his divine stature through correct social behaviour, economic security, political success, or artistic creation. Charity for the needy may be a corrective for selfishness, but cannot be the ultimate goal of his soul's craving.

This ritualistic conception of virtue in the *Vedic* tradition was significantly modified in the *Dharmasastras*, 'treatises on *Dharma*' composed from about 600 BC onward. The most famous of which is the *Manu Dharmasastra*, Laws of Manu. The correct performance of rituals is still important, but the highest *Dharma*, according to this literature, is 'good conduct' in the broadest sense: 'Neither austerities nor the study of the Veda, nor the performance of the *Agnihotra* or rite, nor lavish liberality to priests can ever save him whose conduct is vile and who has strayed from the path of *Dharma*' (*Vasista Dharmasutra*). Nevertheless, "the *Dharma* still fundamentally involves doing (and avoiding) certain things; it is implicitly defined as the adherence to certain norms, specifically, the norms of the ancient Indian society that referred to itself as 'the *Aryas*', which transmitted the *Vedic* literature."[74]

Thus, the renunciation is part of the scheme; it is still to be undertaken only at a certain time and in a certain way, and so falls under the rubric of duty. The *Manu Dharmasastra* states, "A twice-born man who seeks final liberation without having studied the *Vedas*, without having begotten sons, and without having offered sacrifices, sinks downwards."[75] For the *Brahman* order in particular, the *Dharmasastras* spell out numerous restrictions intended to preserve its unique 'purity' – the avoidance of polluting agents, especially contact with people of lower orders, the avoidance of certain foods, and so forth. They also specify rules bearing on marriage and inheritance and other matters of civil law. They prescribe various sacraments to be undergone at certain junctures of life, the most important being the investiture of the sacred thread at the beginning of the period of studentship. They go into a plethora of matters of etiquette, even prescribing how to have sex and answer the calls of nature as part of expiation.

But the *Dharmasastras* speak of, besides the *Dharma* of the specific *Varnas,* 'the *Dharma* common to all orders' (*Sarvasrama Dharma*). That includes such things as forgiveness, self-control, not stealing or lying, nonviolence, restraint of the senses, compassion, patience, freedom from anger, envy and avarice, and so on. Thus, while there is indeed a lack of reflection on the nature of virtue in general in the *Dharmasastras,* or for that matter in Indian thought as a whole, a step in that direction can be seen in the attempt to identify these more general duties - which, however, are considered to apply only to *Aryas*; other 'barbarian' societies are condemned simply for being non-Aryan.

Morality and Duty in Various Schools' of Hinduism

The various Hindu schools of philosophy engaged in an extensive discussion of the nature of the scriptural injunction (*Vidhi*) that commands one to carry out or avoid a certain act. Nyaya philosophers held that the injunction makes one aware of a means of the *Dharmic* act by which a certain desirable purpose can be achieved; that is, it motivates the hearer to act by implicitly appealing to the hearer's self-interest, whether it be spiritual or hedonistic. In general, a *Dharmic*, pious life was considered to be conducive to happiness and prosperity on earth and the attainment of heaven after death; but, as we shall see, it was also considered instrumental in attaining ultimate salvation in the form of liberation from the cycle of rebirth.

Bhatta Mimamsa philosophers, on the other hand, believed that the *Vidhi*, specifically, the ending of the optative verb of the injunctive sentence, actually impels the agent towards acting by virtue of its own peculiar efficacy referred to as *Sabdabhavana*. At the same time, an awareness of some purpose to be achieved through the act is also necessary. Prabhakara's Mimamsa philosophers, finally, held that a *Vidhi* motivates one to act neither by causing one to act through the potency of its language, nor by persuading one to do so by suggesting the achievement of a desired end, but simply by making one aware of an obligation (*niyoga*) that one feels bound to carry out; it is followed for its own sake, without regard for the result of the act it prescribes. Understood in this way, the scriptural injunction resembles the Kantian categorical imperative. This theory also implies that the will of the agent who carries out an injunction is free.

The *Bhagavad Gita*, perhaps the single most important Hindu text that relates to ethics, can be seen as an attempt to reconcile the two ideals of duty and renunciation.[76] Contained in the epic poem the *Mahabharata* (200 BC - AD 200), traditionally attributed to (Vyasa), the *Gita* relates a dialogue between Krsna (Krishna), an incarnation of the Supreme Being Vishnu, and the warrior Arjuna. The issue of the dialogue is whether Arjuna should participate in the great battle that is about to take place, against his own cousins leading the opposing side. Arjuna knows that his cause is just - his cousins are violent and despotic; they have deprived him and his brothers of their due portion of the kingdom - but he feels that it would be a violation of *Dharma* to be an agent of the destruction of his own friends and relatives, no matter how wrong they are. Filial duty has come into conflict with Arjuna's duty as a prince (ksatriya) to preserve order in society and defend it against its enemies. In response to Arjuna's quandary, Krsna does not enter into a discussion on the nature of virtue or universal principles of right action (as perhaps Socrates would have done) but tells Arjuna to cultivate yoga, which will enable him to rise above his situation.

Yoga will provide Arjuna with clarity and equanimity, so that he is no longer confused about his duty which Krsna suggests is obvious, anyway: to defend society against evil or overcome with remorse about the pain he must inflict in doing what he must do. It will bring about a state of calm and centeredness from which he can carry out right action undistracted by passion; 'Yoga is skill in action', says Krsna. Moreover, it will transform the personality, so that Arjuna will no longer act as an individual agent but yield to the forces of nature - ultimately, to God - acting through his body: 'He who thinks this self is a killer and he who thinks it is killed, both fail to understand; it does not kill, nor is it killed'. The *yogin* is not 'bound' by what he does; his actions do not necessitate further rebirth.

Thus, the *Gita* works out a synthesis of the ideals of duty and renunciation, proposing a new ideal of renunciation in action. Especially in the third, fourth and fifth chapters, the theme of renunciation is taken up. True renunciation is the state of inner yoga, a condition of complete calm, contentment and detachment. This is compatible with acting to carry out one's responsibilities in the world, even with observing the specific prescriptions of the *Dharmasastras* - indeed; the *Gita* upholds the *Varnaasrama* system. In reality, all creatures are driven to act as far as they are part of nature, which are subject to constant change in the fluctuations of 'the three *Gunas*' (basic ingredients of material nature).[77] Krsna, the Supreme Being, refers to his own case: 'These worlds would collapse if I did not perform action'. It is stressed, however, that action should be undertaken only for its own sake, out of a sense of duty: 'You have a right to action alone, not the fruits of action. Thus, the state of yoga is essential for right action, because only in that state is one not driven by inclination. It is the detachment of yoga that makes it possible for one to act only for duty's sake. The *Gita* also describes this state of mind in terms of considering one's actions as a sacrifice and surrendering one's actions to God.

Concept of Morality in Contemporary Hinduism

According to Vivekananda, goal of life is freedom and freedom is the basis of morality. Morality and code of behaviour are based on this goal. Vivekananda upholds the idea of *Vedanta*, and says that "we may reach the same goal by different paths."[78] He generalised these paths into four—viz. those of work, love, psychology, and knowledge. These divisions are made in accordance with the type or the tendency that may be seen to prevail in a man. We have found that, in the end, all these four paths converge and become one. All religions and all methods of work and worship lead us to one and the same goal.

According to Vivekananda, most of the movements and struggles are only for the achievement of freedom. The whole universe is in fact the result of this struggle for freedom. In all combinations, every particle is trying to go on its own way, to fly from the other particles; but the others are holding it in check. Everything has a tendency to infinite dispersion. All that we see in the universe has for its basis this one struggle towards freedom; it is under the impulse of this tendency that the saint prays and the robber robs. When the line of action taken is not a proper one, we call it evil; and when the manifestation of it is proper and high, we call it good. But the impulse is the same, the struggle towards freedom. The saint is oppressed with the knowledge of his condition of bondage, and he wants to get rid of it; so he worships God. The thief is oppressed with the idea that he does not possess certain things, and he tries to get rid of that want, to obtain freedom from it; so he steals. Freedom is the one goal of all nature, sentient or insentient; and, consciously or unconsciously, everything is struggling towards that goal. The freedom which the saint seeks is very different from that which the robber seeks; the freedom loved by the saint leads him to the enjoyment of infinite, unspeakable bliss, while that on which the robber has set his heart only forges other bonds for his soul.

There is to be found in every religion the manifestation of this struggle towards freedom. It is the groundwork of all morality, of unselfishness, which means getting rid of the idea that men are the same as their little body. When we see a man doing good work, helping others, it means that he cannot be confined within the limited circle of "me and mine." There is no limit to this getting out of selfishness. All the great systems of ethics preach absolute unselfishness as the goal. Supposing this absolute unselfishness can be reached by a man, what becomes of him? That little personality which he had before is now lost to him forever; he has become infinite, and the attainment of this infinite expansion is indeed the goal of all religions and of all moral and philosophical teachings.

According to Aurobindo, the basis of morality is condemnation or approval. The "ethical being escapes from all the formulas of utilitarian or hedonistic theories that refer all virtues to pleasure and satisfaction to mind, to social sense and to a rule direction of the social impulses."[79] Utility is a fundamental principle of existence. And all fundamental principles of existence are in the end one. Therefore, "it is true that the highest good is also the highest utility, but simply the good of others and most widely the good of all is the one ideal aim of our ethical practices, good, not utility must be the principle and standard of good."[80]

In the first two stages, nature acts impartially and the secret will behind it creates and destroys according to the truth of being. The conscious force in man struggles for expressions and hence whatever helps that expression is good and whatever retards it is evil. In the beginning man was attracted by that which helped him to live or to progress and disliked that which threatened and injured him. Later the feeling of like or dislike to approval or disapproval. This is the origin of the sense of ethical values. This ethical impulse is the means by which man struggles to reach the higher stage of harmony and universality from the lower harmony. In the final super ethical stage man need not need the ethical codes as all the problems of harmony gets resolved in final reconciliation. Thus, in the three stages of evolution, infra-ethical, ethical and supra-ethical, only one stage is ethical.

For Gandhi, morality is quite inseparable with the conception of God and religion. Morality represents the essence of religion. Religious ideal are the realisation of truth or God. If unities are inclusion of selfish consideration and love for others, then God is the essential unity of everything. This act of self-transcendence is nothing but morality. God can be discovered by trying to find him in his creation and that would be possible only by loving all and by serving all. D.M. Datta observes that "The path to the realisation of the true self or God, therefore, lies through the love of others and the performance of duties towards others as love demands. Morality, thus, becomes the essence of religion."[81]

In the conception of morality, Gandhi makes clear that all action cannot be considered as moral. There are unmoral and 'non-moral' actions also. No action that is not voluntary can be called moral. So long as we act like machines, there cannot arise any question of morality. If we call an action moral, it means that it has been done consciously and as matter of duty. According to Gandhi, self-transcendence or love constitutes the essence of morality. Love according to Gandhi, is divine. Performance of duty convinced people. But love at time, tends to be blind. This may lead to dogmatism and even to barbarism and fanaticism. Therefore, Gandhi says that morality does not consist in loving blindly; it is loves with full-consciousness and knowledge of love. Thus, along with love, he puts knowledge as an essential aspect of morality.[82]

According to Radhakrishnan, one must begin with a faith- a faith in religious experience. Religious experience alone is capable of making man realise spirituality and this religious experience is not merely a form of knowledge as other ordinary experiences are, it is not just expressible in a body of certain codes and rules of behaviour. It produces an objective awareness - an apprehension of real coupled with an enjoyment.

According to Radhakrishnan, it is only through religious experience alone that man can attain salvation. But it is not easy to have this experience. It involves a struggle within a fight against oneself. This fight can be carried out in two stages, one is preparatory stage and other is final assault. The first stage consists in bringing about certain changes in intellectual emotional and ethical make up of man. The second stage is the stage of meditation, contemplation and love.[83]

Concept of Morality in Buddhism

The relationship of man to man, the attitude of compassion and the spirit of human love is stressed in Buddhism. According to Buddhism, man's aptitude for goodness, observance of the *Dhamma* and compassion for other beings is the essence of man. To the question what is good, the Buddhist answer is a "set of attributes - love (*metta*), compassion (*karuna*), sympathy and joy (*mudita*), impartiality (*upekkha*) and forgiveness (*khanti*)."[84] To achieve these goods "desires are to be eradicated completely."[85]

The chief characteristic of Buddhist ethics is that, it is based on a sound theory of human nature. Buddhism clearly understands the human psychology that men have a desire or last towards existence, even though it gives lot of suffering. Buddhism uncovers the nature Nietzsche contradiction of the human nature. It is just as a journey, which gives lots of suffering and sorrow but still Men, has a kind of eager desire towards that journey. Therefore, one Buddhist proverb says, life on earth is a pilgrimage in a strange land which the true knower is not anxious to prolong. Buddhism analyses the moral personality of man and finds the principle of moral causation operating in its growth. The doctrine of *karma* or moral causation exhibits all existence as born of desire.

Redemption from suffering is the motive of Buddha's teaching. Escape from the pervasive evil of existence is the goal of moral life. While *nirvana* is the highest goal, all forms of conduct, which lead to it positively or bring a day of rebirth are birth of good and their opposites bad. The good of the life determines moral theory of Buddhism. The moral principles are the means to achieve the good of life and nirvana.

Apparently, the conception of good of life can be considered as a metaphysical one. But the deeper understanding of Buddhism gives us the insight that, the question of good of life itself arises from the ethical basis. Ethical concerns are the basis of philosophical formulation of Buddhist theories.

Buddhist version of will of human being can be interpreted as assigning an absolute value to the good will. Buddha would say that the only thing in the world, which possesses an absolute value, is the good will, the will freely determined by the moral law. Without the notion of 'will' the notion of ethics would be impossible in Buddhist school of thought. According to Buddhism, 'will' is man's distinctive endowment by the virtue of which he is an ethical being. By the inclusion of will, actions ceases, consequently individuality also. Action ceases when delight of the senses in objects ceases. The delight ceases by the recognition of the transcending of life. Fresh formulations are the breaking up of the composite self, which helps us to prevent from saying away from the path of *nirvana*.[86] Escape from the chance of rebirth into the bliss of life eternal is the ideal of Buddhism.

Kamma: The notion of *kamma* has a very important role in the Buddhist ethics. *Kamma* is an act both intellectual and volitional. Psychologically every act consists of three sides: Volitional preparation, act itself and back of the act, i.e., outcome of the act, the feeling of remorse which follows the act. This third factor of '*action*' is crucial in '*kamma*' relation with ethics. Some acts have their relation (outcome) immediately, some after a time, perhaps in the next existence.

Based on the retribution of action, we can distinguish acts in two broad categories: pure and impure. Pure acts means the acts free from passion, desire and ignorance, they do not entail any retribution and do not lead to fresh individual existence. Impure acts only lead to destruction individual existence. Good acts are those which lead to the conquest of passions, desires and illusions of the ego. Bad acts are those which lead to unpleasant retributions. The same classification of acts can be done because of the first aspect of act, volitional preparation, i.e., intention or resolve. Good acts are those done with the motive of happiness in the world hereafter, bad acts are those done with the idea of gaining happiness here below. Even though mainly we can say that in Buddhism the acts are evaluated by understanding the consequence of the acts, but at the same time, it does not deny the role of intention. i.e., good acts are destroying desire and lead to a cancealing of the rewards of other acts. Good acts possess three features: absence of lust, absence of hatred and absence of delusion.

According to Buddhism, there are two extreme paths, both of which are not desirable. One extreme path is the self-mortification or ascetic life, which most of the Indian spiritual systems advocates. And the extreme is the habitual devotion to the passion, to the pleasure of sensual things, to which usually people are attracted. As we have mentioned earlier, Buddhist ethics has not only the base of philosophical analysis, but also of the sound psychological analysis. Both these bases come from the soundness of understanding. Buddhism rejects these two extremes. "It should be emphasised that the Buddha recommends the doctrine of dependent origination as the middle way which avoids the two dogmatic extremes of eternalism and *annihilationism*."[87]

Buddha insists not on an abolition of will or a turning away from the world, but on a hot contest with desire. Passion or emotion is not paralysed in Buddhist ethics, instead of that it is controlled and guided. Buddha does not want a suppression of emotion and desire, but asks for the cultivation of true love for all creation. A state of consciousness is never good in itself, but good or bad by its efforts. If the effect is well-being, we have *sukha*, if ill-being, we have *dukha*, because good/ bad is intrinsic.

It is clear that Buddhism takes the ethical problem in a deep way, that's why, it could present a unique way of reconciliation between descriptive moral life of human and normative understanding of moral life of human life. Buddhism understood that in descriptive level, moral life of human is mostly directed towards the extreme of sensuous pleasure. Buddhism has not denied this life of sensuous pleasure with a presupposition that sensuous life is wrong. Instead Buddhism understands that, the very nature of human psychology itself has some kind of lineage towards the world of sensuous pleasures. At the same time Buddha understood that desire towards the world of pleasure, is the sense of suffering, which has to be removed.

Morality of Buddhism has an eye on both the goal and descriptive realm of human world and his/her psychology. Buddhist ethics, adopts what are quite necessary for the achievement of soul, but apart from the necessary condition for the achievement of goal, a fully developed picture of Buddhist ethics was developed by understanding the descriptive realm of human beings. The ethical system enunciated by Buddha is free from the extremes of self-indulgence and self-mortification. For Buddha, "true way cannot be attained by one who has lost his strength."[88]

Buddha has shown the way of eight-fold middle path: *Right beliefs*: Buddhism holds that wrong actions stem from wrong beliefs therefore right beliefs are quite necessary in an ethical living. *Right aspiration*: Aspirations of the human being are the intentions or resolve of human actions. For Buddhism, one must be longing for renunciation, the hope to live in love with all, the aspiration of true humanity. Right aspirations must find expressions in right speech, right action and right living. *Right speech*: Right speech is the abstaining from rude language, falsehood and frivolous talk etc. *Right conduct*: Right conduct is unselfish action. By the word 'action', it does not mean rituals and sacrifice. Buddha does not believe in those. According to him "Better homage of a man grounded in the *Dhamma* than to *Agni* for a 100 years."[89] Thus, Buddhism revolutionarily redefined the notion of action, "neither abstinence, nor shaving the head, nor a rough garment, neither offerings to priests, nor sacrifices to Gods will cleanse a man who is not free from delusions."[90] According to him, 'Anger, drunkenness, deception, envy, these constitute uncleanly-ness; not the eating of fish.

Right mode of livelihood: Right action leads to right living. *Right effort*: Right effort consists in practicing control of passion, to prevent the rise of bad qualities. Right effort means effort for the subjective purification. Right effort means an inhibition of the bad and a reinforcement of the good by mental avoidance and concentration. *Right mindedness*: Right effort cannot be isolated from right thinking. To avoid mental unsteadiness, the mind that plays and roves is to be controlled. Right rapture: The joyful one characterised by the rise of the thought of truth.

Ethics of Mahayana

Buddhism split into two groups after Buddha's demise, one is Hinayana Buddhism and another one is Mahayana Buddhism. The ethical ideal of Mahayana is the Bodhisattva, as distinct from the art of Hinayana. Bodhisattva literally means "one whose essence is perfect knowledge. But historically it means one who is on the way to the attainment of perfect knowledge, is to become a future Buddha."[91] A Bodhisattva out of the abundance of his love for suffering humanity stops short of nirvana. Weak man in times of stress and sorrow requires a personal guide, and these lofty beings, which can tread the path of nirvana, engage themselves in the task of leading men into the way of knowledge.

Buddhist Criticism of Moral Arguments

According to Buddhism, the moral argument stresses the idea that the sense of moral obligation felt by humans implies the existence of God. In other words, the moral obligation possesses a supernatural source and anyone seriously committed to moral values should believe in the reality of a trance - human source. If the belief in God makes a person moral, then Buddhists don't have any problem at all. But the fact of moral perfection on God's part cannot be used as an argument for his existence. Morality could then be a means of approaching God, not a proof of existence of God.

Thus, to sum up, the Indic religions and philosophical systems, are able to see that the notions like God, Self and Ethical principles are not quite independent. *Vedic* religion and Hinduism follow similar kinds of patterns. Each of these notions influences each other in their construal. Each systems or religions define these concepts in particular patterns. This pattern would be the deciding factor in the construal of all its major concepts. These patterns consist of certain metaphysical and epistemological assumptions. Therefore, the basic metaphysical and epistemological assumptions are the crucial ones in the analysis of each of these principles.[92]

Major critiques that we can raise against both these traditions are epistemological, that is mainly related to the methodology of their metaphysical concepts. The epistemological concern clearly involves only in this context only. Moreover, Hindu ethics are not in accordance with these pre theoretical intuitions, because the purpose of ethical construal is absent in Hindu ethics. That is why Hindu ethics end up in justifying the inequalities of present society like division among human beings on the lines of *Varna*. Whatever may be the justification given to *Varna* system, it ends up in justifying the inequalities and causes undesirable situations. On the basis taking the present system as standard, they find justification for *Varna* system. That is, certain people have a tendency or disposition to justify *Varna* system using various means. That is why they agree on inequalities by bringing such justification. Buddhism can be considered as a philosophical system, which is predominantly ethical. The basic reason behind this is that the basic questions or the driving force behind the construal of entire philosophical system is ethical. Human suffering is the basic question, which Buddhism addresses throughout in its philosophical construal.

References

1. Bishop, D.H., *Indian Thought: An Introduction*, Wiley Eastern Private Limited. New Delhi, pp. 33-34.
2. Chatterjee and Datta, *History of Philosophy Eastern and Western*, (Ed)_S. Radhakrishan, et al. London: George Allen & Unwin Ltd, Vol. I, 1984, p. 64.
3. Bishop, D.H., *Indian Thought: An Introduction,* Wiley Eastern Private Limited, New Delhi, pp. 26-27.
4. Radhakrishnan S., *Indian Philosophy*, London; George Allen & Unwin Limited, Humanities Press Inc, New York, 1977, pp. 73-75.
5. Hajime Nakamura, *A Comparative History of Ideas*, Motilal Banarsidass Publishers, New Delhi, 1992, pp. 32-33.
6. Chattopadhyaya, D., *Indian Philosophy: A Popular Introduction,* People's Publishing House, New Delhi, 1975, pp. 48-50.
7. Mahadevan, T.M.P., *Invitation to Indian Philosophy*, Sterling Publishers Private Limited, New Delhi, 1981, p. 103.
8. Bishop, D.H., *Indian Thought: An Introduction,* Wiley Eastern Private Limited, New Delhi,1975, p. 99.
9. Radhakrishnan, *Indian Philosophy*, Vol. I, Geroge Allen & Unwin Limited, London and Humanities Press Inc, New York, 1977, p. 331.
10. *Ibid.*
11. Puligundla, *The Heart of Jainism*, ed., *Fundamentals of Indian Philosophy*, Mahabhodi Publishers, Mumbai, 1975, pp. 18-19.
12. Radhakrishnan, *Indian Philosophy*, Vol. I, London: Geroge Allen & Unwin Ltd, Humanities Press Inc, New York, 1977, p. 331.
13. Puligundla, *The Heart of Jainism*, ed., *Fundamentals of Indian Philosophy*, Mahabhodi Publishers, Mumbai, 1975, p. 20.
14. Dandekar, R. N., *Insights into Hinduism,* Ajanta Publications, New Delhi, 1979, pp. 133-136.

15. Mahadevan, T. M. P., *Outlines of Hinduism*, Chetana Private Limited, Bombay, 1977, pp. 99-116.
16. Mahadevan, T. M. P., 2006. *The Philosophy of Advaita,* Published Bharatiya Kala Prakashan, New Delhi. p. 57.
17. *Ibid*, p. 62.
18. *Ibid*, p. 67.
19. Chattopadhyaya, D, *Indian Philosophy: A Popular Introduction,* People's Publishing House, New Delhi, 1975, pp. 49-50.
20. *Ibid*, p. 53.
21. Chattopadhyaya, D, *Indian Philosophy: A Popular Introduction,* People's Publishing House, New Delhi,1975, p. 54.
22. Srivastava, *Contemporary Indian Philosophy*, Sarda Publications, Ranchi, 1984, p. 17.
23. Swami Vivekananda, *Complete Works, II*, ed, Lal B.K.,*Contemporary Indian Philosophy*, Motilal Banarasidass, New Delhi, 1987, p. 236.
24. Radhakrishnan, Sarvepally and Charles A. Moore, *A Source Book in Indian Philosophy,* Princeton University Press, New Jersy, p. 578.
25. Aurobindo, Sri, *The Life Divine*, Book II, Chap. 2, Sri Aurobindo Ashram, Pondichery, 1949, p. 26.
26. *The Philosophy of Sri Aurobindo*, Banaras Hindu University Press, Banaras, 1945, p. 13.
27. Lal, B.K., *Contemporary Indian Philosophy*, Motilal Banarsidass , NewDelhi, 1978, p. 94.
28. *Ibid*, p. 95.
29. Mahadevan, T.M.P., *Contemporary Indian Philosophy*, Sterling Publishers Pvt. Ltd. New Delhi, 1981, p. 247.
30. Lal, B.K., *Contemporary Indian Philosophy*, Motilal Banarsidass, New Delhi, 1987, p. 262.
31. Jayatillek, K.N., ed, Ninian Smart, *The Message of the Buddha*, George Allen and Unwin, London,1975, p. 99.
32. *Ibid*, p. 60.
33. *Ibid*, p. 111.
34. Aravind Sharma, The term is from '*Dhamma Pada*'. Initially, this term captured the essence of Buddhism but later developed into "*Dhamma – Sanyata*' *The Philosophy of Religion – A Buddhist Perspective*, Oxford University Press, New Delhi, 1995, p. 13.
35. The term is used not in its usual normative flavour. It connotes to anything that is an element of being (*Dhamma*). The constituent of existence, *Ibid.*
36. Basham, A.L., *The Wonder that was India*, Oxford University Press, Oxford, 1975, p. 270.

37. Radhakrishnan S, "*Indian Philosophy*," Vol. I, McMillan Company, New York, 1962, p. 457.
38. John, Hick, "*The Philosophy of Religion*, third edition; Englewood Cliffs, Prentice-Hall Inc, New Jersey, 1983, p. 19.
39. Sharma, Chandradhar, *A Critical Survey of Indian Philosophy*, Rider and Company, London, 1960, p. 139.
40. Sharma Arvind, *The Philosophy of Religion*, A Buddhist Perspective. Oxford University Press, New Delhi. 1995, p. 34.
41. *Ibid*, p. 35.
42. *Ibid*, p. 36.
43. Ramaiah, Sundara G. *Nature and Destiny of Soul in Indian Philosophy*, Oxford University Press, New Delhi, 1995, p. 21.
44. Bishop, D.H., *Indian Thought: An Introduction*, Wiley Eastern Private Limited, New Delhi, p. 59.
45. Radhakrishnan, S, *Indian Philosophy*, George Allen & Unwin Limited, London,1977, p. 320.
46. Jaini, J.L. *Outlines of Jainism*, Cambridge University Press, London, 1916, p. 77.
47. Tatai Natumal, *Studies in Jaina Philosophy*, P. V. Research Institute, Jainashram, Hindu University, Varanasi, 1951, p. 230.
48. *Ibid*, p. 231.
49. *Ibid*, p. 232.
50. Ramaiah Sundara, G, *Nature and Destiny of Soul in Indian Philosophy*, Oxford University Press, New Delhi, 1995, p. 21.
51. Matilal, B.K. (1977), *Nyaya-Vaisesika*. Otto Harrassowitz, Weisbaden. p. 73.
52. Nakamura, Hsjime, *A Comparative History of Ideas*, Motilal Banarsidass Publishers Private Limited, New Delhi, 1992, p. 269.
53. *Ibid*. p. 269.
54. Puligandla, R, *Fundamentals of Indian Philosophy*, Mahabodhi Publishers, Mumbai, 1975, p. 63.
55. Chattopadhyaya, D, *Indian Philosophy: A Popular Introduction*, People's Publishing House, New Delhi,1975, p. 129.
56. *Ibid*.
57. Radhakrishnan S, *Indian Philosophy*, George Allen & Unwin Limited, London, 1977, p. 111.
58. Chhanda Chakraborty, *Common Life in the Rig – Veda and Atharvana Veda*, Punthi Pustak, Calcutta, 1977, pp. 78-79.
59. Radhakrishnan, S, *Indian Philosophy*, George Allen & Unwin Limited, London, 1977, p. 111.

60. *Ibid*, p. 79.
61. Bowes Pratima, *The Hindu Religious Tradition; A Philosophical Approach*, Allied Publishers Private Limited, Bombay, 1976, p. 75.
62. *Ibid*, pp. 76 - 80.
63. Puligandla, R, *Fundamentals of Indian Philosophy*, Mahabodhi Publishers, Mumbai, 1975, pp. 48-49.
64. Bhattacharya, H. S. (1976). *Jain Moral Doctrine*. Jain Sahitya Vikas Mandal. Mumbai, p. 47.
65. Bishop, D.H. *Indian Thought: An Introduction*,Wiley Eastern Private Limited, New Delhi,1975, pp. 86-87.
66. *Ibid*, p. 87.
67. Radhakrishnan S, *The Indian Philosophy*, Vol. I, George Allen & Unwin Limited, London, 1977, p. 326.
68. Charles T. Gorham, *Ethics of Great Religions*, PRIRUP Prakashan, New Delhi, 1986, p. 25.
69. Saral Jhingran, (1989), *Aspects of Hindu Morality*, Motilal Banarasidass Publishers Pvt Lmt, New Delhi, pp. 73-75.
70. *Ibid*, p. 76.
71. Radhakrishnan, S. (1960). *Brahma Sutra, The Philosophy of Spiritual Life*. Greenwood Press, New York. p. 264.
72. *Ibid,* p. 265.
73. *Ibid*, pp. 266-267.
74. *Ibid*, p. 270.
75. Radhakrishnan S. (1960). *Brahma Sutra, The Philosophy of Spiritual Life*. Greenwood Press, New York, pp. 268-269.
76. Charles T. Gorham, *Ethics of Great Religions*, PRIRUP Prakashan, New Delhi, 1986, pp. 29.
77. *Ibid*, pp. 30-32.
78. Mahadevan, T.M.P., *Contemporary Indian Philosophy*, Sterling Publishers Private Limited, New Delhi, 1981, pp. 116-117.
79. *Ibid*, p. 177.
80. Aurobindo, Sri, *Sri, The Life Divine,* Book II, Chap. 2 Vol. 19, Sri Aurobindo Ashram, Pondichery, 1971, p. 139.
81. Lal B.K., (D.M. Datta, *The Philosophy of Mahatma Gandhi*, p. 83) *Contemporary Indian Philosophy*, Motilal Banarsidass, New Delhi, 1978, p. 132.
82. *Ibid*, p. 134. (last para)
83. Radhakrishnan, S, *Indian Philosophy*, Vol. II, George Allen & Unwin Ltd, 1977, p. 614.

84. Rhys Davids, (1976). *Buddhist Psycology and Ethics*, Oxford University Press, Oxford, p. 120.
85. *Ibid.* p. 122.
86. Rhys Davids, (1976). *Buddhist Psycology and Ethics*, Oxford University Press, Oxford, p. 124.
87. *Ibid*, p. 123.
88. *Ibid*, pp. 125-26.
89. Joshi Lal Mani, *Studies in the Buddhistic Culture of India*, Motilal Banarasi Dass, New Delhi,1977, pp. 101-105.
90. *Ibid*, p. 106.
91. *Ibid*, p. 242.
92. Rhys Davids, (1978). *Outlines of Buddhism*, Oriental Books Reprint Corporation, New Delhi, p. 127.

Chapter – IV

Ambedkar's Critique of Religion and Morality in Semitic and Indic Traditions

The aim of this chapter is mainly to discuss Ambedkar's critical comments on the place of religion and morality in Semitic and Indic traditions. He considers that the altruistic nature of Judaism was under suspicion because of its special preference to Israel. He understood that, the preference might be because the Jew community has been under the slavery for long time. In that sense, he appreciates the notion of Lord with the Oppressed. Ambedkar was very much enthusiastic and appreciative on the life of Jesus and the principles of Christianity. However, he disagrees with them mainly on the affirmation of speculative ideas of the religion and other superstitions in the practice. Moreover, his main criticism is that the principles of equality and other valuable things are withered by church in its practices. His complaint against Islam was mainly for its intolerance, which develops from the persistent affirmation of only one true God.

Ambedkar's analysis and criticism mainly concentrate on the nature of Hinduism and Buddhism. Ambedkar appreciates the democratic, equalitarian aspect of Buddhism and its realistic and scientific attitudes. He criticises Hinduism for its attempts to provide justification to the present hierarchical order of the society.[1] Ambedkar understood that caste and its division is not ailment/evil, which intrudes in the Hinduism, but he analyses that caste and its division is the very part and the basis of the Hindu Religion. Thorough analysis reveals that each shift and changes are clearly supported with many other original records and writings. One of the major emphases of his work is that Ambedkar's attempt to justify morality without reference to transcendental religious beliefs is a first step to make the realm or morality an autonomous one. Thus, external considerations are no longer above moral principles. Ambedkar makes such a morality as the basis of religion, which he construes as Dhamma. That is qualified as the 'Copernican Revolution' in the realm of morality. With regard to Jainism, he had different opinion on its unpractical attitudes, especially regarding its position on *Ahimsa.*

Ambedkar's Critique on Judaism

The conception of morality that is depicted in Judaism is highly valuable and altruistic one. Indeed, God is described as clothing the naked, nursing the sick, comforting the mourners, burying the dead, so that man may recognise his own obligations. In addition, all the human beings asked, as He (God) is merciful and gracious, so be you merciful and gracious. As He is righteous, so be you righteous. As He is holy, strive to be holy. Sin/wrong is ultimately deliberate disobedience or rebellion against the divine sovereign.

One of the major problems with Judaism is that its ethical system is not a dynamic one. In certain sense, it experiences the stagnation and exists without further kind of development. It is because morality is defined as following the path of God, or in the image of God. Here, the problem is that the motive of ethical practice is absent. Questions like, "why I am trying to follow the God or be the image of God have to answer in non-ethical way."[2] According to this, the ethical concerns are the consequence of following God. Another subsequent question is about the motive of being ethical. Ambedkar thinks that this can be explained only by self-consequentialism, which is either the desire of heaven or the fear of hell. Thus, the motive of ethical behaviour reduced to the matter of self. What is more crucial than this in the Judaism is the immobility of the ethical system. According to Judaism, "being ethical means being the follower of God or being the image of God."[3] Ambedkar poses the basic question that how can we strive to be the image of God? He says that the primary thing is that we must have some idea of what God is then, only one should be able to adopt the qualities of morality.

Major question regarding the Jews is: how a certain community/ tribe is privileged in front of God. How the people of Israel can be considered as the people of God. The spiritual leaders of the Judaism have conquered other people on the justification about the particular place given to them by God. Moreover, the scriptures only describes Israel as the chosen people, they did not provide any rationale for it. It is really a suspicion mark on the altruistic nature of Judaism.

He further asks how these conceptions were generated. Although the scriptures are providing information regarding the unique character of the God, they are unchallengeable. They are always undeviating and permanent. They never provide any new information according to changes of times. Thus, Ambedkar tried to say that the ethical system of Judaism has not been an independent one. By description it self, the ethical system of Judaism depends on the characterisation of God in the scriptures. The scriptures are immobile and stagnant in their content.[4] Therefore, this immobility involuntarily transmitted to the ethical system also. Ambedkar opined that by the very definition itself, the ethical system should be lively and ever changing. It is because ethics deals with the standardisation of human relation. According to him, human relation contains many complexities and various natures which changes from time to time. Then the static system of ethics would be ineffective to guide the human actions. He argues that the normative system would be unable to guide the human actions.

Ambedkar questions, what would happen to the other factors, which are the subjective and, presently prevailing social values? What extent do they determine to the direction of ethical principles? As a result, do the ethical principles end up as unchallenging one to the present social values, which would be in accordance with the current social structure? Ambedkar raises all these questions on the notion of religion and morality in Judaism.

Ambedkar's Critical Views on Islam

In Islam what one can observe is that there is relentless affirmation of one and only true God. Most of the stories and myths of Islam insists on the point that there is only and truly one God who will be the judge to decide the fate of all human beings. The affirmation is good in the sense of providing energy and confidence in the practice of religious and ethical principles. However, this affirmation is in way contempt against other religions, and then it would be highly problematic. Then 'the affirmation towards the one and only God prompts one to be intolerance towards other beliefs.'[5] It would prompt one to deny the democratic space of other believers.

Moreover, ethical principles are mostly concentrated on certain impositions of social manners and practices or customs. In addition, ethical principles are most of the times considered as imposition on group. The fear of hell became the major motive of the ethical principles. That is, following certain customs and manners in order to avoid undesirable consequences. However, Ambedkar thought that they overlooked the role of the transformation of mind and purifying process of mind is less emphasised in the Islamic philosophy.[6] Consequently, many good principles are practiced in different manner.

The question is that if some people force the other faiths to accept their philosophy through swords, then what will happen. There shall be total unrest, lot of bloodshed, killing, looting, destruction of properties; miseries, pollution, diseases, contaminations, famines and death to all the people i.e. end of human race. Is this acceptable to an Islamic believer, can anybody give a guarantee to a hungry and destitute person a paradise after his death. Moreover, where is the paradise located, has anybody seen that place. Can anybody produce a solid proof of that paradise, if not; people are misled in false pretension.

According to Ambedkar, Islam is very conservative and fundamentalist in its outlook in some respects. He understood that the religion "itself is moulded in the way of allowing no other exposure to the other world. That's why social exclusiveness is part and parcel of Islam which ended up in degradation of women, lack of education, social backwardness etc."[7] This reluctance to reform and reconstruction within itself is understood by Ambedkar as paving the way for caste like features in them. And Ambedkar understood that the focal point of "Islam is the conservative idea and retention of traditional values rather than the social concerns. Therefore, it lacks the spirit of social service and social reform and reconstruction and fosters social stagnation."[8]

Ambedkar rejected Islam on the basis of its approach to women. He upholds equality as a basic principle. He considered that women in

Islam are deprived of mental and moral nourishment owing to the *Purdah* system. Ambedkar observes that this is a religious way of implementing social segregation. "As a consequence of *Purdah* system, a segregation of Muslim woman is brought about. Being deprived of healthy social life, the process of moral degradation set in. Being completely secluded from the outer world, they engage their mind in petty family quarrels, with the result that they become narrow and restricted in their outlook."[9] Thus, women in *Purdah* system in particular become helpless, timid and unfit for any fight in life. A social system, which cuts off all contact between the two sexes, produces an unhealthy tendency towards sexual excesses and unnatural and other morbid habits and ways.

Brotherhood of Islam is generally put forward as its plus point. But exploding the myth, Ambedkar says that, "Islam is a close corporation —the Brotherhood of Islam is not the universal brotherhood of man. It is the brotherhood of Muslims for Muslims only. There is the fraternity but its benefit is confined to those within that corporation. For those who are outside the corporation there is nothing but contempt and enmity. Islam is a system of social self-government and is incompatible with local self government, because the allegiance of Muslim doesn't rest on his domicile in the country which is his but on the faith to which he belongs."[10] In addition, he observes that Islam and its personal laws promote slavery, which is unthinkable in the case of religion, which promotes equality. Moreover, Ambedkar observes that Islam always puts itself against the scientific attitudes and methods.

Ambedkar's Critique of Christianity

In Hindu society, marginalisation, oppression, poverty and ignorance attributed to the cycle of birth which are sanctioned by religion. People blame their birth for their low status. However, in the context of the Christian concept of incarnation, the idea that God became man suggests the nature of these values. By identifying himself with the poor, the lepers, widows the outcastes and sinners, God revealed his intention for the liberation of the oppressed in all societies. By taking birth as a man, he destroyed all fatalistic and domestic socio-religious values, which keep people obedient under the yoke of oppression.[11]

Ambedkar on 14th October 1956 on the event of the great mass conversion of *Dalits* in a long speech in Nagpur during public *Deeksha* ceremony function said, "From the study of comparative religion he could say that two personalities could captivate. These were the Buddha and Christ."[12] Jesus' solidarity with the lowly was the main reason for Ambedkar's admiration and reverences for Jesus. He argues that the free social order stands on the foundation of the fundamental tenet, that an individual is an end in him with inalienable rights and distinctive moral responsibility.[13] According to the book of Ezekiel, "Behold all souls are mine: as the soul of the father, so also the soul of son is mine: the soul that *sinneth*, it shall die - the son shall not bear the iniquity of the Father, neither shall the father bear the iniquity of son. The righteousness of righteous shall be upon him, and wickedness of the wicked upon him."[14]

Further, to explicate what Ambedkar means by fraternity he takes maxims from Christian's sources: "Fraternity is the name for the disposition of an individual to treat men as the object of reverence and love and desire to be in unity with his fellow beings. This was well expressed by Paul when he said 'Of one blood are all nations of men, here is neither Jew nor Greek, neither bond nor free, neither male nor female; for yet are all one in Christ Jesus."[15]

Though Ambedkar takes favourable position to the principles of Christianity, he was disappointed by the Christian Churches in India, which are not following the approach of Jesus and allowed the caste distinctions to divide them and discriminate the lower castes in their fold.[16] Ambedkar still defends the egalitarianism of Christianity and Islam in his famous "Conversion speech" at Bombay in 1936. "Although the castes exist in Muslims and the Christians alike it will be meanness to liken it to that of the Hindus. There is a great distinction between the caste systems of the Hindus and that of the Muslims and Christians. Firstly, it must be noted that though the castes exist amongst the Christians and the Muslims, it is not the chief characteristic of their body social.....there are some differences between the caste-system of the Hindus and that of the Muslims and Christians; the caste system in Hindus has the foundation of religion. The castes in other religions have no sanction in their religion- Hindus cannot destroy their castes without destroying their religion. Muslims and Christians need not destroy their religions, for eradication of their castes. Rather their religion will support such movements to a great extent."[17]

The God of liberation always leads His people from bondage to liberation and not from bondage to bondage. As He says, 'No oppressor shall again overrun them.'[18] God recognised the faithful Israelites who were in bondage from the time of Joseph. In addition, the God of oppressed heard their voice. In Christianity, God is portrayed as God of oppressed. In addition, the Bible starts with the assertion that God is the creator of all living and non-living beings of this universe.

However, at the end of 'Genesis' (The First Chapter of the Bible) it is clear that God as the protector and father of the Universe is reduced to the protector and father of certain tribe or community. Then the Bible depicts that God sanctions the Chosen people to kill and conquer other tribes. Jesus is also born in the same tribe. Moreover, the New Testament begins the genealogy of the tribe, and Jesus' mission clearly begins with in the confinement of certain community. Nevertheless, the specialties with Jesus' efforts were that they always tended to overcome the limits of the tribes and it always challenged the prevailing authority of Judah Community. He appeared as a reformist and dissident leader.

Jesus' missionary work, according to Ambedkar, always tends to identify itself with the downtrodden, poor and outcastes, even though its main missionaries belongs to Judah Community (12 disciples of Jesus are from Judah Community). The identification with the downtrodden happens because the Judah Community was captivated as slaves at that time. In addition, they were under the captivity of Babylon for fourteen generation. The social situation of the Judah community makes them to think in a revolutionary and pro-downtrodden manner.[19] If Jews were the rulers at that time, then it would not have such a progressive and revolutionary theology. That is the reason for the basic difference between the Old Testament and New Testament. Thus, Ambedkar pointed out that the social situation of the community, which practices certain religion, has clear impact on the construal of moral principles.

In those days, religious philosophy used to be the most powerful and solemnly affirmed. Since there was no scientific test available in those days, religious mysticism was accepted. Now due to advancement of science and its tested theories, the real light of all natural phenomenon and the dark age of mysticism, superstitions and hypocrisy in the name of religion have been exposed. The unscientific and unproven theories of religions have no basis in the modern awakened world.

Critical Analysis on the Role of Church

Ambedkar says that the accessibility of god is a debatable issue. The privileged status of the mediating body in providing the access to god makes Christianity distanced from an all community-activity like Judaism where the keys to the accessibility of god rests even with elderly people who know the texts. According to him, "the idea of '*accessibility of god*' itself is very different in different periods of Christianity. Some of the interpretations say that it is through personal effort, hard work and spiritual practices by which an individual gets access."[20] However, certain other interpretations rely solely on the initiative of the mediating body for accessibility of divine or god.

In his opinion, the idea of '*love*' and '*compassion*' made people to embrace the Christian belief and faiths in more popular passion. The practice of *compassion* and *love* alone are sufficient for the accessibility of god, but still their interesting point is that, how do we properly understand God's path. Here, again the church plays an immense role.[21] There are the certified authorities who clearly know the path to god and expect that every man is capable of achieving this. Hence, it could be argued that is the man-god relationship, there is a certain dynamics that the mediating body plays, they are;

> Man-to-god accessibility does not exist independently of a mediating body. The ontology that a Christian possesses is the ontology revealed by this mediating body. His or her beliefs depend on this ontology.
>
> The active god or the very 'activeness' of god, rests with people who believing in a particular ontology. Moreover, this is impossible without a mediating body because it is their duty to make people believe in the faith of Christianity.

It is clear that "the worldview of Christianity provides an unavoidable place for the mediating body."[22] Hence, when it comes to the practice of a faith, it is obvious that the regulating body can have their stakes. Ambedkar also had the view that one of the major shortcomings of Christianity as many thinks, is the privileged status of clergy and the body that regulates it. Even in the Protestant version of Christianity, there are visible instances of such regulating bodies of certain kind.

However, Ambedkar did not take position regarding the existence of supreme absolute being. Ambedkar's position was that these are the matters, which cannot be verified; therefore, one cannot hold it as a reasonable one. However, he admits the space for beliefs. One can hold beliefs that God exists, even though it is not that much rationally founded. Then that belief should be a tool to reform the society and which assures equality among people. That belief based on rationality, and there is no basis for claiming the existence of God, but Ambedkar did not insist that every belief should be rational. Some unverifiable beliefs also one can be held but should have some purpose and that purpose should be abolition of inequality among human beings. He unified both these strands. Regarding the unverifiability of beliefs, he criticises Christianity and favours Buddhism since it denies permanence of any absolute entity. Nevertheless, regarding the useful purpose of beliefs he favours Christianity and Buddhism other than Hinduism.

Ambedkar's Critique of *Vedic* and Hindu Tradition

Ambedkar's critique of *Vedic* and Hinduism is based on philosophical and sociological aspect that appeared in his article 'Philosophy of Hinduism.' In this article, he also spoke of the philosophy of religion. This article gives both his general critique of Hinduism as well as philosophy and sociology of religion. His analysis begins with his working definition of religion, "I take religion to near the propounding of an ideal scheme of divine governance the aim and object of which is to make the social order in which men live a moral order."[23] From this definition, it is very clear how deep an understanding he had about the religion. It would illuminate through the comparison of other thinkers and philosophers of religion. The major point which is so obvious is that he is considering the notion of religion in a positive manner i.e. religion as something which is essential and which is to be maintained. Moreover, he considers it as ideal scheme of divine governance. The purpose of this ideal scheme is making a particular kind of social order. Then he relates this social order into morality.

The important points which we can perceive in this definition is that, on the one hand he reforms the nature of religion in an ideal and divine manner, on the other hand, he insists that it is meant for making and maintaining of certain social order. One can question this notion that if the purpose of the scheme which is called religion is only for maintaining a particular social order, why an ideal and divine scheme is needed. A sociological analysis is realistic and a mechanism, which is able to addresses those, are enough. In this juncture, one can understand how Ambedkar's interventions are philosophically much relevant even though he addresses the concrete and direct problems of the society.

The outcome of the contract between ideal conception and concrete contact through his analysis of religion is traced back by a comprehensive vision. Moreover, his position is understood as the emphasis of the conception of this ideal scheme. However, he differs from the other idealists by insisting that, this ideal scheme is translated or transformed by looking on context. This is the way, in which he defines how the religion as an ideal scheme governs the society. That is, within the context by looking at the goal, it is possible to derive certain conditions, which enable us to make the society closer to this ideal scheme. Here Ambedkar envisions the ideal scheme as guiding principle. It is possible to explain adequately what the ideal scheme means especially, when its concern is social.[24]

According to Ambedkar, there is an objectionable role of *Supreme Being* in the construal of morality in *Vedic* tradition and virtue or morality is in conformation with cosmic order (*rta*). Morality is being in accordance with the supreme entity or being. In addition, various interpretations of *Vedic* morality depend on the construal of the conception of supreme, absolute entity.[25] However, essentially all of them admitted that there is a *Supreme Being* and the virtuous life is something, which is in conformation with the characteristics of the supreme entity.

There are crucial problems, which lie in relation with the construal of morality in relation with the *Supreme Being*. One is that since "morality is standardisation of the human relation, how the notion or characteristics of *Supreme Being* would enable to define what is norm or standard of human relation."[26] This amount to a situation where normative account which is completely detached with the descriptive realm. This is the violation of basic principle of normative construal, which tells that normative construal should be consistent or compatible with descriptive realm. Thus, the difficulty regarding the incompatibility of *Vedic* ethical construal with descriptive realm is a dilemma, which all religious construals have been facing.

Moreover, one even claims that there is no need of proper understanding of descriptive realm (In this context descriptive realm means relation among humans) to formulate a normative account, since normative account concerns only about goal which one has to achieve. The objection has rightly pointed out that to develop a normative account, the idea of goal and its understanding is the necessary condition. Normative account means to achieve a certain goal what would be highly suitable or best which one has to follow. Here, our thinking on the best possible way of achieving the goal is constrained by the information, which is available to us. In normative account, we can only claim if this is the case, then to achieve the particular goal, certain way is best one.[27] How can we find out certain way as the path, which one ought to follow to reach the goal? It is by formulating by certain conditions, and if the path to be accordance with the conditions then that would be the normative path. It is true that the necessary conditions are formulated by defining the goal.

However, necessary conditions are solely insufficient to determine which path would be the right one. Therefore, along with the necessary conditions, sufficient conditions are also inevitable. Moreover, in formulating the notion of sufficient condition, the understanding about the particular is indispensable. Formulations of sufficient condition are purely contextual. For example, by looking on the goal, if one formulates '*love*' as necessary condition, but the notion '*love*' does not have any unified meaning in different contexts, *love* of mother to her child, in some how one can consider as purely personal and related to affection, care, touching, etc. *Love* to the people, is quite different from this notion, here it receives an entirely different form that which is related to their welfare, equality, peace etc, that is the term is related to more social aspects.[28] Even though the concepts are same, it implies different senses in different context. Therefore, what is quite important regarding the religious and moral principles are the specification of the necessary conditions in relation with the contexts. In addition, thorough analysis shows that all religions throughout the ages specified what exactly they meant. All the religions define their principles in accordance with their specific social situation and with the social values, which they hold.

Ambedkar tries to argue that the social situation of the community, which practices certain religion, has clear impact on the construal of moral principles. In addition, how one can, philosophically understand the influence of certain social elements in the construal of normative principles. Ambedkar says that the distinction of necessary and sufficient conditions of a normative account is useful to understand the role of social elements. In Hinduism, according to him, we can find the influence of the social situation, especially the caste-hierarchy.

According to Ambedkar, the *Vedic* morality concentrated on a more specific problem, which is faced only by the *Vedic* morality or its consequential systems. That is, how much sufficient is the *Veda's* conception of *Absolute* or *Supreme Being* to define the notion of morality.[29] This question mainly arises because *Vedas* consider the Absolute as indeterminate. Beyond the indeterminacy, it is not able to provide feasible description of the *Barhman*. If a goal became that much intangible or ambiguous, how one can provide certain adequate conditions or standards for the achievement of goal. The whole idea, on which Ambedkar worked out as criticism to 'the *Vedic* morality is mainly guided by the idea that normative construal can be analysed based on goal means relation or all goal-means relations, is what all-normative construal talk about. *Vedic* morality identifies metaphysical absolute entity with high esteemed ethical principle that is if one entity is supreme one, then that alone is perfect good or virtue.'[30]

One major consideration that Ambedkar wants to explain is that this idea cannot be defended adequately. Moreover, this idea clearly points out the intrusion of power into the ethical realm. That is how one can claim *Supreme Being* is to *Supreme Being*, the absolute good. Here what happens is that one's own ethical domain clearly subordinates the metaphysical presuppositions. We can take certain possibilities regarding the world and the *Supreme* other than what is usually conceived. Suppose this world is created with certain purpose. Even if, the purpose is a 'vicious' one, is created by 'evil'. Consider the purpose of creation as need of few to serve or praise the supreme. At this point, how one can claim that supreme is identical as highest good.[31] Here one would be able to see that there is a presupposition behind the claim that supreme is identical to highest good.

The presupposition is that whatever is given is ethically best. The world and its purpose of creation is a highly esteemed one. Here what one can see is that the claim of supreme is identical to highest good, can be justified by the presumption that only the highest ethical principle can be supreme one. What obviously makes this argument invalid is its circularity. The two propositions, the supreme is identical to highest good and only the highest good can be the supreme, are dependent on each other for their validity. This leads to the circularity. The nature of circularity is not itself sufficient to reject those claims from the realm of ethics, since circularity is a logical flaw, and ethics cannot be considered as discipline, which is not predominantly a logical one.[32] Nevertheless, "my cause of worry is mainly not about its illogical nature but one of its consequent."[33] That is a circular argument does not explain anything or it is not adding anything new. In relation with concern of ethics, then what we loose is the specification regarding the nature of supreme good.

Further, the argument that the high ethical principle can be the *Supreme Being* has defined by the metaphysical principle. However, since metaphysical principles and ethical principles belong to different realm, the next problem is that of confusion of categories. Thus, another pertinent question is how one category would be sufficient to explain the other category? In addition, the other major problem is of sufficiency of conditions. That ethical principle is considered as supreme, and then the challenge in the normative construal is that this notion of supreme has to be defined in terms of ethical principles. That is what would be a supreme in human relations. That is, we admit with the normative *Vedic* construal that by the definition of ethical principles it is possible to formulate certain necessary condition or standards for the feasible ethical principles for human beings. How can one formulate sufficient conditions? That is from the conception of highest good as the supreme, one can formulate certain necessary condition that, then highest good is omnipotent or omniscient etc. Nevertheless, from that how one can formulate that highest good is loveable, therefore love is a quality, which every one has to practice. Those are the conditions, which have practical ethical discipline possible. Here without sufficiency of condition one can tell that ethical discipline did not hit the target.

Ambedkar says that the Hindu ethics largely talks about the significance of the duty. 'The notion of duty is an important idea among all religious and non-religious ethical construals.'[34] However, the Hindu-*Vedic* specific notion of duty cannot be a considered as equivalent to the other ethical theories. The notion of duty is defined in relation with the *Karma* theory. Ambedkar explained that the *Karma* theory says that we will reap the fruits of our own deeds and that is what determines our future. Our destiny depends upon our deeds. The most interesting thing, which is related to *Karma* theory, is that *Karma* theory does not tell what exactly it meant.[35] Concisely, we can say that our past actions determine our future and present life. What we are experiencing is the consequence of the past actions. Past actions mostly mean the actions in the past life or in previous birth, which is quite unknown to us. Then the remaining option is only that determine the deeds in the previous life by looking at the consequence of present or justifying the present status of life by claiming that it is the benefit or detriment of the past actions.

That is, virtually *Karma* theory ends up in a kind of exercise, which upholds the validity, or justification of the present status on the name of unknown past. Justifying the present social order became the undertaking of the metaphysical and ethical principle. Ambedkar argues that the notion of duty is defined in Hinduism according to *Varna* (caste) which she/he belongs. Birth in a particular caste is due to the consequence of the deeds of the previous life and Hinduism does not hold on the general theory of human duty. It is always considered in the fragmented level. He posed questions, as it would be wondering, that why a normative construal fails to overcome the divisions in the society, and how an ethical principle became in accordance with present unequal social status.

Ambedkar's main criticism to the Hindu ethics is that it is not sensitive to the basic facts of life. Hindu ethics mainly denies the plurality of the nature. Hindu ethics, which focuses on the monolithic nature, is a kind of extension of Hindu metaphysics. In certain sense, one can say that the chief characteristic of the Hindu philosophy is that of absence of plurality.[36] According to Ambedkar, the Hindu philosophy is not comprised of one strand of thought, therefore, any one Hindu system of thought process can be considered as the representative of the Hindu tradition. Nevertheless, the analysis of the Hindu philosophy shows that the absence of pluralism is a prevalent characteristic of all Hindu philosophical traditions. *Advaita* tradition completely denies the existence of plurality. For them, plurality is a false notion, which is evoked by *Maya*. In addition, there is only one absolute entity, which is the *Barhman*.[37] Even though dualistic Hindu philosophy accepts that individual, self is quite distinct from the absolute entity. They also emphasise the supremacy of the absolute over the individuals and emphasises that all diversity stems from the supreme absolute. One can argue that denying the independence of plurality in the level of dualistic philosophy is a common factor to all the religious traditions. That is true also, but the strong denial of pluralism from the side of Advaita tradition is unique only to Hindu tradition.

Ambedkar argues that, denying the space of plurality and affirming the importance of unity or homogeneity has disastrous consequence. Mainly there are two aspects regarding the notion of homogeneity in Hinduism. We cannot say that Hinduism is advocating homogeneity in the sense of equality or impartiality. It is because no other religion explicitly defends the division among the humans and stand for the different notion of duty to human being according to their caste. However, in metaphysical sense no other religion like Hinduism advocates the uniformity of nature. That is all creatures and humans are identical, there is no difference among them. There is only one entity, which is *Barhman*.[38] It is surprising that the same religion, which talks about the identity of the all nature and world and of God, on the other hand talks about distinction and division among human beings.[39] Here what it reveals is that the real implication of the homogeneity of Hinduism and the uniformity emphasises that there is only one supreme entity or there is only one supreme god, all other is in some way or other subordinate to this supreme. The uniformity means reduction, reducing all plurality into one claimed standard of good or existence and this construal of the standards to one particular entity is claimed as the standard to which level all others are required to rise. That is in the normative understanding; it denies the standard existence of the plurality.

At this juncture, it would be helpful to understand how Jainism gives importance to pluralism and how they treat pluralism without reducing into something else. The problem with the homogeneity, which Hinduism advocates, is that it principally stands in the supremacy of one factor and it advocates all other factors to be like the claimed standard. That elimination of plurality is actually the consequence. Ambedkar notes that what has formed the basis for the unity of India is Brahmanical culture- its ideas, values and customs. However, ethnically all people are heterogeneous.

Ambedkar criticises Hinduism for defining the caste system without looking into the basic facts of caste in India. Hinduism tries to defend it firstly on the premise that the division among the human on caste line is not human creation.[40] It is a divine creation. The distinction, which is thrust on the society, is something, which is determined by the divine absolute, and something, which is evolved with the human creation. This construal makes the distinction among human beings unquestionable and even if anybody has a kind of dissatisfaction, that distinction is not something, which can be changed because it is divine. Ambedkar insists on the necessity of sociological analysis rather than speculative one.

Ambedkar gives a sociological reading of the famous hymn *Rig Veda* X, 90 and he explains its content as well as form. The organic metaphor- the social body is as if the human body- is both politically and socially significant. "The equation of the different classes to different parts of the body is not a matter of accident. It is deliberate. The idea behind this plan seems to be to discover a formula which solves two problems, one of fixing the functions of the four classes and the other of fixing the gradation of the four classes after a preconceived plan."[41] There is only one possible good form of society, the one where its different parts are interdependent on each other by their respective functional specialisation, and hierarchically ordered for their statuses and dignities-the body metaphor (opposing the head to feet) expressing immediately and in itself the will to refuse 'equality of dignity by birth of all the four classes. Thus, "The organicist and functionalist model of society emphasising the harmonious interaction of the separate parts of society can only be the ideology of a dominant class."[42]

The *Vedic* religions are made to prevail their notion of purity and sacredness through out all its matters, purity by keeping away certain things. Mainly we can understand that purity is something, which is produced by certain external conditions, by not touching certain things and by avoiding certain things. The real concept and real practice of religious preaching are when the believer starts cleaning himself from inside. If inside is unclean or corrupt, he cannot attain purity by any dress, painting of body, hairstyles or bathing in any water. Therefore, religion does not prevail outside the body. Sins and good deeds are committed by the inner voice of the individuals. They cannot be washed out by any degree of bathing, dress or prayers, ceremonies, festivals and rituals. These sins, crimes committed, or good deeds are not the dirt on the body, which can be cleaned by clothes, prayers and bathing.[43]

The lower *Varna* people and all the women or those who oppose the existence of *Barhma* are labelled as impure and ignorant. Further, it imposed severe penalties such as death if they take part in the sacrificial ceremonies. Ambedkar says that the highly ignoble persons can only record such hypocritic statements. Notion of purity is associated with the supremacy of *Barhman* and Infallibility of them. That is unchallengeable. Supremacy and Infallibility in some sense can be considered as the denial of the democratic sphere. Indians believe in Brahmanism who are so much mesmerised to think that *Vedas*' knowledge is God's gift, which others do not have even those they know that they have been produced neither by God nor by man. These *Vedas* and allied books are called "*Sruti*" which means 'heard' when revealed' so "they are infallible, unquestionable and unchangeable i.e. they are absolute" and can only be heard by Brahmins and no other *Varna* people because the *Vedas* are supreme. The other group called "*Smriti*" is of inspired human authorship, can be "*seen*", is written by other human beings, seers, *Rishis*, and can be transmitted to the public. It is claimed that *Vedas* are directly connected with *Barhman*. So this word "*Barhman*" is so sacred which is supposed to be restricted with in Brahmins circle who are the only offsprings of *Barhma*/Brahmin. So due to the fear and possibilities of transmitting this word to non-Brahmins, the Brahmins did not write the complete *Vedic* philosophy so that they can keep it restricted to the Brahmins only.[44]

Ambedkar says that, according to Buddha, "Everything is questionable, till we find the truth and validity, in this world. Man must have the freedom of thought and if any religious philosophy prohibits any human being then that philosophy is obnoxious."[45] Ambedkar observes that the Brahmins have declared that the *Vedas* were not only sacred but in point of authority, they were final. Here Ambedkar clearly observes that the notion of sacredness is strongly linked with the power, especially in its hierarchical manner. That is why Ambedkar's main position is that the principles and ideas of a particular religion cannot be analysed in isolation. The ideas along with its social consequences formed a particular sphere. Ambedkar is quite aware of how the notion of infallibility works as a dangerous notion, which develops as, threat to the very democratic space itself. According to him, there is a transition from sacredness to final authority and from there to infallibility.

Ambedkar writes, "Buddha was totally opposed to the Brahmins on this point. He denied that the *Vedas* were sacred. He denied that whatever *Vedas* said was final. He denied that the *Vedas* were infallible.....In the *Tvijja Sutta* the Buddha declared that the *Vedas* were a waterless desert, a pathless jungle, in fact perdition. No man with intellectual and moral thirst can go to the *Vedas* and hope to satisfy thirst."[46] Ambedkar makes it clear that the notion of infallibility is rejected not simply because of certain disagreements with the *Veda*; the notion of infallibility itself is a methodologically invalid. "As to infallibility of the *Vedas*, he said nothing is infallible, not even the *Vedas*. Everything, he said, must be subject to examination and re-examination."[47]

The possible criticism that rose against the rejection of the notion of 'infallibility' is that these kinds of rejections are quite simplistic in philosophical way. The notion of Infallibility is quite necessary in epistemological basis, in the absence of it, all the philosophical systems would end as clashes of relativistic ideas. The danger of relativism is purposefully invited by these rejections. In relativistic sphere, it is difficult to assert certain principles as normative, good, and ideal. Consequently, this leads to anarchic social situation where certain principles are absent to guide human beings into better or higher social order.[48] Ambedkar's position is that the rejection of final, infallible authority does not necessarily imply the discharge of anarchism and relativism. There are certain comprehensible, non-dogmatic authorities rather than dogmatic imposition of final authority to certain persons or to certain text.

Ambedkar makes it clear that appeal to reason is the one, which saves us from the situation of a cluster of relativistic ideas. Here one has to understand that conceding the authority of the *Vedas* is simply certifying certain things as final, rather than in accepting the reason. We do not accept certain doctrines as final, rather than we accept a function of human faculty, which always leaves room for revision. That is why Ambedkar talks about a certain affirmation in a particular point of time, not that certain things are true forever.

One can contest the point that it is absurd to maintain that the use of reason would enable us to reach a particular standpoint by rejecting all others. Contesters argue that the use of reason only increases the number of contesting views. Nevertheless, Ambedkar points out that there is possibility of legitimate and focused use of reason and the use of reason should be in relation with goal, based on this we can formulate certain testing criteria for any religious philosophical ideas, which are the necessary condition of that goal.[49] Ambedkar describes these tests by quoting Buddha's reply to the confused *Kalamas*, "The tests are these, replied the Blessed one; ask yourselves, do we know whether: 'these things are salutatory; these things are blame worthy; these things are reprehended by the wise: theses things being done or attempted lead to ill-being and to suffering."[50]

Ambedkar says that the practice of sacrifice in *Vedic* tradition is unethical and inhuman. In most of the cases, deities in this tradition were so cruel that they not satisfied with the sacrifice of animals, needed human blood. To get human blood, no Brahmin, Kshatriya and Vaishya was ready to sacrifice himself, so only weaker sections of the society the Sudra was the target victim. The poor Sudras were slaughtered and blood spilled over the fire to please the deity and the body of the victims used to be thrown away for vultures or given back to the families.[51]

While attacking on the inhuman practice of sacrifice Ambedkar heavily drew from the Buddha's teachings. Accordingly, Buddha divided the matter of sacrifice into two sections, one is true sacrifice and second one is false sacrifice. True sacrifice means self-denial for the good of others. False sacrifice means killing of animal or human being as an offering to god or deities for personal benefit i.e. taking life of other living beings for performer's own enjoyments. On examining the facts, Buddha concluded that the *Brahmanical* sacrifice was a false sacrifice. By killing somebody, the victim could get salvation or his/her soul will get liberation. That is all hypocrisy. Therefore, there were 62 religious cults at the time of the Buddha, and all the other cults opposed that practice of sacrificing animals to please the gods and the idea of salvation of the soul of the victims. On this, the opponent used to say, "If the victim's soul can get salvation, why not the Priest sacrifice himself or his own family members to get quick salvation and send his soul to heaven?"[52]

In the theory of *Varna*, the division of society was obnoxious to Ambedkar. He said that freedom is the birth right of all humans including all living beings. Life is most precious to all living beings. He advocated for an open and free society. Man must be recognised by his virtues and action and not by birth. If a born Brahmin becomes a scoundrel then he is not worthy of any respect. In addition, if a born *Sudra* becomes a virtuous man, then he deserved to be a respected. Fixing everything based on birth and not changing or improving is a most heinous theory. How in the world is that, a woman who gives birth to a Brahmin becomes the lowest and the Brahmin, the most superior in the *Varna*. This is just a fraud on the part of society. Moreover, when there is such a partiality of grading one too high and others to the lowest, it might be the source of perpetual conflict and tension in the society. In such a society, there will never be a common goodwill, coexistence, unity and common interest for the nation.

Ambedkar while reviewing the fourth clause of *Varna* system for occupation, that one once born in one *Varna* has to continue the same occupation as of his forefathers were doing i.e. no change in his status, Ambedkar took the position of Buddha. According to Ambedkar, the Buddha said, "it does not serve the interest of all and welfare of the masses. Indeed the Brahmins made this theory to benefit them and restricted the non-Brahmins for any advancement for generations to come. In that system, man was made to serve a class of self-styled superman. The only purpose of such restrictions was to exploit the weak and ignorant masses in a state of complete subjugation."[53]

Another important concept that lacks the morality, according to Ambedkar is the *Jati* or Caste system, first time described in *Manusmriti*. The masters of *Vedic* philosophies further claimed that those who do not understand the power of *Barhman* are impure e.g. Sudras and all women. These impure have to approach the holy power at the risk of injury or even death, and may participate in its radiant power only indirectly e.g. these impure Sudras and women can not take part when the sacrifice is performed. For those sanctified by knowledge or status, its uses range from magical (invoking it to destroy those whom one hates or to increase one's material wealth) to the mystical (achieving union with the cosmic power itself). The lower *Varna* people and all the women, those who are opposed to the existence of *Barhma* are labeled as impure and ignorant. Further, it imposed severe penalties such as death if they take part in the sacrificial ceremonies. According to Ambedkar, highly ignoble persons can only record such hypocritic statements. All human beings are equal and freedom is the fundamental right of all. The statements and claims of the *Vedic* philosophers are puerile.[54]

The theories of *Barhman* as were not handed down even at the time of the Buddha, they all communicated orally from Brahmin to Brahmin. Had they written down, some day their legitimacy would have been put for questioning. Therefore, every non-Brahmin is kept in the dark. Secondly, it mentioned that the super knowledge is hidden in *Vedas* and *Upanishads*, but those literatures are not open to all the people, barred to read, write and listen to those scriptures.[55] Therefore, existence of that kind of restricted knowledge has no value for the masses of India and hence that is useless. In comparison to these crude, inhuman postulated theories of the *Vedas* and *Barhman*'s, the Buddha and his disciples spent their entire lives spreading the message of equality, compassion for all living beings, morality and spiritual cultivation. The instructions given to *Sigala* concerning social ethics is clear evidence of Buddhism's deep concern for society as a whole and the welfare of the people.

The *Upanishads*' main concern was how *Barhma* and *Atman* (soul) are related to each other. "They claimed that *Atman* and *Barhma* were the same but *Atman* did not realise that it is *Barhma* because of *Upadhis* (superimposed attribute that veils what lies behind it) in which the *Atman* was entangled."[56] This soul matter was a carry on problem from their ancestors Aryans "Scythian nomads" who also did not know anything about it, themselves either. The Buddha could not find any proof of *Barhma* nor of *Atman.* Therefore, Ambedkar rejects the theory of *Atman* and *Barhma. Upanishads* are grouped in the philosophy of purely speculative thinking in India. As we noted before, all the *Vedic* related philosophies are based on speculations, myths, fiction, and fables, which is not based on scientific or natural truth and facts.

Contrary to the above, the Buddhists doctrines are based on Natural and scientific facts. Moreover, the philosophy of *Upanishads* was based on *Barhma* and *Atman*, which are just figments of human mind and therefore have no value for human beings in practical and spiritual life.[57] Nevertheless, some people in the name of authorities are misguiding the innocent public and enjoying themselves. Moreover, with today's scientific facts such speculations of *Barhman* and *Atman* are the subject of ignorant persons. Moreover, illiterate individuals created those types of speculations, when a scientific research can be used to prove that the theory was non-existent. Therefore, those were the speculations of primitive age people and nothing is to be gain from such philosophies.

According to Ambedkar, "The Brahmins put all their emphasis on knowledge. They taught that knowledge was the be-all and end-all of every thing. Nothing further considered...Besides he (Buddha) was more concerned with the use of knowledge to make than with knowledge itself."[58] In contemporary philosophical discussions, the existence of the pure meaning and pure knowledge as an idea, contested more. Especially later Wittgenstein clearly emphasises that the use of the sentences is the meaning of it. Even in the realm of scientific knowledge, the pure knowledge, which is devoid of context and meaning, is senseless. In view of this, one can understand how philosophically deep and full are the Buddhist doctrines and Ambedkar's Interpretation on it. Further, Buddha analyses that the knowledge must have '*Sila*' (Virtue). According to Buddha, "He said (Buddha) that at one and the same time, no one can know and see everything. Knowledge is never final. There is always something more to be known."[59]

According to Ambedkar, there are not any realistic claims of *Barhma* that, He is the source of knowledge. Even if some one claims that He is the source of knowledge, Ambedkar argues what kind of knowledge they are referring to namely, Spiritual, Scientific, Social, Human, Public affairs, Political, Mathematical, Business, Natural sciences. Because a human being needs all these various special kinds of knowledge for day to day life and future advance. However, no such details about the authors of these *Vedas* and *Upanishads* have been given. If by knowledge they only mean the one limited to spiritual life then such knowledge is not enough because human beings cannot survive only on spiritual knowledge. Moreover, if it is spiritual then it must be open and available to all so that all the people can improve their spirituality and could not only be limited to handful *Vedic* and Upanishad owners. In addition, if it is limited in number and the mass is barred to have that knowledge. In such a case, "*Barhma* is a biased person or identity and such knowledge is no good for the masses."[60]

In the above statements, as claimed the existence of *Barhman* are very vague and flip-flop so that interrogator cannot nail down the statement makers. Absolutely no such entity exists in all the states except the supreme nature and its physical and chemical components whose properties are well known to the scientists in modern era. Thus, Ambedkar argues that such mesmerising and ambiguous statements and claims could only fool the innocent public in the medieval era but certainly not now.

The notion of infallibility is described in the *Origin of Scriptures* in a different way. There is a simple explanation for truth and untruth to verify. If a thing exists in this universe, the creator can describe about its features, shape, size, colour, actions, qualities, properties and other characteristics to certain factual limitations. Because the creator is careful of three factors: firstly, about his own knowledge, secondly, his personal consciousness and lastly, his critics for counter checks. However, when the thing does not exist in the universe, then the creator has unlimited scope i.e., he has no limitation to describe in his own imaginations. The myths, fictions, tales, epics, fables have no limitations. The authors are not controlled by any of three factors as in the case of describing the "Truth". This is how *Barhma*, *Atman* and other religious characters are invented through myths, fictions, fables, Epics and other gullible.

Moreover, gullible public, by following the concepts in scriptures do not get any benefit but definitely, the authors and enforcement administrators get rewards for their mental creation through this literature in terms of monetary offerings. Ambedkar rejects such theories as speculative. He asserts that, "They are not verified nor are they verifiable. They were the result of imagination let loose. There was no reality behind them. Besides what good were these speculative theories to operate in his relation to men? The Buddha did not believe that the world was created, He believed that the world had evolved."[61] According to Buddha, not all the existing things in the universe are permanent. All of them are continuously arising and dissolving or passing on to make new things.

Ambedkar thoroughly denied the individualistic conception of the social structure, at the same time gave tremendous emphasis to 'self individual' in ethical perspective. It may be a matter of wonder, but it shows his philosophical analysis. His socio-political analysis emphasised on the significance of social structure rather than the individual. According to him, "The atomistic conception of individuals in a society, so greatly popularised, in political orations, to say that individuals make up society is trivial; society is always composed of classes, their basis may differ. They may be economic, intellectual, or social, but an individual in society is always a member of a class. This is a universal fact."[62]

While sticking on to this analysis, he tries to develop an understanding of the human mind. An understanding of human psychology is the factor that prompts him to give an emphasis on ethical aspect. Following parts shows that, how strongly Ambedkar explicates the human psychology aspect of socio-political problems, according to him, "Undoubtedly is an aspect of social psychology; it is a sort of nausea of one group against another group" Ambedkar asserts that "caste is a notion, it is a state of the mind but it is also a disease of the mind, as he repeated everywhere and all his life."[63]

Understanding socio-political situation and its deep-rooted causes, usually leads one to describe or reduce everything into that particular framework of analysis. The grand-narrative model is the chief characteristic of the most of the systematised political thought. The most typical example of these kinds of attitude is of Marxism.

Marx's distinction of superstructure and base structure is quite crucial in most of his analysis. Base-structures that consist of class relations are the one, which has caused efficacy in human affairs. Superstructure that includes man's behaviour, man's belief in religion is only the product of the base structure. Change in the base structure will end up in the change of supperstructure.

Amidst of these theories one would be able to clearly comprehend the significance of Ambedkar who clearly balances the emphasis on both individual and structured social aspects. The distinction makes him to give more space to ethics. According to Ambedkar, the balancing of the individualistic ethical and social ethical aspects were not mere pragmatic one, rather it is philosophically rigorously defined. Ambedkar criticises the Western social movements and theories for neglecting the significance of individualistic ethics. For him, what the West was not able to achieve was not equality or liberty, but fraternity. Ambedkar says that, "In producing equality society cannot afford to sacrifice fraternity or liberty. It seems that the three can co-exist only if one follows the way of the Buddha."[64]

Ambedkar's Critical Views on Jainism

According to the Mahavira's doctrine of "*Ahimsa Paramo dharma*"[65] non-killing is the greatest philosophy of religion, but that is an extreme end and impossible to practice so far as man is living on this earth. Similar quotation is cited in Mahabharata the *Barhmanic* religious epic *Ahimsa* is *Paramodharma*. Whereas in the same Mahabharata it is said that in 18 days there was a war between two cousin groups and several million people were killed. Jainism is totally against any kind of killing in any circumstances. They put non-violence into practice as a rule, which we have to follow. However, the critic points out that this is a simplistic insistence. Some time one has to do small-scale violence to avoid occurrence of large-scale violence and destruction. The critic's points out that usually nobody will contest the intention of the principle of '*Ahimsa*'. The intention is the well-being of all living being. However, to implement this intention, such a straightforward way like complete insistence to *Ahimsa* would not help. It is because the living situation is more complicated.

The Buddha's *Ahimsa* doctrine states "*love* all, so that you may not wish to kill anyone."[66] This is a positive way of stating the principle of *Ahimsa*. From this it appears that, the Buddha's doctrines of *Ahimsa* do not say, "Kill not. It says love all." In the light of these statements, it is quite easy to have a clear understanding of what the Buddha meant to make a distinction between will to kill and need to kill. He did not ban killing where there was need to kill. What he banned was killing where there was nothing but the will to kill. According to Ambedkar, "Buddha points out that the Barhmanism has in it the will to kill. Jainism has in it the will never to kill. Buddha's *Ahimsa* is aligned in the middle path. According to Buddha, *Ahimsa* is certainly a valuable principle but it cannot be celebrated as a rule. A principle leaves freedom to act. A rule does not. Rule either breaks you or you break the rule."[67]

According to Ambedkar, asceticism is the practice only to torture the body and not improving the mental qualities of humans. All good and bad actions are the products of the mind. Therefore, Buddhism emphasised that right training of the mind always does good and think right. Buddha, according to Ambedkar, said that, when man is in problem he goes to mountains, forests, woods, water for refuge, but such refuge cannot give permanent shelter to bring real happiness or salvation. When comparing the extreme asceticism of Lord Mahavira, Buddha said, "Hunger is the worst disease. Health is the greatest of gifts, contentedness the best of riches; trust is the best of relationships, *Nirbbana* is the highest happiness."[68]

From the Buddhist point of view, Ambedkar questioned the philosophy of the Mahavira's strict asceticism and *Tapascharya*, which subjugate and uproots man's instincts and desires to become better persons by his own thoughts and noble actions. Let us assume the philosophy of Lord Mahavira that asceticism is the only and sure way to get liberation. The whole population is entitled to get total liberation from all sufferings and are not fettered at all, and also be free from *Samsara* cycle i.e. birth, sickness, old age and death. However, contrary to the above presumptive theory they live in extreme destitute conditions in this very life and no hope of any light throughout their life expectancy. Both Buddhism and Jainism believe that life is full of sufferings. To end the sufferings Jainism preaches that liberation is brought about by strict asceticism and inaction. While Buddhism preaches that, the suffering can only be ended through right actions throughout one's lifetime.

Like Buddhism, Jainism also is an atheistic religion. Nevertheless, Jains still believe in many gods, deities, sages, demigods and demons of the mythical Brahmin inventions. Jains also believe and worship the demigods and personal deities such as Vishnu, Shiva and *Sakti*. This adoption may be due to heavy threat on Jains by Brahmins after Buddhism was chased out from its homeland. Brahmin writers are influential advisers of the *Vedic* kinds from Chandragupta III and IV onwards. Such acts had nothing to do with any spirituality or true fundamentals of good religion, but merely on politics of power, hierarchy and monetary gains.[69] Jainism was unacceptable to Ambedkar, as he felt that it is not advocating the principles in practical form. Especially, *Ahimsa* propagated by Jainism is too rigid to follow. He criticises this view extensively in his famous text on the *Buddha and His Dhamma*.[70]

Ambedkar's Approach to Buddhism

Ambedkar, found "*Karuna*-love for human beings and even more *Maitri*, love for living beings only in Buddhism."[71] The following features of Buddhism seem to have attracted Ambedkar: first, Buddhists emphasise on reason as against faith or superstition. Second, the Buddhists rejection of dogmatic beliefs such as God and soul, which are accepted by most of the other religions. Third, the Buddhist's strong opposition to the caste system. Lastly, Buddhism emphasised morality as an essence of good life. "The morality according to Buddhism was essentially human centric and had no reference to soul or to God."[72]

Ambedkar restricted Buddhist beliefs and practices to this world and this life; he refuted the beliefs in other worlds and past and future lives. He also rejected the existence of consciousness independent of the body. Similarly, Ambedkar posted scientific rationality as the core of Buddhist approach to the nature of the world and the individual. According to Ambedkar, Whatever that transgressed the authority of experience and reason is non-Buddhist in essence. Ambedkar sought to eliminate mystical elements from Buddhism. Accordingly, he rejects the elements such as *Dhyana* and *Samadhi* (meditation and concentration) as the central. The relation between religion and morality underwent radical change in Ambedkar's reconstruction.

Ambedkar says that the Buddhism is religion rooted in morality, however, in most religions; belief in transcendent entities such as God,

Atman and other worlds became the boss or morality. In Ambedkar's words "Every religion preaches morality, but morality is not the root of religion."[73] In his argument, Ambedkar makes morality the root of religion. "In *Dhamma* morality takes place of God, although there is no God in *Dhamma*. Morality is the essence of *Dhamma*."[74] To put it crudely, the "religions have put religious beliefs at the centre and morality are supposed to rotate around them. In Ambedkar's reconstruction of Buddhism, morality is placed at the centre and religious beliefs are supposed to rotate around it."[75]

At this point one would be able to comprehend how deeply and substantially Ambedkar is different from the religious people and from atheist people. Ambedkar strongly differs with the atheist people that, man is not purely a materialistic being and the needs are not purely material. Therefore, any kind of socio-political problems can analyse and works out in a purely materialistic manner. Ambedkar was able to comprehend the role of spirituality in man's existence better than the atheists which includes spirituality, also the nourishment of human life in holistic manner.

The redefinition of morality consequently leads to radical redefinition in the notion of religion. Ambedkar's analysis makes it evident that based on this notion of *Dhamma*; it is possible to divide the notion of religion into two categories. The Religion, which is *God-centric* and secondly, the Religion, which is *Dhamma centric*. Former emphasises the relation between the individual and God and undermines social relations, it also paves ways to superstitions. The *Dhamma*, on the other hand is essentially moral, social and rational. In addition, Ambedkar asserts that the purpose of religion, which is Dhamma - centric, is to make the world and kingdom of righteousness. The distinction is something more than different type. He says that these are descriptive and normative distinctions respectively. Ambedkar's reinterpretation mainly lies on the point to cut out the religions' and moralities' link with transcendental entities. Since Ambedkar's attitude is not outrightly rejecting, but engaging with the discourse and understanding the limits and reinterpreting the notions, one should take extreme care to distinguish Ambedkar's religious notions and traditional religious notions.

Ambedkar also consider's morality as sacred one. M.P. Rege when he points out the limits of Ambedkar's Buddhism says, "According to Ambedkar, *Dhamma* means morality and normality means *Dhamma.* However, morality, which is *Dhamma,* should be sacred. In this context, '*sacred*' can mean only transcendent. Morality springs towards this transcendent and is rooted in the transcendent."[76] But, Pradeep P Gokhale when he counters this argument points out that by the word 'sacred' Ambedkar meant only something which cannot be violated not that something which is related to transcendental entities. However, still the question that is remaining is how one can claim certain principles as something that cannot be violated. What should be the basis of the claim of impossibility of the violation? When certain principles are described as should not be violated, it can be justified in the framework of normative construct. However, the impossibility of how one can be justified is still in question.

The one important point that one can raise is that Ambedkar's interpretation of Buddhism is methodologically justifiable or not. Obviously, there are certain kinds of social and political reasons for Ambedkar's interpretation of Buddhism. However, due to socio-political reasons, he did not overlook mythological aspects in the reinterpretation of a philosophical system. Buddha's reinterpretation is a philosophically founded one. Usually, Ambedkar's question of centrality of the doctrine of the four noble truths is to be considered along with his interpretation which is methodologically justifiable. However, "A doctrine such as that of the four Noble Truths, which is generally regarded as the core of Buddhism, becomes the subject of critical examination and consequent dialectical negation in the *Madhyamika* philosophy of Nagarjuna. *Sunyta* is accepted as the framework here and other Buddhist doctrine are adjusted in a deconstructed form within this framework."[77]

There is lot of discussion regarding the reinterpretation of Buddhism as methodologically justifiable or not. To what extent one can consider that methodology of interpretation, which prevailed, in spite of the obvious political social context. This discussion mainly sums up Ambedkar's interpretation of four noble truths and of *Karma*. According to Ambedkar, "The Buddha's law of *Karma* applied only to *Karma* and its effects on the personal life. There is however an extended doctrine of *Karma*. According to it, *Karma* included *Karma* done in past lives. This is a most pernicious doctrine. This doctrine is often found to be attributed to the Buddha."[78] One can clearly understand the strong motive behind Ambedkar's rejection. Because the principles like *Karma* upheld as metaphysical justification for the social oppression, views the sufferings of the downtrodden as punishment for misdeeds in former lives. However, at the same time, Ambedkar found certain merits in the *Karma* theory, especially in the element of causality. "No Buddhist will deny that everything is under the sway of causality. Unless all humankind is treated as linked together as parts of one universal whole, we cannot perceive the full significance of the doctrine of *Karma*. Not only are the murderer and thief responsible to society, but society is equally responsible for breeding such characters."[79]

Ambedkar considers four noble truths as a leader monkish accretion; for Ambedkar, the four noble truths as presented in the Canonical account of the Buddha consist of the first Sermon, (*Dhammachakka Pavattana Sutta*) was problematic for their attribution of suffering to the ignorance and craving of sufferer. Ambedkar's main objections to the four noble truths are as follows: Since suffering is a material reality, or at least predominantly a material one, any kind of valid account should mainly focus on the material aspect of it, i.e., socio-political aspects of the suffering. Social conditions should be considered into the main account of suffering. However, the four noble truths treat suffering in a purely psychological way. According to it, the mental state of the suffering is the cause of suffering. Virtually sufferer and his mental state is the cause of suffering. According to Ambedkar, this kind of psychological explanation of suffering is spreading permission in the suffering. He wrote in the introduction of his work, 'the four Aryan truths deny hope to man and make the gospel of Buddha a gospel of pessimism.'

According to Ambedkar, "The centre of religion lay not in the relation of man to God. It lay in the relations between man and man. The purpose of religion is to teach man how he should behave towards other men so that all may be happy."[80] Ambedkar uses the word *Dhamma* as synonymous to true religion. The purpose of religion is to explain the origin of world. The purpose of *Dhamma* is social teaching. The purpose of religion is closely associated with the removal of people's misery. Ambedkar considers misery as the result of people's inequality to others. To remove misery, each one must learn to be righteous in his conduct in relation to others, and thereby make the earth the kingdom of righteousness.

Ambedkar heavily emphasised on '*Saddhmma*', in the interpretation of '*Dhamma*'. For Ambedkar, Buddhism is *Saddhamma.* Ambedkar says, "Men are born unequal, some have more capacity, and others have less. All have to enter into what is called a struggle for existence. If inequality were recognised as the rule of the game, the weakest will always go to the wall. Should this rule of inequality be allowed to be the rule of life? Some answer, in the affirmative on the ground that results in the survival of the fittest. The question, however, is, is the fittest best from the point of view of society. No one can give a positive answer. It is because of this doubt that religion preaches equality. For equality may help the best to survive even though, the best may not be the fittest however, what one wants is the best, not the fittest. This was the view point of Buddha and it was because of this, that he argued that a religion which does not preach equality is not worth having."[81]

Ambedkar considers Buddhism as a democratic system and Buddha as a great democrat. Ambedkar argued that, "(*Bhikkhu Sanghas*) were nothing but parliaments. They knew and observed all the rules and parliamentary procedure known to modern times the rules applied by Buddha to the meeting of *Bhikkhu Sanghas*, he must have borrowed them from the rules of the political assemblies functioning in the country in his time."[82]

References

1. Raghavendra Rao, K. (1993). *Babasaheb Ambedkar*, Naveen Shahdara Publishers, New Delhi, p. 27.
2. Louis Green Span and Stefen Andersson, ed, *Russell on Religion*, Routledge. New York, 2006, pp. 206-207.
3. *Ibid*, p. 208.
4. Rajasekhar Setty, V.T.(1983). *Ambedkar and His Conversion*, Dalit Sahitya Academy, New Delhi, p. 66.
5. *Ibid*, pp. 233-235.
6. Jatava, D.R. (1993). *The Critics of Dr. Ambedkar*. Surabhi Publications, New Delhi, p.194.

7. Anand, Telthumbde, *Ambedkar on Muslims (Myths and Facts)*, VAK Publications, Mumbai, 2003, p. 23.
8. *Ibid*, p. 24.
9. Surendra Ajnat, *Pakistan or Partition of India*, Buddhist Public House, Jalandhar, 1986, pp. 220-221.
10. *Ibid*. p. 221.
11. Peter Vander Veer, (1996). *Conversion to Modernities: The Globalisation of Christianity,* Lagos Evangelical Publishers, Germany, p. 99.
12. Keer, Dananjay, *Dr. Ambedkar: Life and Mission*, Popular Prakashan, Bombay, 1991, p. 299.
13. Gauri Viswanathan,(1998). *Outside of the Fold: Conversion, Modernity and Belief*, Princeton University Press, New Jersey, p. 609.
14. Moon, Vasnt,ed, *Ambedkar B. R., Writings and Speeches*, Govt. of Maharashtra, Vol. III, Bombay, 1989, p. 99.
15. *Ibid*, pp. 95-96.
16. Gauri Viswanathan,(1998). *Outside of the Fold: Conversion, Modernity and Belief*, Princeton University Press, New Jersey, p. 610.
17. Moon Vasant, *Why go for Conversion?* trans., Dalit Sahitya Akademy, Bangalore,1987, pp. 19-20.
18. *Ibid*, p. 21.
19. Rajasekhar Setty, V.T.(1983). *Ambedkar and His Conversion*, Dalit Sahitya Academy, New Delhi, p. 67.
20. Louis Green Span and Stefen Andersson, ed, *Russell on Religion*, Routledge, New York, 2006, p. 89.
21. Jatava, D.R. (1993). *The Critics of Dr. Ambedkar*, Surabhi Publications, New Delhi, p.195.
22. *Ibid*, p. 90.
23. Moon, Vasnt,ed, Ambedkar, B.R. '*Philosophy of Hinduism*' in *Ambedkar Writing and Speeches*, Govt. of Maharashtra, Vol.VII, Bombay, 1990, p. 32.
24. Dinesh, S. Anand, *Origin of Scriptures*, Blumoon Books, New Gyan Offset Press, New Delhi, 2002, p. 70.
25. Jatava, D.R. (1993). *The Critics of Dr. Ambedkar*, Surabhi Publications, New Delhi. p. 25.
26. *Ibid*, p. 26.
27. Dinesh, S. Anand, *Origin of Scriptures*, Blumoon Books, New Gyan Offset Press, New Delhi, 2002, p. 71.
28. Ambedkar, B.R, (1991). *The Buddha and His Dhamma,* Siddharth Publications, Bombay, p. 159.
29. Jatava, D.R. (1993). *The Critics of Dr. Ambedkar*, Surabhi Publications, New Delhi, p. 222.

30. *Ibid*, p. 223.
31. *Ibid*, pp. 223-224.
32. Moon, Vasnt,ed, *Ambedkar B. R., Writings and Speeches*, Govt. of Maharashtra, Vol.III, Bombay,1989, pp. 247- 248.
33. Dinesh, S. Anand, *Origin of Scriptures*, Blumoon Books, New Gyan Offset Press, New Delhi, 2002, p. 35.
34. Moon, Vasnt,ed, *Ambedkar B. R., Writings and Speeches*, Govt. of Maharashtra, Vol.III, Bombay, 1989, p. 232.
35. Jatava, D.R. (1993). *The Critics of Dr. Ambedkar*, Surabhi Publications, New Delhi. p. 99.
36. *Ibid*, p. 255.
37. *Ibid*, p. 426.
38. *Ibid*, p. 427.
39. Ahir, D.C. (1996). "*The Pioneers of Buddhist Revival in India*", Blue Moon Books, New Delhi, p. 150.
40. Michael Mahar J, (1972). (ed)., *The Untouchables in Contemporary India*, Tucson, The University of Arizona Press, Arizona, p. 231.
41. Ambedkar, B.R., *Who were the Shudras,* Govt. of Maharashtra, Vol. 7, Bombay, 1990, p. 32.
42. Pradeep, P. Gokhale, *Reconstructing the World. 'Universal Consequentlism: A Note on B.R. Ambedkar's Reconstruction of Buddhism'*, Sri Satguru Publications, New Delhi, 1993, p. 45.
43. Dinesh, Anand. *Origin of Scriptures*, Blumoon Books, New Gyan Offset Press, New Delhi, 2002, p. 171.
44. *Ibid*, p. 52.
45. Ambedkar, B.R., *Buddha and His Dhamma*, Siddhartha Publications, Bombay, 1991, p. 275.
46. *Ibid*, pp. 275-276.
47. Ambedkar, B.R., *Buddha and His Dhamma*, Siddhartha Publications, Bombay, 1991, p. 277.
48. *Ibid*, p. 278.
49. *Ibid*, p. 279-280.
50. *Ibid.*
51. Dinesh Anand, *Origin of Scriptures,* Blumoon Books, New Gyan Offset Press, New Delhi, 2002, p. 55.
52. *Ibid*, p. 61.
53. *Ibid*, p. 62.
54. *Ibid*, p. 91.
55. Qanauji Lal Gautama, (2002). *Dr. Baba Saheb Ambedkar and Brahmanism*, B.R. Publishing Corporation, New Delhi, p. 6.

56. *Ibid*, p. 27.
57. *Ibid*, p. 28.
58. Ambedkar, B.R., '*The Buddha and His Dhamma*', Siddhartha Publications, Bombay, 1991, p. 272.
59. *Ibid*, p. 273.
60. Dinesh Anand, *Origin of Scriptures*, Blumoon Books, New Gyan Offset Press, New Delhi, 2002, p. 81.
61. Ambedkar, B.R. '*The Buddha and His Dhamma*', Siddhartha Publication, Bombay, 1991, p. 271.
62. Moon, Vasnt, ed, *Ambedkar, B.R, Writing and Speeches*, Govt. of Maharashtra, Vol. I, Bombay, 1989, Castes in India, p. 37.
63. Moon, Vasnt, ed, Ambedkar, B.R., *Writing and Speeches*, Govt. of Maharashtra, Vol. III Bombay, 1989, p. 68.
64. Moon, Vasnt,ed., *Ambedkar, B.R., Writings & Speeches*, Govt. of Maharashtra, Vol. III, Bombay, 1989, and Buddha or Karl Marx, p. 462.
65. Keer, Dhananjay, (1987). *Dr Ambedkar: Life and Mission*, Sangan Books, London, p. 512.
66. *Ibid*, p. 513.
67. *Ibid*, p. 514.
68. *Ibid*. p. 515.
69. Dinesh S. Anand, *Origin of Scriptures*, Blumoon Books, New Gyan Offset Press, New Delhi, 2002, p. 124.
70. Ambedkar, B.R. '*The Buddha and His Dhamma*', Siddhartha Publications, Bombay, 1991, p. 324.
71. Moon, Vasnt, ed., *Ambedkar, B.R., Writings & Speeches*, Govt. of Maharashtra, Vol.II, Bombay, 1991, p. 271.
72. Pradeep, P. Gokhale, *Reconstructing the World*, '*Universal Consequentilism: A Note on Ambedkar's B.R.,Reconstruction of Buddhism*',Sri Satguru Publications, New Delhi, 1993, p. 46.
73. Moon, Vasnt,ed, *Ambedkar, B. R., Writings & Speeches*, Govt. of Maharashtra, Vol. I and IV, Bombay, 1989 - 1991, p. 4.
74. Ambedkar, B. R. *The Buddha and His Dhamma*, Siddharth Publications, Bombay, 1987, p. 322.
75. Pradeep, P. Gokhale, *Reconstructing the World*,'*Universal Consequentilism: A Note on B.R Ambedkar's Reconstruction of Buddhism*',Sri Satguru Publications, New Delhi, 1993, p. 126.
76. Ambedkar, B.R. '*The Buddha and His Dhamma*', Siddhartha Publication, Bombay, 1991, p. 325.
77. Pradeep, P. Gokhale, *Reconstructing the World* , '*Universal Consequentilism: A Note on Ambedkar's Reconstruction of Buddhism*', Sri Satguru Publications, New Delhi, 1993, p. 128.

78. Ambedkar, B.R, '*The Buddha and His Dhamma*' Siddhartha Publications, Bombay, 1991, p. 338.
79. Ahir, D.C., *The Pioneers of Buddhist Revival in India*, Blue Moon Books, New Delhi, 1996, p. 238.
80. Ambedkar, B.R. '*The Buddha and His Dhamma*', Siddhartha Publications, Bombay, 1991, p. 181.
81. Ambedakr, B.R. '*Buddha and His Dhamma*', Siddhartha Publications, Bombay, 1991, p. 221.
82. *Ibid*, p. 184.

Chapter – V

Ambedkar's Views on Philosophy and Religion

This chapter tries to highlight the importance of Philosophy of religion in the society that has been interpreted by Ambedkar. He gave paramount importance to the problem of 'Religion'. For Ambedkar, religion is vital to the social life of a society. Religion generally means belief in god, belief in soul, worship of god, curing of the erring soul, propitiating God by prayers, ceremonies, and sacrifices. There are many religions in this world such as Christianity, Islam, Hinduism, and Judaism, which are God-centric. Every religion has its own philosophy, a set of practices, rituals, customs and rules. Ambedkar's notion of religion is entirely different. For him religion is not *God-centric* rather it is *man-centric*. According to him the role of religion is to discover truth and build peaceful and harmonious society through human values. These values form the bedrock of egalitarian society based on the principles of equality, liberty, fraternity and justice in which human dignity assumes significant place. This chapter tries to highlight the following issues like the nature and necessity, functions, scope and authenticity of religion from Ambedkar's point of view.

Ambedkar while tracing the relation between philosophy and religion opined that the philosophy is something that is universal whereas religion is specific and defined. He says that "religion is something definite, there is nothing definite as to what is to be included in the term philosophy."[1] In Ambedkar's view, Religion is very much essential to the existence of mankind. He says that "some people think that religion is not essential for society. I do not hold this view. I consider the foundation of religion to be essential to the life and practices of society."[2] "He had strong religious sentiments regarding the formation of religion, but he had no faith in Hinduism as he hated hypocrisy that existed in it."[3] In his opinion, Religion in India acts as a social force in the lives of people and most of the decisions are influenced by the Religion. Ambedkar desired a religion, which instructs people to establish a society based on liberty, equality and social order in which men live with moral values. This will be the science in which we shall be using the term Religion in the following discussion.

Analysis of Religion

According to Ambedkar's analysis of religion,[4] every religion contains primarily a system of ideal scheme and means to attain the same. Every religion proposes an ideal scheme to its followers as the good to be achieved as the sacred goal and divine ultimate aim in life. All religions may not stress equally all values and some may even neglect essential values. Even if some religions were to emphasise the same ideals, it means that they often would differ. This method of studying and analysing the religions can easily be extended also to the ideologies such as Marxism. Theologian, R. Panikkar, and Liberation theologian, J.L. Segundo, have employed a similar method to the study of religions and ideologies.[5]

The questions regarding religion, that haunt and taunt the social activists and the militants involved in the fight for human rights, or the liberation of the oppressed poor, have been satisfactorily answered by Ambedkar by his own life and clarified in his writings.[6] He has demonstrated beyond doubt that religion has a role to play in the liberation of untouchables or *Dalits* and the non-persons existing in Hindu culture. Religion and revolution need not be opposed to each other; rather religion can serve as the motivation force for revolutionary struggles. Those who deem religion to be the opium of the masses, a projection of the human desires and needs, an infantile fixity or a superstitious hang over of the savage past, have a good guide in the writings of Ambedkar, who dispels their doubts about its necessity and importance. Many social scientists have confirmed the revolutionary potential of religion.[7]

Ambedkar has shown the vital need of religion for the individual as well as for the society at large. By presenting sacred ideals and humane values, and by reinforcing them in the society, religion helps the development of the persons and the progress of the society. Religion thus preserves, protects, and promotes life.[8] Conservation of life by religious consecration is the law of life. Hence, religion is not a burden enforced by the supernatural powers, be they God or his prophets, and heavenly revelations. It is a vital role arising out of the need for protecting the weak in the society, and for maintaining peace among the various groups, tribes, classes, races and castes. Religion is, therefore, nothing but morality that is based on the law of love, which is the law of life.[9]

Ambedkar's theology is based on his own personal understandings in life. He did bear the stigma of untouchability and its insults. He was the victim of exploitation of the caste system. He was refused place to stay, water to drink, vehicle to travel, just because he was born in a particular community. Though a scholar of repute abroad, he had to bear the insults of the ignorant, in his home state just because he was a Dalit.[10] He, like Moses, forsaking the positions that could have been his, opted to lead his people into the land of freedom. Unto the last, he struggled for this mission. His theology/philosophy was therefore pathos-praxis based. His commitment to the liberation of *Dalits* prompted his critical reflection, motivated and inspired all his studies and writings. He was no armchair philosopher/theologian; praxis-reflection was his methodology.

Ambedkar's reinterpretation of religion, Buddhism and the Philosophy of Religion reveal his hermeneutical skills. His hermeneutical suspicion went beyond the Marxian suspicion, which failed to grasp the evil consequences of caste oppression and caste alienation. His reinterpretation of Buddhism, in accordance with modern scientific principles and socialistic revolutionary thrust is remarkable.[11] Ambedkar's thinking and interpretation was also highly critical. He insisted that Philosophy of Religion should not only be descriptive but also critical. His Dalit Critical Principle was *radical* in its depth and extent. It sought the root causes of the problem, without stopping the diagnosis at the level of symptoms. And in its extent, the critique of Ambedkar targeted all the political parties, ideologies, religions, social reform movements and the eminent social and political activists, even if they are popularly hailed as *mahatmas,* freedom fighters and social reformers.[12] The theology of Ambedkar is based on the principles of love and wisdom, which is like two wheels of his theological caravan. He emphasises the necessities of both the Buddhist discerning wisdom and Christian loving service.

In his Theology "wisdom meets love", which explains to enlighten as well as empower us, to serve and struggle with detachment and compassion.[13] His theory is not only in its integral synthesis of Christian love and Buddhist wisdom. But there is also an integration of the secular scientific enlightenment of the East and West; where in the modern rational enlightenment and the ancient Buddhist religious enlightenment were happily married. This is a new paradigm highly recommended to the Indians of secular democracy.[14] The dualisms between science and religion, secular and sacred, politics and spirituality, involvement and detachment, action and contemplation, material and spiritual, works and faith, social reality and the divine Kingdom, do not exist in Ambedkar's new integral holistic theological paradigm.[15]

Philosophy of Religion

Ambedkar's Philosophy of Religion at the outset of his book, *Philosophy of Hinduism,* takes up the argument on the meaning of "Philosophy of Religion."[16] Owing to two facts, he confesses that he is unable to get a clear idea about it. Firstly, there is nothing unambiguous about what is incorporated in the term philosophy. Secondly, philosophy and religion have been adversaries and hostile to each other which makes the unhappy choice of the title, "Philosophy of Religion" confusing. Ambedkar, in his *The Buddha and His Dhamma* describes the accepted perception of religion held by common people and advocated by European theologians, who hold Religion that connotes "belief in God, belief in soul, worship of God, curing of the erring soul, propitiating God by prayers, ceremonies, sacrifices, etc."[17] He shows that the origin of religion was never fixed. From time to time the word, "religion", is an imprecise word with no unchanging meaning: "It is a word with many meanings. This is because religion has accepted through many stages. The impression has not had the same meaning which it had at the prior stage or is likely to have at the succeeding stage."[18]

Ambedkar gives an historical account of the evolution of the concept of religion in the three stages from the primitive to the present form of religion. In the first stage of hunting, rain and floods and the events in which the primitive man could not explain. Any strange performance done to control the observable fact was called magic. Religion therefore, in primitive stage, came to be identified with *magic*. In the second stage, the progression of religion came to be identified with beliefs, rituals, ceremonies, prayers and sacrifices. This outset of religion is imitative. The essential point in religion starts with the belief that there exists some power, which causes these phenomena which primal man did not know and could not understand. Magic lost its place at this stage. This power was originally malicious. But later it was felt that it could also be compassionate. Beliefs, rites, ceremonies and sacrifices were necessary to both propitiate a benevolent power and also to placate an angry power. In the historical process, the power was called God or the Creator. The last and the third stage saw this strong belief of God who created this world and also man. This was followed by the belief that man has a soul and the soul is perpetual and is answerable to God for all the man's actions in the world.[19]

Pringle-Pattison's definition of philosophy of religion is, in fact more pertinent for "comparative religion" whose endeavour is to discover the common principle in the varied manifestations of religion.[20] Differing with the sense and aim of philosophy of religion as outlined by Pringle-Pattison, Ambedkar gives his own explanation and the goals of philosophy of religion. Ambedkar viewed the Philosophy in its innovative sense which was of dual nature. It meant the teachings like that of the philosophy of Socrates or the philosophy of Plato. In another sense, it meant that the critical base was used in passing judgments upon various things and different events. Proceeding on this basis, Philosophy of Religion appears not merely a descriptive science. He regarded it as living being both descriptive as well as normative one. As long as it deals with the teachings of a Religion, Philosophy of Religion becomes a descriptive science. In the same way, so long as it involves the use of critical reason for passing judgment on those teachings, the Philosophy of Religion becomes a normative science.[21]

For Ambedkar, Philosophy of Religion is both a descriptive study as well as a normative study judging the value of a meticulous religion.

Each religion promotes "good" and advocates a particular philosophy of life. That is why he states, "I do not think there can be such a thing as a general Philosophy of Religion. I believe that each religion has its particular philosophy. To me there is no Philosophy of Religion. There is a philosophy of a Religion."[22] The social order on which a particular religion sanctifies, legitimises, spiritualises, promotes and sets up as a sacred ideal which should not be debated, being the norm of the divine ascendancy is the essence, the main purpose of the religion. For Ambedkar, the aim, set of goals or value-system which he calls "the ideal scheme", held up by a pernickety religion, governs people through its institutions influencing the political structures more powerful than often the Law and the Government of a society.

Ambedkar clearly emphasises that the main aspect of normative account and its critical nature. The Philosophy of Religion of Ambedkar is one of the best that we have in India. He has made it clear that a Philosophy of Religion should not only be descriptive but also be critical.[23] The experts in the Phenomenology of Religion, Sociology of Religion and even the Comparative Religion and History of Religions do not go beyond the description of religion. This could be due to their objectives and methodology. But the philosophers and theologians of religion have no excuse not to be critical of religions. They often turn apologists than critical thinkers. The insistence of Ambedkar is that religion is basically a social phenomenon and that humans may not need a religion if they were to exist individually is also to be noted.[24] Many religious leaders and priests, who overemphasise only the individual salvation of *soul*, of personality *mukti* and *nirvana* are only exploiting religion for their interests. Any religion that fails to emphasise the social dimension, the social responsibility and the need of social commitment, according to Ambedkar, is a false religion.

The divine governance of people through religion is also affected by the control of the religious ideals that exercise over the minds of the people, who are thus motivated to obey or submit to sacred principles more than the practical secular principles or their instinctual desires. Ambedkar defines religion in a brief statement, "*That which governs people is Religion.*"[25] For the same reason, Ambedkar considers the ascertainment and examination of the ideal scheme of a particular religion, with which a religion governs, is an important dimension of the Philosophy of Religion. According to Ambedkar, three proportions are involved in the study of Philosophy of Religion, whose proper definition, ascertainment and assessment are necessary for this science. They are: The explanation of Religion, the ideal scheme for which Religion stands and, "the criterion to be adopted for judging the value of the ideal scheme of divine governance for which a given Religion stands."[26]

Another facet of the Philosophy of Religion is that "to know the ideal scheme for which a religion stands" which follows logically from Ambedkar's elucidation of religion. To define what is fixed, everlasting and foremost part in the religion of any society and to separate its essential character from those, which are expendable, is often very complex. Distinguishing between the *primitive* religions and the *positive* religions, he adjudicates that the task is not so difficult in case of the latter. The primary characteristic of *positive* religions is that they have not grown up like primitive religions under the action of cataleptic forces operating silently from age to age, but trace their derivation to the teaching of great religious innovators who wrangle as the organs of a divine revelation. Being the result of conscious formulations, the philosophy of a religion which is *positive* is unchallenging to find and easy to state.[27]

He argued for the reorganisation of Hindu religion, and listed out the following the necessary items. According to him, there should be one and only one standard book of Hindu Religion, acceptable to all Hindus and recognised by all Hindus. This of course means that all other books of Hindu religion such as *Vedas, Shastras* and *Puranas,* which are treated as sacred and authoritative, should end to be so, and the preaching of any doctrine, religious or social that are restricted in these books should be penalised.

No ceremony performed by a priest who does not hold a *sunad* shall be deemed to be valid in law and it should he made penal for a person who has no *sunad* to officiate as a priest. A priest should be the servant of the state and should be subject to the disciplinary action by the State in the matter of his morals, beliefs and worship, in addition to his being subject along with other citizens to the ordinary law of the land. "The numeral of priests should be limited by law according to the requirements of the State as is done in the case of the Christianity."[28]

Ambedkar required Hinduism based on a set of moral principles, which are appropriate equally to all the participants of the society. And only these moral principles would sustain the society.

The criticism that levelled by Ambedkar on Hinduism was not accepted by M.K. Gandhi, even though he accepted some weakness in Hinduism and he claimed that Hinduism had not only bad elements, it also had some good elements and criticisms should be on the best side. Ambedkar, in response to Gandhi's comments, says that, "Religion must be judged not by its worst specimens but by its best, which is true enough but, does it dispose the matter? I say it does not. The question still remains—why the worst numbers are many and the best so few?"[29] Ambedkar tried to explain the various reasons for considering Hinduism as a false religion.

According to Ambedkar, the Hindu society, introduced the caste system and permeated it deeper and deeper. The upper class is considered sacred and divine whereas the lower class is considered polluted and supposed to serve these upper classes. As a net result the society had gradations: Those who were in the higher position commanded due respect whereas those at the bottom lived under the mercy of the top line people. Manu's code of conduct is taken into the concept of *Dharma.* It advocated the compulsory duties and obligations of the different castes. In other words, in the Hindu religion there was calculated division of labourers and labour. Those who did menial jobs were not even regarded as citizens and they were not allowed to come up in life by the religious doctrines. There are some groups within the society that could enjoy all the facilities, and can develop themselves, and some groups who are not entitled to use that opportunity because of religious sanctions. Ambedkar attacked the caste system based on occupation and said that, "the Hindu social order is an order based on classes and not on individuals. It is a command in which classes are graded one above the other. It is an order in which status and function of the classes are determined and fixed."[30]

Ambedkar argues that the Hindu religion, its concept of God and its allied religious principles and customs that tend to preserve the caste system intact. Religious doctrine made the untouchables, presently called as *Dalits*, to believe that they are born to be slaves and that they are fit only to the menial jobs. For him, a Hindu means a caste and his responsibility and loyalty is restricted only to his caste. The *Virtue* and moralities have become caste bound and there is no possibility for sympathy, charity and appreciation of the deserving. The untouchables or *Dalits* were not allowed to get the same status with others in the Hindu religion. Ambedkar finds significance of religion only in their principles but condemns the religion, which is guarded by its rules and codes. He feels that Hindu religion is meaningless to the untouchables because of its rigidity. Hindu religion has got several codes of conduct. For the untouchables some were strictly adhered. Violating them by the untouchables led to severe punishment and excommunication.

The philosophy of Hinduism as a part of the philosophy of Religion it is necessary to examine the *Upanishads*. The philosophy of the *Upanishads* has been well summarised by Buxley. He says that the *Upanishad* philosophy agreed that, "supposing the existence of a permanent reality, or 'substance', beneath the shifting series of phenomena, whether of matter or of mind."[31] The substance of the cosmos was '*Brahma*' that of the individual man '*Atman*'; and the latter was separated from the former only, if I may so speak, by its phenomenon envelope, by the casing of sensations, thoughts and desires, pleasures and pains, which make up the illusive phantasmagoria of life. This the ignorant, take for reality; their '*Atman*' therefore remains eternally imprisoned in delusions, bound by the fetters of desire and scourged by the whip of misery.

Lala Hardyal says that, "The *Upanishads* claim to expound' that, by knowing which everything is known."[32] This quest for 'the absolute' is the basis of all the spurious metaphysics of India. The treatises are full of absurd conceits, quaint fancies, and chaotic speculations. And we have not learned that they are worthless. We keep moving in the old rut; we edit and re-edit the old books instead of translating the classics of European social thought. Indian pundits and graduates seem to suffer from a kind of mania for what is effete and antiquated. Thus, an institution, established by progressive men, aims at leading our youths through *Sanskrit* grammar to the *Vedas* via the Six *Darshanas*. According to Ambedkar, it is a false move in the quest for wisdom.

Religion is concerned with the love of truth, whereas Philosophy is stagnant and Religion is dynamic. These differences are merely two aspects of one and the same thing. Philosophy is static because it is concerned only with knowing of truth. Religion is dynamic because it is concerned with love of truth. Unless religion is dynamic and begets in us the emotion of love for something, then it is better to be without religion; as religion is a perception of truth and if our perception of truth is not accompanied by our love for it, then it is much better that the religion is not seen at all. This is the outcome of all transcended philosophies which have no influence on the way of life. As Blake said, "Religion is philosophy and philosophy is Brotherhood. Philosophy must become Religion i.e., it must become a work Ethic."[33] It must not remain mere metaphysics. As Mr Plowman says, "If religion were a Metaphysic and certain, it would never be the concern for men. To keep it wholly in the realm of Metaphysices is to make non-sense of it. Believing in religion as something which is not directly and vitally effective in politics is ultimately belief that is strictly speaking idiotic; because in the effective sense such a belief makes no difference, and in the world of time and space 'what makes no difference does not exist."[34] It is for these very reasons that the philosophy of the *Upanishads* proved so ineffective.

It is, therefore, incontrovertible notwithstanding "the Hindu Code of Ethics and not withstanding the philosophy of the *Upanishads*, because not a little or not a jot did abate from the philosophy of Hinduism as propounded by Manu. They were ineffective and powerless to erase the infamy, preached by Manu in the name of religion. By not withstanding their existence one can still say "Hinduism? Thy name is inequality."[35] Ambedkar new philosophy of religion led him to leave Hinduism and convert to another religion. Religious leaders from other religions too invited him to join in their religions. Time and again Ambedkar emphasises that "*Religion is for man,' man is not for religion.* And he substantiates his argument with the following analysis. If you want to gain self-respect, change your religion. If you want to create a cooperating society, change your religion, if you want power, change your religion. If you want equality, change your religion, if you want to make the world in which you live happy, change your religion. Why should you remain in a religion that does not value your manhood? Why should you remain in a religion that does not let you enter its temples?"[36] Why should you remain in a religion that does not give you water to drink? Why should you remain in a religion that bars you from good jobs? Why should you remain in a religion that dishonours you at every step? He still informs, "I am sorry, I will not be with you. I have decided to change. This is not the place to give reasons."[37] But, in "the conversion speech" he refused even to be a well-wisher of Hinduism and suggested means for its change helping it to reform. He categorically stated, "You must make your effort because *Hindu society is neither our aim nor our field of action. Our aim is to gain freedom we have nothing to do with any thing else.*"[38]

The Philosophy of Religion of Ambedkar also, in the same stratum, proposes justice and social welfare as the criterion to judge the religions. Paul Knitter, a liberation theologian of religion, has taken up the debate on the need for a criterion, to evaluate religious practices. He has, in dialogue with Liberation Theology, proposed the critical principles. While Knitter's suggestion still remains a proposal, Ambedkar's Dalit Critical Principle had been put to use and proved to be effective as the criterion to judge religions and ideologies. The promotion of justice to the *Dalits* and the oppressed is the best criterion to judge religions, ideologies or political and social events and activities.

Ambedkar holds that Hinduism like Judaism, Christianity and Islam is also a positive religion. Like Christianity that has its Bible, and the other positive religions have their own holy Books, accordingly does Hinduism too. The Bible of Hinduism is called the *Manu Smrti,* "a divine code which lays down the rules which govern the religious, ritualistic and social life of the Hindus in minuscule detail."[39] The ideal design of divine governance, the social moral order and the principles projected and consecrated for the same, can easily be ascertained from the sacred codes promulgated and enforced by the sacred books of the positive religions which include the norms of the founders or innovators of particular religions.

The third dimension in the Philosophy of Religion is the criterion to be adopted for judging the value of the ideal scheme of divine governance for which a given religion stands. Religion must be put on assessment. That leads to the description of the norm. Of the three dimensions, this third one is the most difficult one to be ascertained and defined."[40] Ambedkar disagrees with those who hold that this dimension is not a part of Philosophy of Religion. D.S. Adam makes it clear that some students of the Philosophy of Religion seem to regard the first two dimensions only in the field of Philosophy of Religion. They do not identify the third dimension as part of the study of the Philosophy of Religion. He disagrees with this view. The difference is probably due to the fact that he regards the Philosophy of Religion as a normative study and as a reminiscent study.[41]

Religion as Social Revolution

Ambedkar suggests that a philosophy of a religion must be judged, based on its revolution because the mother of Philosophy is revolution. So Ambedkar held the view that, "As for myself I think it is safe to proceed on the view that to know the philosophy of any movement or the institution has undergone. Revolution is the mother of philosophy and if it is not the mother of philosophy, it is a lamp, which illuminates philosophy. Religion is no exception to this rule. The best method to ascertain the criterion of which to judge the philosophy of (any) religion is to study the Revolutions which religion has undergone. That is the method I propose to adopt."[42] Further he says, "To me the best method to ascertain the criterion by which to judge the Philosophy of Religion is to study the Revolutions which religion has undergone."[43]

Ambedkar says that the religion must be taken seriously because, through that a proper socio-economic and political change can be brought about only through a cultural-religious revolution. Ambedkar not only insists that social and religious problems have a suggestion to politics but also persuasively demonstrates that political revolutions are brought about, or at least proceeded by, socio-religious revolutions which first guide in a cultural revolution. For instance, the Religious Reformation started by Luther was the forerunner of the political liberation of the European people. In England, Puritanism led to the establishment of political liberty which later on led to the foundation of a new world. It was Puritanism which had won the war of American Independence and Puritanism was a religious movement. The same is true in the case of Muslim Empire. Before the Arabs became a political power they had undergone a thorough religious revolution started by the Prophet Mohammad. Even the Indian History supports the same termination. The political revolution led by Chandragupta was preceded by the religious and social revolution of Buddha. The political revolution led by Shivaji was preceded by the religious and social reform brought about by the religious reformers of Maharashtra.

The political revolution of the Sikhs was preceded by the religious and social revolution led by Guru Nanak. However, the Gautama Buddha is the first social revolutionary in history claims Ambedkar.

By taking these historic instances Ambedkar says that the emancipation of the mind and the soul is a necessary preliminary for the political expansion of the people.[44] Religion is needed to wage any kind of revolution in the society, since it mentally engineers the minds of the people. Religion, thus, plays no inconsequential role in the emancipation of the mind and soul of the people, which is a preliminary requisite for the socio-political transformations of society. According to Ambedkar, revolutionary social change needs religion as an important motivating, concretising, empowering and energising factor.

Ambedkar reminds us of great prophets like Buddha, Jesus and his predecessors like Amos, Isaiah who condemned religious practices that exploit the poor and smack of hypocrisy. Ambedkar lashes out at wrong concept of religion and said, "Our religion today has neither God nor morality. I have no doubt that this is a much degenerated state of human mind; and it is a task for the future generation to restore religion in the purer and nobler form."[45] He proceeds to enumerate the stages of its degeneration: He added that in his day in India there was no religion except the worship of idols, whether they were of *Sadhus*, *Saints*, or miracle-makers. Ambedkar attacked the real character of the Hindu Religion, in short, "so long as we remain in a religion which teaches a man to treat another man as leper, the sense of discrimination on account of caste which is deeply rooted in our minds cannot go. *For annihilating castes and untouchability from among the untouchables, change of religion is the only antidote*."[46] "I tell you, religion is for man and not man is for religion. If you want to organise, consolidate and be successful in this world, change the religion."[47]

Ambedkar, by captivating support from Robertson Smith and Crawley, analyses the differences and similarities in the norms between the savage and the civilised society which he again divides in to antique society and Modern society. It is consequently clear that savage and civilised societies agree upon one aspect. That is, in both the societies, the inner interests of religion, namely, the life processes by which individuals are preserved and the race maintained are the same. There is no real difference between the two. At the same time they are different in two other important respects. In a savage society, God comes in the scheme of Religion, and in a civilised society, morality becomes consecrated by religion.[48]

To determine the norm of judging the Philosophy of Religion, Ambedkar takes up a chronological survey of the 'ruling concepts of religion' as a scheme of divine governance, centuries down from the ancient society to the modern society. He also analyses the important revolutions.[49] And the character of these revolutions is of dual nature. One is an *external revolution*, caused by the scientific revolutions such as the Copernican revolution, and the Darwinian revolution caused by the emergence of sciences like Medicine and Psychology, which shattered the empire of religion bit by bit restraining its field and authority. It was a revolt of science against the extra territorial jurisdiction assumed by Religion over a field, which it did not belong. The second one is *internal revolution, which was* a real Revolution or may be compared to any other political Revolution such as the French Revolution or the Russian Revolution, "which involves a constitutional change. By these kinds of Revolutions, the scheme of divine governance came to be distorted, amended and reconstituted."[50]

The *internal revolution* must be paid more attention in order to determine the model for judging the philosophy of religion for it "touches the nature and content of ruling of perceptions of the relations of God to man, of society to man and of man to man. How great this revolution was can be seen from the differences which divide savage society from civilised society."[51]

In the savage society, religion is without God, and its morality is self-governed by the religion. The change that has occurred in the civilised society is the first stage in the internal religious revolution. The second stage of Religious Revolution would take place within the civilised society. As a result of which the civilised society was split into antique and modern society. This second stage of revolution is far greater than the first, as it brought about prominent differences in the conceptions regarding the relations between God, Society and Man. Ambedkar demonstrates about ten differences in the relationship between God and Man, Society and Man, and Man and Man which was very much evident in the Antique and Modern society. Quoting from R. Smith, he finally sums it up saying, "By this Revolution, God has ceased to be merely the protector of society and social interests, in gross, he has also ceased to be the center of the divine order. Society and man have distorted the places which were the centers of this divine order. It is man who has become the center of it."[44]

From the analysis of religious revolutions, Ambedkar ends with a note that individual justice and social utility must serve as the norms for judging the value of the varied ideal schemes of divine governance proposed by different religions. The religion that helps greater promotion of individual justice and equality, presents itself with the divine and spiritual religious ideals, and also maintains a moral social order which in turn promotes social utility and progress, that kind of religion should be judged as the better religion.

Ambedkar sums up his historical survey of the norms by quoting that, 'we began with the distinction between antique and modern society, which differed in the type of their divine governance that they accepted as their religious ideals. At the one end of the Revolution, first it was antique society where in, its primary focus was on society as part of its religious ideals. At the other end, during the period of modern society, the main focus was over individual as part of its religious ideals. To put the same fact in terms of norms, it can be said that the norm or the criterion, for judging a particular act 'right and wrong' in the antique society was *utility,* while the norm or the criterion for judging 'right and wrong' in the modern society was *justice.* Thus, the Religious Revolution was not a revolution in the religious organisation of society, if it results in the shifting of the center from society to the individual. It was a revolution in the norms."[52] Here Ambedkar explains his meaning of justice, "I want to explain what I mean by the principle of justice, if all men are equal, all men are of the same essence and the common essence entitled them to the same fundamental rights and to equal liberty. In short, justice is simply another name for liberty, equality and fraternity."[53] For Ambedkar, fraternity and liberty are really derived notions. The basic and fundamental conceptions are equality and respect for human personality. Fraternity and liberty take their roots in these two fundamental conceptions. Equality is the original notion and respect for human personality is a reflection of it.[54]

Is there an intimate relationship between the two norms of *justice* and *utility* chosen by Ambedkar to judge the religions? Here he brings out their interrelationship and connection relying on the significance of justice given by J.S. Mill who has pointed out, "there is no obligatory antagonism between justice and utility. In other words what is unjust to the individual cannot be useful to society."[55] Ambedkar uses to pass judgment concerning a religion by ascertaining whether a meticulous religion is a religion of rules or of principles. According to him, a religion that does not lay stress on the principles and has developed into only a set of rules has already degenerated. He considers this principle to judge religions to be important, and so he explains the same with minute details, viewing why the religion of principles is better:

> The imperative may be right but the act is automatic. A religious performance may not be an accurate act but must at least be an accountable act. To permit this task, religion must chiefly be a matter of principles only; it cannot be a subject of rules. The moment it degenerates into rules, it ceases to be a religion, as it kills responsibility, which is the real meaning of a religious act. A religion of rules must give way to the religion of principles. A religion like Hinduism which according to him advocates the ancient rules of life must reinstate them with a religion of principles. The principles that must replace the rules are again the identical principles, which are resultant from justice, which is also one of the norms for judging the religions. They are liberty, equality and fraternity, in short, democracy.[56]

For Ambedkar, religion is not a worship of God by man, or a relationship between God and man, nor is it the deliverance of soul after life. For him, religion is a social institution of ethics that sanctifies the proper association between the individuals in the society, and the welfare of the individual and preservation of the egalitarian society.[57] This constitutes the important aspect of Ambedkar's philosophy of religion. Yet, some people claim that religion is a relationship between God and the human beings. It cannot be accepted that "all religions are equal," in the giving of this goal and the ability to attain the same. Hence, we still need a measure to evaluate religions. Ambedkar strongly disagrees with the affirmation that all religions are equal and hence "equal respect" is to be paid to all religions. "Ambedkar strongly advocated that one must give a new doctrinal basis to religion—a basis that will be in consonance with liberty, equality and fraternity and democracy."[58]

According to Ambedkar, a religion should be a matter of principle only but shouldn't be a matter of rules. When it degenerates into rules it ceases to be a religion because it destroys the responsibilities of the true religion. He added that the caste has almost disorganised and demoralised the Hindus. Another reason for Ambedkar to find problem with Hindu religion is its dual role. On the one hand for Hinduism the principles of Freedom, Equality and Fraternity are irrelevant. On the other hand he finds that Hindu religion divides the people permanently because of its inbuilt character of caste stratification. He wanted a religion, which is not duplicitous in the name of religion and teaches his followers to relate with others on the basis of liberty and fraternity. But there is no fraternity or equality among the Hindus and the caste system continued to exist. According to Ambedkar, the outcast is a by-product of caste system and there will be outcastes as long as the caste system exists. So nothing can redeem the outcaste except the annihilation of caste system.

Assuming the aim of religion is to reach God. Every road is that sure to lead him which will perfect religion that is still to be discovered. But the fact is that religions are not all true and hence, the adherents of one faith have a right, indeed a duty, to tell their erring friends what they conceive to be the truth. This argument again appears in another essay of Ambedkar titled, "*Away from the Hindus*" that discusses the reasons for conversion and disproves the objections raised against the move. The second objection for conversion is that it is not needed since all religions teach the same truth, namely, to seek goodness. Granting that all religions may teach to adhere to the "good", yet, they hold opposing views in what they propose as good. Ambedkar perceives that, "Religions may be alike in a way that they all teach that the meaning of life is to be found in the pursuit of 'good'. But religions are not alike in their answers to the question, 'What is good?' In this they certainly differ. One religion holds that brotherhood is good, another caste and *untouchability* is good. Some religions advocate the method of violence while others absolutist non-violence. This shows that all religions are not the same."[59]

Ambedkar says that there are three important characteristics, which form the subject matter of a philosophical analysis of religion both in natural and social theology. They are (a) The existence of God (b) God's providential government of the universe and (c) God's moral government of mankind. For him the philosophy of religion needed to be seen in terms of three perspectives, "its doctrine of God and of the divine as an integral part of its *theory* of nature; the ideal scheme for which a religion stands; and the specification of the criterion to be adopted for judging the ideal scheme of divine governance portrayed by a religion."[60] As far as Ambedkar is concerned philosophy of religion is normative science and regarded the specification of a set of criteria for judging the philosophy of a particular religion and by implication of all religions. After this basic explanation Ambedkar attempted to specify the meaning of religion.

Ambedkar measured religion as a system of values and as a science of social reconstruction. He said that the foundations of religion were indispensable to life and practices of life. He regarded religion as an essential one for single-minded human relationship. His view of religion in terms of character of his community could be understood from his fear of so-called denationalisation of the depressed classes. He felt that the acceptance of Buddhism by his community would raise its politico-cultural status and bring them on par with the Hindus. He discarded the Hindu religion because of moral incoherence and also on the grounds of logical incoherence. He looked at religion not as a road to salvation but as the basis for social interaction.

Ambedkar holds a perception that religion is a vital force, a scheme of moral governance and foundation for human society. He also says "While I condemn a religion of rules, I must not be understood to the opinion that there is no necessity for a religion. It is the foundation of society, the basis on which all true civil governments rest and both their sanction. Consequently, "when I urge that these ancient rules of life be annulled, I am anxious that a religion of principles, which alone can claim to be a true religion, shall take its place."[61] For Ambedkar, religion is necessary as a system of values and as a science of social reconstruction. Religion is necessary for the over all development of an individual and it is a system of such socio-cultural values, which would carry all the individuals on equal plane and would create an equal status for all communities. He looked at the religion not as a road to salvation but as the basis for social interaction. Ambedkar wanted a religion, with morality in order to build up nationalism with the association of Indian culture. He always wanted a religion with complete Indian culture and nature. He also emphasised that a religion should be free from exploitation, and true religion does not justify exploitation.

According to Ambedkar, the ideal of religion always wins over the secular practical ideal. This shows how great the difference in the force and sanction of these two ideals over the human mind. A religious ideal never fails to work so long as there is faith in that ideal. There is a criticism against Ambedkar that says that Ambedkar was against religion and wanted to destroy the religion, on the contrary, one should remember that he called for the destruction of religion of rules and not of principles.[62] On such principle, he tries to impress upon the necessity of religion. Thus, he condemns a religion of rules. Here, Ambedkar agrees with Burke that, 'True religion is the foundation of society, the basis on which all true civil government rests, and both their sanction."[63]

Ambedkar deems religion to be essential to personal as well as social life. Religion exercises a great pressure of moral power over a person's heart and mind, builds up the person's character, it is a powerful driving force for human activity and it instills hope. According to Ambedkar, religion can only satisfy the human being who is not satisfied with material things. A liberative religion alone can renovate the human minds of those who are socio-culturally enslaved. Ambedkar pertinently illustrates "the dominion which religion exercises over the minds of men."[64]

Ambedkar says that the true religion holds together society based on the moral force that exercises over the members. Its ethical power prevents social evils, crimes and atrocities, thus, religion alone can cultivate equality, liberty and fraternity and the enforcement of justice and order. Thus, religion is an important governing principle in the society. For Ambedkar, "That which governs people is Religion. That is the true definition of Religion." [65] For him, religion is also an important source of power in the society. Ambedkar recognised the influence of religion over people and its function as effective power-source in Indian society. And, he rejects the view that the religion to be idiosyncratic worship of God for the salvation of one's soul. His idea of religion is basically social and, it is defined in terms of moral and social order based on its ideal and principles. Consequently, the perception of Ambedkar on religion is based on principles, values and ideals where a society is governed by both individual and society that are preserved, promoted and sanctified.

According to Ambedkar, Hinduism as a religious faith is based on the infallibility of *Vedas*. Ambedkar says that, "The Hindu is not prepared to face any inquiry; there is no act of the Hindu, which is not covered or ordained (his) Religion."[66] He also refutes the idea that Hinduism holds all religions that are good and true. By saying this it wants to avoid the application of reason or the criterion for acceptance or non-acceptance of religion. Ambedkar believes that religion could be either liberative or oppressive; it all depends on various factors. Religion could function as a tool of domination if it propagates infallibility and requires total surrender to its totalitarian perspective. Religion is liberative if it is open for the notion of revolution or change. The social ideal of a particular religion, which is the divine scheme of governance of that religion, decides whether it is good or not good.

On the question of God's existence and the role of religion and morality, Ambedkar says that the religion is necessary for man and society to manage the secular and moral affairs of mankind, but to hold the view that, all religions are equally true and good is to cherish a wrong belief. Most of the existing religions are theistic and metaphysical; but to maintain that God is an essential element of a religion is also to nourish a mistaken faith. Religions, according to Ambedkar, wish to develop the social systems of their own choice to bring men together in peace for progress; but to bestow a divine governance over them so as to prevent the growth of an open society. The religions must preserve their textbooks for guiding the people in right direction; but to believe in their infallibility and divine authority is to mar the growth of free inquiry and critical reason. The eternal soul is unknown and unseen, a mere metaphysical speculation and to say that an individual's aim of life is to achieve its salvation *(Moksha)* is to escape the social responsibility bestowed on him as a member of society.

All the religions develop some sort of prayers and pilgrimages, rituals and ceremonies, as religious duties for men, simply being certain appendages to a religion; but the most integral part of a religion is the morality it professes for the welfare of mankind. The center of religion and Man, the base is morality, the aim is the secular welfare of mankind, and the means is the righteous conduct embedded in social responsibility that all human beings owe towards their fellow-beings living in human society. And lastly, the test of Justice and Utility must be applied to judge the relevance of a religion, and that consists in the trinity ideal of Liberty, Equality and Fraternity to effect the necessary change in its social norms of cruel and dynamical nature."[67]

For Ambedkar, the function of religion is to provide legitimacy to the set of values and rules that would help establish a moral order among human beings. These values and rules could be particularistic, relatively arbitrary and community specific when the communities were small and isolated. Concepts of local deities and of behavioural norms that were thought to please them were an adequate base for a semblance of social order so long as they served the interests of the power elite in the community. But with the changes in technology, in the means of production and the means of communication, isolated human groups were forced into contact with one another, and the need arose for new values and rules which were more universal. Thus, what were needed were a more universal morality and more universal concept of Godhood.

Ambedkar reiterates that the religion is a social force and stands for a scheme of divine governance. The scheme becomes an ideal for society to follow. The ideal may be non-existent in the sense that it is something, which is constructed. But although non-existent, it is real. For an ideal has full operative force which inherent in every ideal. Those who is deny the importance of religion not only forget this; they also forget to realise how great the potency is and sanction that lies behind a religious ideal as compared with that of a purely secular ideal. A religious ideal has a hold on mankind, irrespective of an earthly gain; this can never be said of a purely secular ideal. A religious ideal never fails to work so long as there is faith in that ideal."[68] For Ambedkar, God who permits the survival of immoral social divisions in the society like caste is no God. Ambedkar objects the worship of God who permits the existence and survival caste system.

Advocating Buddhism he discarded the *Shastras,* and also their authority as did by the Buddha and Nanak.

The *Dhamma* as True Religion

The final rejection of all religions and "religion" as such, as understood in the theistic sense, took place when Ambedkar chose the non-theistic Buddhist *Dhamma* as the true religion. In his book that he wrote for the Neo-Buddhism titled, *The Buddha and His Dhamma,* denounces "religion" and contrasts it with the *Dhamma* of Buddha which is not considered a "*religion*" by all the European theologians. Here by religion he means a theistic religion: "This is what religion has come to be and this what it connotes-belief in God, belief in soul, worship of God, curing of the erring soul, propitiating God by prayers, ceremonies, sacrifices, etc."[69] Stating that *Pradanya* and *Karuna* are the corner stones of Buddha's *Dhamma*, Ambedkar explains the difference between the subject matter of religion and the subject matter of *Dhamma:* "The two are poles apart. The purpose of religion is to explain the origin of the world. The purpose of *Dhamma* is to reconstruct the world."[70]

Ambedkar equates *Dhamma* with morality. He regrets that in non-*Dhamma* religions morality is not given prominence nor is it effective. He asks the question that what the place of morality in *Dhamma* is and gives the simple answer that morality is *Dhamma* and *Dhamma* is morality. In other words, in *Dhamma*, "morality takes the place of God although there is no God in *Dhamma*. In *Dhamma* there is no place for prayers, pilgrimages, rituals, ceremonies or sacrifices."[71] Morality is the essence of *Dhamma*, without it there is no *Dhamma*. "Morality in *Dhamma* arises from the straight necessity for man to love man. It does not involve in the sanction of God. It is not to please God that man has to be moral. It is for his own good that man has to love man."[72]

The rational and scientific principle is the other pillar on which *Buddha-Dhamma* of Ambedkar needs to be stressed and substantiated. Being a man of science and a philosopher, who was influenced by secular scientific rationalism that swept the West, Ambedkar, was cautious to avoid anything that would smack of superstition, and verge on the border of the irrational. Nothing that cannot be proved rationally and argued logically can be part of his philosophy. The influence of Western Philosophy on his modern scientific mind was great. Not solely a single school of thought, but various trends in philosophy such as the secular humanism of Renaissance and Enlightenment, Socialism, Marxism, Positivism, Liberalism, Utilitarianism, engaged his attention and left their marks on his mind.[73]

In the light of all these, Ambedkar strove hard to make his new religious sect thoroughly rational. He hinges his arguments unshakably in the Buddha's rational epistemology of "dependent origination", that is, things are related to each other in cause and effect relationship in the ceaseless change of reality.[74] Accordingly, the speculative and supernatural beliefs in God *(Brahman)* or the eternity of the *Soul (Atman)* or heaven *(Moksha)* do not enter his scheme. *Dhamma* is not a belief in the supernatural being but the striving for a moral humane fraternal social life. *Dharma* in the *Vedic* Brahminic religion was to offer sacrifices *(Yagnas),* rituals and prayers to worship God (*Brahman*). These praises, offerings and sacrifices are offered in order to gain heavenly benefits hereafter, along with the earthly gains.

Ambedkar lays stress on the Buddha's reinterpretation of *Dhamma* as morality and his rejection of Brahminic understanding of *Dharma* as sacrifices and prayers. Thus, Ambedkar comes to reject all the theistic religions and the age-old Hindu beliefs, the existence of God *Brahman* is an *Atman,* S*oul*, *Samsara* theory of transmigration, the *Karma* theory of the effects of past, affecting the present life, and the *Moksha* theory of life after death. Infallibility of *Vedas* is not accepted and *Upanishadic* thought is considered pure imagination.[75] Further, Ambedkar, while accepting the Buddha and his *Dhamma,* presents him as the most rational and enlightened of human beings, and his *Dhamma* as the most scientific system, at least as Ambedkar understands and interprets it.

The Buddha is presented as one who did not force his followers, but who gave complete freedom of thought. He rejected the infallibility of sacred books, divine authority and the revelation. The Buddha, emphasises Ambedkar, unlike the other founders and innovators of religions like Moses, Jesus, and Mohammed does not claim to be of divine origin, nor receiver of divine revelation as a divine prophet. The Buddha claimed to be only in 'Enlightened' human being who, in turn, is a *marga-data,* the finder and giver of the way, and not, as others have claimed to be, a *moksha-data,* giver of salvation.[76] Finally, according to the rational scientific principle, Ambedkar tries his best with all the intellectual calibre that was at his disposal in great store, to clarify and reinterpret some of the accusations against Buddhism, which he calls "misunderstandings." He gives scientific explanations for the same and proves them to be useful to the society.

Ambedkar affirmed the inevitability of a religion. He said that "a man made with hunger did not resort to theft not feared the legal consequences, but because of pressure his religion exercised over his mind". Religion had a direct connection with the laws based on the reason. He often said that whatever good he had in him was the fruit of religion, he also emphasises that, he wanted religion, but did not want hypocrisy in the name of religion. To him, religion is the driving force for human activity. Man cannot live by bread alone. Since he has a mind it needs food for thought. He considered the foundations of religion to be essential to the practices of society."[77] Ambedkar's personal philosophy of life and political involvement was based on religion. His whole philosophy was based on the fundamental principles of liberty, equality and fraternity which borrowed from the teachings of his master, the Buddha.[78]

Herbert Spencer describes religion as "the weft, which everywhere crosses the warp of history." This is true in every society. But religion has not only crossed everywhere the warp of Indian history, in fact it forms the heart and soul of the Hindu mind. From his birth to death, the life of Hindu is influenced by his religion in relation to his food, dress, occupation, marriage, etc.[79] Another reason why Ambedkar lays stress on religion as a social force is that it provides the people with the motivation to realise the same religious ideals that are more powerful than the practical secular ideals. Religion, social status and property are all sources of power and authority, which one man has, to control the liberty of another and also leads to legitimacy.[80]

Ambedkar separated religion from theology, in order to ascertain the functions and purpose of religion. Ambedkar insists that "The primary things in religion are the usages, practices and observances, rites and rituals and theology is secondary, its objective is to rationalise them."[81] In the same way, religion should also be distinguished from what is considered to be supernatural. It is not to think religion as though it was super-natural.[82] It is not right to view religion as an individual, private and personal matter, nor is it to be mistaken as the zenith of the special religious instinct inherent in the individual nature. The correct view is that the religion, like language is social for the reasons that either it is essential for social life or individual has to have it because without it's involvement he cannot participate in the life of the society.[83]

Ambedkar spells out its functions: *Firstly*, from the savage society to our present day the main social function of religion is concerned with life, life processes and the preservation of life. The religious ceremonies are related with the stages of life with events like birth, puberty, marriage, death, sickness, war, drought, pestilence or concerned with the cultivation of food grains and cattle that furnish to human social life.[84] God's place in religion is only as a means for the conservation of life and that the end of religion is the end of conservation and sanctification of social life.[85] In the same way this is true for the present society also, though this essence of religion is hidden or forgotten. "The life and the preservation of life make up the essence of religion even in the present day society are beyond question."[86]

Secondly, Ambedkar asserts that the best statement regarding the purpose of religion given by Charles A. Ellwood who had written that, "Religion projects the essential values of human personality and of human society into the universe as a whole. It unavoidably arises as soon as man tries to take up a valuing attitude towards this universe, no matter how small and mean that universe may appear to him... What the reason does for ideas, religion does then for the feelings. It universalises them; and in universalising them, it brings them into harmony with the whole of reality.[87] As C.A. Ellwood understands 'social values are universalised and also continued to be spiritualised by religion for the realisation of a specific social purpose'.

Ambedkar says that religion emphasises, universalises social values and brings them to the mind of the individual who is required to be familiar with them in all his acts in an order that he may function as an approved member of the society.[88] *Thirdly*, maintaining the social control and social order is the significant function of religion. Religion acts as an organisation of social control by prohibiting the individual's beliefs and practices that go divergent to the good of the larger group. Thus, religion is an influential way of social control, more powerful than the Law and Government. Ambedkar again quotes Ellwood to strengthen his argument, "Without the support of religion, law and government are bound to remain a very insufficient means of social control. Religion is the most powerful force of social gravitation without which it would be impossible to hold the social order in its orbit."[89]

Though, different religions give different theistic explanations about the purpose of religion, Ambedkar rejects them all and offers his own formulation. According to him, the purpose of religion is "To make the world a Kingdom of Righteousness."[90] What does he mean by the Kingdom of Righteousness? What does it entail? What are the means to realise this ideal scheme? Can this goal be reached at all? Ambedkar clears all these doubts in the following verses, which he puts in the Buddha's mouth: To the question "What is the purpose of religion?" The Buddha's answer is very different. He did not tell people that their aim in life should be to reach some imaginary heaven. The kingdom of righteousness lies on earth and is to be reached by man by righteous conduct. What he did was to tell people that to remove their misery each one must learn to be righteous in his conduct in relation to others and thereby make the earth the kingdom of righteousness.[91]

In addition, two other purposes were also added, they are, the training of man's mind, instincts and dispositions and the courage to stand by what is right, even alone.[92] A religion that does not have as its core, morality essential for social order and progress, is anathema for Ambedkar. His religion of Neo-Buddhism is nothing else but the way, the *marga,* which would realise not the kingdom of God here on earth or in the otherworldly heaven, in *moksha*, but a religious path that would usher in the just, moral "Kingdom of Righteousness."[93]

The *Dhamma* would not only enforce morality by detachment,[94] it would purify the mind and cleanse it of all the passions,[95] bring forth harmony, cater to the growth of all the individuals in the society without discrimination, thus fostering equality and fraternity.[96] It would establish proper human relationships essential for happiness,[97] with *karuna* and *maitri*[98] and thus remove sorrow *(Dhukka)*.[99] It would in a special way protect the weak leading their liberation, and stop the class-caste conflicts resulting in a class-casteless society.[100] Psychological revolution is brought about by shedding of the ego and the desires through detachment and enlightenment. But one cannot stop with this. He/she must continue with the social revolution to remove the causes of *Dukkha.* Love, *karuna with maitri,* demands this. Liberation of the oppressed and the *Dalits* is the task of the Enlightened persons.

Religion, Modernity and Nation Building

Ambedkar regarded that religion is necessary for nationalism, since religion is the essence of cultural heritage and value system that are very much necessary for the formation of a civil and political community and, necessary factor for building a powerful nation. Ambedkar was not in favour of the depressed classes converting them selves into Islam or Christianity, as both these religions are alien to Indian culture and therefore they cannot provide the foundations of a political and social community. Ambedkar's theory of religion based on this concept is expressed as, "If the depressed classes join Islam or Christianity they not only go out of the Hindu religion but they also go out of the Hindu culture. On the other hand, if they become Sikhs, they remain within the Hindu culture. This is by no means a small advantage to Hindus. What the consequences of conversion will be to the country as a whole is well worth bearing in mind, conversion into Islam or Christianity will denationalise the depressed classes. If they go to Islam, the number of Muslims will be doubled and the danger of Muslim domination also becomes real."[101]

Ambedkar opens up a big problematic territory here. It had touched the many issues related to the concepts of religion, culture and nation. Ambedkar has evaluated each one of these concepts from the marginalised interest point of view. One might wonder about Ambedkar's differentiation of the terms 'Hindu religion' and 'Hindu culture'. His coinage of the term Hindu culture seems to be thoroughly equivalent to Indian culture. Scholars ought to differ from Ambedkar's equation of Hindu culture with that of Indian culture. But we may accept with his implied view that culture is a broader category than religion. The second issue dealt by Ambedkar is the question of conversion. While preferring conversion into Indian religions such as Buddhism and Sikhism, Ambedkar discards conversion into Islam and Christianity on the ground that they are not Indian in origin.

Here Ambedkar's option could be named as soft, moderate or limited conversion. The reasons behind this limitation may be his nationalistic concern and his fear of alienation of the *Dalits* that he did not want to leave his followers with the risk of losing their national identity. Even after clarifying these aspects, Ambedkar's conclusion remains debatable. It clearly implies that he considered both religion and culture as constituent element of nationalism. That is why he was searching for such a religion within the Indian culture. His concept of religion became not only highly political but came very closer to social living.

The religion can also be tested by yet another set of criteria that Ambedkar has outlined in his article, 'Buddha and the Future of His Religion.' B.A.M. Paradkar gives an astute summary of these criteria in his essay, "The Religious Quest of Ambedkar': Apart from the classification of religion into a 'Religion of Principles' and a Religion of Rules, Ambedkar maintained four essential criteria as the ways of testing the utility of a religion. Firstly, a society in order to hold itself together, it must have either the endorsement of the law or the sanction of morality. But the part played by law in this respect is very small. It is proposed only to keep the minority within the range of social discipline. "The majority is left out and has to be left out, to sustain its social life by the postulates and sanction of morality. Religion, in the sense of morality must therefore remain the governing principle in every society."[102] Secondly, in order to function, religion must exist with reason, which is merely another name for science. In other words, an understanding between science and religion should not be preposterousness. Thirdly, moral code is not enough for religion, but its moral code must recognise the essential canons of social life, namely liberty, equality and fraternity and finally, religion must not consecrate or ennoble poverty. Ambedkar said, 'Renunciation' of riches by those who have, it may be a blessed state but poverty can never be. To announce poverty to be a blessed state is to misrepresent religion, to perpetuate vice and crime, to consent to make earth a living hell.[103]

According to him, most important of all, "The problem for the Depressed Classes was to find a solution along the lines which would preserve their national homogeneity with in Indian culture. While seeking a definable religious identity, they had to strive for national and political unity."[104] It should also be stressed, as explained below, that finally Ambedkar's choice fell on Buddhism because he had rejected all other theistic religions as irrational and superstitious, and because it belongs to Indian culture. This seems to be reason why he preferred to revive a degenerated and profligate Buddhism, than to join any of the live religions readily available now in India.

While discussing the reasons for the conversion, Ambedkar goes into the societal functions of religion, namely, the protection of life and the social control which are achieved by religion, by spiritualising and sanctifying the values of life as final.[105] These social functions can also serve as the criteria to judge the value of a religion. To some extent, a particular religion is able to fulfill the social function of a religion, only to that extent, it can be deemed to be good religion. Ambedkar himself favourably uses this criterion and questions the usefulness of Hinduism. He asks whether it acknowledges the personal dignity and equality, strives for justice and promotes the social advancement.

The untouchables or *Dalits* need three possessions: "First thing that they need is to end their social isolation. The second thing is, to free them from their lowliness complex. The third thing is, Will conversion meet their needs?"[106] Again he asks, "Can religion alter this psychology of the untouchables? Will conversion raise the general social status of the untouchables?"[107] These questions also serve as the criteria to judge the value of a religion in the line of Ambedkar's thought.

Moreover all the religions may not possess identical nature. Besides being an authority, which defines what is good, religion is a motivating force for the promotion and spread of the 'good'. Are all religions approved in the means and methods they advocate for the promotion and spread of good? The Philosophy of Religion, as Ambedkar defines it, differs much from the comparative Religion. All the religions are equally true and good, but not in the field of Ambedkar's 'Philosophy of Religion'. In his view Philosophy of Religion begins where the Comparative religion ends. He accuses comparative Religions for creating the impression that all religions are equally good and true, and that there is no need of discerning between them. According to him, this belief is positively and perceptibly wrong and there is no greater error than this.

He also elaborates that religion is an uncertain phenomenon, it can be constructive or harmful, it can help to promote the good of society or it can bring adversity, it can also be liberative or oppressive. For instance, particular religion is more ready to lend a hand than others, or a religion can cause more harm compared to the others. It is a fact of experience, and it is to determine this fact properly that we need a norm to judge the value of various religions. To dismiss the false ideology that all religions are good and to point out that religion can also be harmful or helpful. Ambedkar quotes Prof. Tiele's vivid survey of the progress as well as destruction caused by a religion.[108] A force which shows such a strange difference in its result can be accepted as a good religion without examining the form it takes and the ideal it serves. It all depends upon what kind of social ideal that a given religion, as a divine scheme of governance, holds out. This is a question, which is not answered by the science of comparative religion. Indeed, it begins where comparative religion ends. "The Hindu is simply trying to avoid it by saying that although religions are many, they are equally good."[109] "Ambedkar strongly condemns this ideology that all religions are true."[110]

According to Ambedkar, God is a human creation. In the primitive period the primitive man regarded anything as divine power, which he was not able to understand. "This power was originally malevolent, but later on, it was felt that it could also be benevolent. Later the power was called God or the creator."[111] So man developed the theory of God to explain natural phenomena. Ambedkar raised a question that if God was benevolent then why his own creations are considered untouchables. In his perception, God was an embodiment of hatred and injustice because it was said that the unjust social structure, which gave birth to Untouchability, is a God given one hence it cannot be changed. Hence, Ambedkar rejected the idea of God created by religion.

The efforts of Ambedkar to engage into a hypothetical and practical analysis of the Hindu social and philosophical order, attempted to build counter-ideology in order to re-construct Indian society, to cleanse impurity, to unify the untouchables, to give an identity and a goal, to fight for devising ways of advancing the social, political and economics conditions of the downtrodden. Ambedkar's analysis on the Hindu social order seriously questions the centrality of caste system and its viewpoint of social domination and successive oppression and intolerance. Ambedkar asserted the pathway of social resistance to the debasing Hindu social order. He said, "however sympathetic you may be to our cause, the fact of your being orthodox Hindu, your being part and pillar of the orthodoxy, deprives you of any right to advise us... this is a question of power, of caste, of self-interest and partiality. This is not a question of knowledge, intelligence, of the reason this you should desist from preferring us. Say what you may but we are not willing to tolerate this injustice."[112]

Ambedkar's criticism of Hindu social order is based on his understanding of the democratic heritage of the western society. His hypothetical beginnings are derived from the clarification and rational tradition of modern Europe. From that tradition, he had inherited the values of liberty, freedom, equality and fraternity and he measured the Indian society on the foundations of these values. According to Ambedkar, the indispensable future of a social order is that it should be built on the initial notion of freedom. Freedom as both philosophy and practice is the basis of human society, as human beings naturally possesses the freedom of will. As they grow and progress, so would be the social order, which must be flexible as to allow newer changes according to the science of the times and human progress.

The other important concept in Ambedkar's direction of good social order is that it should distinguish the individual in the society. By recognising the individual, a good social order together recognises the good of the community. The individual is not to be sacrificed for the sake of collective. So, the chief role of a good society is accepted as a person and not a cog in the wheel turned for the purpose of social mobility alone. He/she needs to be respected in the society for the reason that he is a human person.

Ambedkar emphasises that the human existence is not to be treated solely in the physical sense alone, but it has to be valued in the sense of something higher than that. According to which every human being has a spiritual super-existence through knowledge and love. In Ambedkar's ideology, respecting the every individual devoid of any caste or class stratification is sacred. "The inviolability is at the core of the concept of liberty."[113] According to Ambedkar, three important kinds mark the principle of a reconstructed social order. Human society is to be built on the foundation of freedom or liberty, equality and fraternity. These values are based on the notion that an individual is not a means but an end itself. While the notion of liberty emphasises the inviolability of the human person, the concept of equality insists the right of the individual to be treated as an equal and to be respected as a complete member of the society irrespective of his attainments. According to Ambedkar, fraternity is the "disposition of an individual to treat men in reverence and love and dignity and the desire to be in unity with other fellow beings."[114] It strengthens the society and it gives vigour for the individuals to commit for the welfare of all. According to Ambedkar the Hinduism comprises of caste social order in hierarchy. "'*Sanskritization*'[115] is impossible that one can not change his caste and fraternity must also be sacrificed as the proper climate for the change of caste status, merely by adopting the behavioural development of personality."[116]

Ambedkar is of the opinion that the non-Aryan depressed classes are "the broken-men", who eventually came to be treated as marginalised, belonged to Buddhism. Ambedkar's theory is that the contempt of Buddhism and beef-eating is the root of unsociability in Hinduism. It was his disputation that the outcastes, by converting themselves into Buddhism were only improving their original dignity "which was earlier clouded by the 'horrible and vicious dogma' of caste and untouchability."[117] Ambedkar held that *Dalits*, the broken people, who fled from the villages after the tribal wars and came to be expelled from the *Chaturvarna* social system of the *Vedic* Brahmins and later, came to be treated as the depressed classes were Buddhists by religion.[118]

Ambedkar's theology of religion is praiseworthy on many counts. It has emphasised the *social* function of religion without neglecting to emphasise its necessity for *personal* growth. It laid more stress on *orthopraxis,* the right moral conduct based on love, than doctrines, cults, rituals and devotional practices. Many magical trappings of religion and doctrinal binding chains have been broken down by his theology. He has emphasised the liberative, prophetic, critical dimension of religion.

Ambedkar's Theology is *humanistic and anthropological*, his thought is Social Humanism.[119] Ambedkar's main concern was to regain the full humanity deprived of caste oppression and sex discrimination, which are not only economic alienations but also primarily anthropological alienations. In his theology, Ambedkar gave importance to the common good, and the establishment of a humane social order, a society based on liberty, equality and fraternity of all the people. As a part of it, *Holistic human development* was much insisted upon. He would never take rest only with the fulfilment material well-being, and often reminded his people of the spiritual salvation, mental enlightenment, cultural transformation, social status, unity, love and peace, which are essential for happy and holy life.

Ambedkar's religion is a religion of humanity, a religion at the service of humans to understand the humanness.[120] It is very much *contextual and cultural.* He would not accept wholesale, the imported Marxian theory, which does not take into account caste and religion, which are very powerful and influential factors in the Indian context and culture.[121] He rejected also Islam and Christianity that are foreign and were attached to the anti-national and imperialistic countries. By the revival of Buddhism, Ambedkar did a great service to the *Dalits*. The return of Buddhism not only gives identity and explanation to the *Dalits*, it has also revived the Dalit Dravidian, non-Aryan, non-Brahminic "Indian" culture, whose ancient religion was Buddhism.[122] It has exploded the myth of Hindus, who equate Indian culture with Hindu-Hindi culture, and India with Hindustan.

Ambedkar's theological approach was *analytical as well as synthesist.* His writings expose his inquisitive mind, which would not rest content with simplistic understanding but would reach to the heart of the matter. Posing one question after another that takes him deeper, and deeper Ambedkar comes up with the real causes and reasons for the matter in argument.[123] At the same time his theology exhibits many points of synthesis. Steering clear of the existing "*isms*", ideologies and schools of thought, and assimilating the best from them, Ambedkar offers an original synthesis that follows the Buddhist middle path.[124] As already mentioned, there is a synthesis of the clarification of the East and the West in his thought. Similarly, in his Theology we find salient features of American Liberalism and Russian Socialism, individualism and collectivism, materialism and spiritualism, scientific positivism and religious wisdom, which blend together in his synthesis. His liberative praxis also uniquely combined in its scheme both the Gandhian *Satyagraha* and Marxian class struggle. The social analysis of Ambedkar was again a blend of the economic analysis including Dialectical Historical Materialism, and the cultural analysis of religion, culture and social institution of caste.[125] His Dalit revolution included both the cultural Revolution and social revolution.

Ambedkar's Theology is essentially *stereological and eschatological.* Its aim and dream was to build up the Kingdom of Righteousness and *Dhamma Raj* by perfecting the social order gradually. To begin with, socio-religious reform for equality, national independence, democratic constitutional forms of government and state socialism are to be realised. The transformation of the social relationships and attitudes, based on the new value-system of liberty, equality and fraternity, is the foundation of the new just egalitarian society. Justice, social, economic and political, is to be secured for every member of the national and the human family. Only then can humane divine state of love and peace can reign in the universe, with blessedness and happiness for all creatures, the humans and the nature. With this eschatological hope, the Ambedkar spiritual struggle for the *Dhamma Raj* strives ahead. Another striking feature in Ambedkar's theology is non-dogmatism and provisionalism. As his guru, the Buddha, he strives hard to influence us to be rational and scientific, and not to believe anything on the word of someone else, because so and so said it, or because it is claimed to be a divine revelation. He made it very clear to his people that he does not want blind followers, and also that nothing of what he has written is perennial, infallible and dogmatic.[126] Instead, he calls attention many times to the Buddhist principle of impermanence and constant change.[127] Hence, "Ambedkar was also ready to admit, 'There can be no finality in thinking."[128] A responsible person must be ready to learn and rethink, and not to get enslaved by consistency, which is a '*virtue of an ass*'; he wants neither himself nor us to belong to that category.[129]

At the same time, we also find his theological approach *universalistic in nature.* It wishes the welfare of all people. It wants the end of class-caste struggle, so that all can live in peace and prosperity. Ambedkar urged the *Dalits* to strive not only for their own welfare, also for universal liberation and peace. The benefits of growth and social reform, according to Ambedkar, must not be usurped by the minority but accrue to all.[130] Ambedkar's Theology emphasised the common good, the just social order that will secure justice and equality for all the citizens. It strives for the universal peace of the Kingdom.

Religion and Science: Critical Appraisal

Religion has its basis in faith whereas Science has its basis in reason. Science probes in matter in rationalistic way, Religion says things are as they are because of faith. And faith can't answer the problems of life while science does in rationalistic way. So as science advances man's control our nature expand and life becomes more comfortable. This is because science becomes a part and parcel of productive forces. In that way, it contributes for the development of material things, instead of this religion basis its survival on faith and to the extent science expance it fields gets narrower. Psycological force or generally confused with spiritualism but mental strength is not something supernatural it bounds are with in the parameters of science because brain is the highest form of development of matter so far. The role of faith in religion is faith has its own role to play in life based on proper thinking. Like faith of attachement among the people, one should have faith in love, family and friendship and human values. It should be bind people together.

References

1. Moon Vasanth, *Dr Babasaheb Ambedkar's Writings and Speeches*, Vol.III, Govt of Maharastra, Bombay, 1989, p. 8.
2. Dhananjay Keer, *Dr. Ambedkar's Life and Mission*, Popular Prakashan, Bombay,1987, p. 259.
3. Jatava D.R., *Ambedkar's Philosophy of Religion*, INA Shree Publishers, Jaipur,1998. p. 76.
4. Guenter Lewy, *Religion and Revolution*, Oxford University Press, New York, 1974, Section 2. 4.
5. Panikar R and Koothothil A, "*Man and Religion*," Jeevadhara 11, 61(1981), pp. 7-11; and Segundo J. L. *Faith and Ideologies*, Orbis Books, New York, 1977, pp. 25-30.
6. Guenter Lewy, *Religion and Revolution*, Oxford University Press, New York, 1974, Section 2. 2.

7. Otto Maduro, *Religion and Social Conflicts*, Orbis Books, New York, 1982, Section 2. 2. 4.
8. *Ibid*, Section 2. 2. 3.
9. Anthoniraj, Thumma, *Prema Yoga*, ISPCK, New Delhi, 1999, Section 3. 3. 3.
10. Jatava, D. R, *The Political Philosophy of B. R. Ambedkar*, Popular Prakashan, New Delhi, 1991, pp. 1-2.
11. Jatava, D.R. *The Political Philosophy of B. R. Ambedkar*, Sections 5. 3. and 6. 4.
12. Jatava, D. R, *The Political Philosophy of Ambedkar*, Phoenix Publishing Agency, Agra, 1965, p. 6.
13. Pieris, A, *Love Meets Wisdom: A Christian Experience of Buddhism*, Orbis Books, New York, 1988, Sections, 5. 4;
14. Paulos Mar Gregorios, *Enlightenment East and West: Pointers in the Quest for India's Secular Identity*, Simla, I. I. S. A., 1989, p. 151.
15. Jatava, D.R., *The Social Philosophy of B. R. Ambedkar*, Agra, Phoenix Publishing Agency,1965. pp. 256–260.
16. Moon, Vasanth, *B.R. Ambedkar's, Writings and Speeches,* Vol. III, Govt. of Maharashtra, Bombay, 1989, p. 3.
17. Ambedkar, B. R, *The Buddha and His Dhamma*, Siddharth Publications, Bombay (1957), 1991, p. 226.
18. *Ibid*, p. 225.
19. *Ibid*, p. 226.
20. *Ibid*, p. 5.
21. Moon, Vasant, ed., *Dr B.R. Ambedkar's, Writings and Speeches,* Vol. III, Govt. of Maharashtra, Bombay, 1989, p. 5.
22. *Ibid.*
23. Ambedkar, B. R, *The Buddha and His Dhamma*, Siddharth Publications, Bombay,1991, Section, 2 . 3, p. 226.
24. *Ibid*, Section 2. 4. 2, p. 226.
25. Moon, Vasant, *Why Go for Conversion*? Dalit Sahitya Akademy, Bangalore, 1987, p. 16.
26. *Ibid*, p. 8.
27. *Ibid*, p. 7.
28. Moon, Vasant, ed, *Babasaheb Ambedkar's Writings and Speeches*,Vol. I, Govt. of Maharashtra, Bombay, 1989, pp. 76-77.
29. *Ibid*, p. 88.
30. Gore, M. S. *The Social Context of an Ideology – Ambedkar's Political and Social Thought*, Sage Publications, New Delhi, 1993, p. 262.

31. Moon, Vasant, ed, *Babasaheb Ambedkar's Writings and Speeches*, Govt. of Maharashtra, Vol. III, Bombay, 1989, p. 85.
32. *Ibid.*
33. *Ibid.*
34. *Ibid.*
35. *Ibid*, p. 86.
36. Eleanor Zelliot, "*Religion and Legitimation in the Mahar Movement*," in Bradwell L. Smith, ed., *Religion and Legitimation of Power in South Asia*, Leiden, E. J. Brill, Princeton University Press, 1978, p. 102.
37. Moon, Vasant, ed., *B.R. Ambedkar's Writings and Speeches*, Vol.I, Bombay, Govt. of Maharashtra, 1989, p. 78.
38. Moon, Vasant, *Why Go for Conversion*? transe, Dalit Sahitya Akademy, Bangalore, 1987, p. 18.
39. Moon, Vasant, ed., *B.R. Ambedkar's Writings and Speeches,* Vol. III, Govt. of Maharashtra, Bombay, 1989, p. 8.
40. *Ibid.*
41. *Ibid.*
42. *Ibid*, p. 6.
43. *Ibid.*
44. Moon, Vasant ed., *B.R. Ambedkar's, Writings and Speeches*, Vol. I, Govt. of Maharashtra, Bombay, 1989, pp. 43-44.
45. Keer, Dananjay, *Dr. Ambedkar: Life and Mission*, Popular Prakashan, Bombay, 1990, p. 452.
46. Moon, Vasant, *Why Go for Conversion*? trans. Dalit Sahitya Akademy, Bangalore,1987, p. 17.
47. Keer, Dananjay, *Dr. Ambedkar: Life and Mission*, Popular Prakashan, Bombay, 1990, p. 275.
48. Moon, Vasant, *B.R. Ambedkar's Writings and Speeches*, Govt. of Maharashtra, Vol. III, Bombay, 1989, pp. 11-12.
49. *Ibid*, pp. 9-21.
50. *Ibid*, p. 21.
51. *Ibid*, p. 9.
52. *Ibid*, p. 21.
53. *Ibid*, pp. 21- 22.
54. *Ibid*, p. 25.
55. *Ibid*, p. 66.
56. *Ibid.*
57. Moon, Vasant, ed., *B.R. Ambedkar's Writings and Speeches*, Vol. I, Govt. of Maharashtra, Bombay, 1989, p. 77.

58. Moon, Vasant, ed., *B.R. Ambedkar's Writings and Speeches*, Vol. V, Govt. of Maharashtra, Bombay, 1989, pp. 420 - 421.
59. Gore, M.S, *The Social Context of an Ideology – Ambedkar's Political and Social Thought*, Sage Publications, New Delhi, 1993, p. 237.
60. Moon,Vasant. ed, *B.R. Ambedkar's Writings and Speeches,* Vol. V, Govt. of Maharashtra, Bombay, p. 405.
61. Gore, M. S. *The Social Context of an Ideology – Ambedkar's Political and Social Thought*, Sage Publications, New Delhe, 1993, p. 231.
62. Moon, Vasant, ed, *B.R. Ambedkar's Writings and Speeches,* Vol. III, Govt. of Maharashtra, Bombay, 1989, p. 73.
63. *Ibid*, p. 75.
64. *Ibid*, p. 76.
65. *Ibid*, p. 77.
66. Ambedkar, B.R, *Why Go for Conversion*?, Dalit Sahitya Academy, Bangalore, 1987, p. 16.
67. *Ibid*, p. 22.
68. Keer, Dhananjay, *Dr Ambedkar's Life and Mission*, Popular Prakashan, Bombay,1991, pp. 494-495.
69. Moon, Vasant, ed., *Dr. Babasaheb Ambedkar's Writings and Speeches*, Vol. I, Govt. of Maharashtra, Bombay, 1989, p. 68.
70. Ambedkar, B. R., *The Buddha His Dhamma*, Siddhartha Publications, Bombay, 1991, p. 226.
71. *Ibid*, p. 227.
72. *Ibid*, pp. 230-231.
73. *Ibid*, p. 231.
74. Jatava, D. R, *The Social Philosophy of B. R. Ambedkar*, Phonenix Publishing Agency, Agra, 1965, pp. 41-43, and 267-268.
75. Ambedkar, B. R, *The Buddha His Dhamma*, Siddhartha Publications, Bombay, 1991, p. 247.
76. Lederle, M, *The Untouchables' Claim to Human Dignity*, Journal of University of Poona, Humanities Section, Poona, 1976, pp. 71-72.
77. Keer, Dananjay, ed., *Dr. Ambedkar's*: *The Buddha and His Dhamma*, Siddhartha Publications, Bombay, 1991, pp. 151 – 157.
78. Kuber, W. N., *B.R. Ambedkar*, Publication Division, Ministry of Information and Broadcasting, Govt. of India, New Delhi,1990, p. 80.
79. Keer, Dananjay, *Dr. Ambedkar*: *A Memorial Album*, Popular Prakashan, Bombay, 1982, p. 459.
80. Moon, Vasant, ed., *Dr. B.R. Ambedkar's Writings and Speeches*, Vol. III, Govt. of Maharashtra, Bombay,1989, p. 23.

81. Moon, Vasant, ed., *Dr. B.R. Ambedkar's, Writings and Speeches*, Vol. I, Govt. of Maharashtra, Bombay, 1989, p. 45.
82. Moon, Vasant, ed., *Dr. B.R. Ambedkar's, Writings and Speeches*, Vol. V, Govt. of Maharashtra, Bombay, 1989, p. 407.
83. *Ibid.*
84. *Ibid*, p. 409.
85. *Ibid*, p. 407.
86. Moon, Vasant, ed., *Dr. B.R. Ambedkar's, Writings and Speeches,* Vol. I, Govt. of Maharashtra, Bombay, 1989, pp. 408-409.
87. *Ibid*, p. 407.
88. *Ibid*, p. 409.
89. *Ibid.*
90. Moon, Vasant, ed. *B.R. Ambedkar's, Writings and Speeches*, Vol. I, Govt. of Maharashtra, Bombay, 1989, p. 411.
91. *Ibid*, pp. 201- 202.
92. *Ibid*, p. 201.
93. *Ibid*, pp. 201-203.
94. *Ibid*, pp. 200-202.
95. *Ibid*, pp. 170 and 296.
96. Ambedkar, B. R. *The Buddha His Dhamma*, Siddhartha Publications, Bombay, 1991, pp. 73-74.
97. *Ibid.*
98. *Ibid*, pp. 146-147, and 178.
99. *Ibid*, pp. 38-39.
100. *Ibid*, p. 83.
101. *Ibid*, pp. 232-234.
102. Moon, Vasant, *Why Go for Conversion*? Dalit Sahitya Akademy, Bangalore, 1987, p. 19.
103. Paradkar, B. A. M., *The Religious Quest of Ambedkar*, Ajay Prahaghan, New Delhi, 1968, p. 51.
104. *Ibid.*
105. *Ibid*, p. 53.
106. Moon, Vasant, ed., *B.R. Ambedkar's Writings and Speeches,* Vol. V, Govt. of Maharashtra, Bombay, 1989, pp. 407-410.
107. *Ibid.*
108. *Ibid*, p. 418.
109. Ambedkar quotes the following perceptive passage of Prof. Tiele; Moon, Vasant, ed., *B. R. Ambedkar's Writings and Speeches*, Vol. V, Govt. of Maharashtra, Bombay, 1989, p. 24.

110. *Ibid.*

111. Ambedkar, B. R, "*The Buddha and the Future of His Religion,*" The Mahabodhi, April-May 1950, p. 203. Cited by Paradkar B.A.M, *The Religious Quest of Ambedkar*, in T.S. Wilkinson and M.M. Thomas, eds., *Ambedkar and the Neo-Buddhist Movement*, Bangalore, CISRS, 1972, p. 52.

112. Keer, Dhananjay, *Dr. Ambedkar*; *Life and Mission*, Popular Prakashan, Bombay, 1991, p. 253.

113. Gore, M. S., *The Social Context of an Ideology – Ambedkar's Political and Social Thought*, Sage Publications, New Delhi, 1993, p. 98.

114. *Ibid*, p. 261.

115. Moon, Vasant, ed., *Babasaheb Ambedkar's Writings and Speeches*, Govt. of Maharashtra, Vol. III, Bombay, 1989, p. 97.

116. Srinivas, M.N., *Social Change in the Modern India,* Orient Longman, Hyderabad, 1988, p. 67.

117. Moon, Vasanth. ed, *Dr. Babasaheb Ambedkar's Writings and Speeches*, Vol. III, Govt. of Maharashtra Bombay, 1989, p. 99.

118. Paradkar, B. A. M, "*The Religious Quest of Ambedkar*," Ajay Prahaghan, New Delhi, 1968, p. 63.

119. Zelliot, E, "*Religion and Legitimation*", Princeton University Press, Princeton, 1969, p. 98.

120. *Ibid*, pp. 4-5, and 261-269.

121. *Ibid*, pp. 265-267.

122. Jatava, D. R, ed, *On contextuality of Ambedkar's thought*, *The Political Philosophy of B. R. Ambedkar*, Phoenix Publishing Agency, Agra, 1965, p. 2. Sections 3. 4. 2. and 6. 4.

123. Jatava, D. R, *The Political Philosophy of B. R. Ambedkar*, Marathi Dalitha Sahitya, *Marathi Dalit Literature Movement*, a unique one of its kind, was inspired by Ambedkar; *for a collected translations of modern Marathi Dalit literature*, Arjun Dangle, ed., Poisoned Bread, New Delhi, Orient Longman, 1992; R. S. Khare, *The Untochable as Himself*; *Ideology Identity, and Pragmatism among the Lucnow Chamars*, New York, Cambridge University Press, 1984; *Ibid.*, pp. 6-8, 139-143, and 150-151; Donald E. Smith, India, *As a Secular State*, Princeton, Princeton University Press (1963), 1967, chapter 13: " *Hinduism and Indian Culture*," pp. 372-378; p. 2.

124. Jatava, D. R., *The Social Philosophy of B. R. Ambedkar*, Phoenix Publishing Agency, Agra, 1965, pp. 39 - 42.

125. Jatava, D. R, *On contextuality of Ambedkar's thought*, (ed) *The Political Philosophy of B. R. Ambedkar*, Phoenix Publishing Agency. Agra, 1965, p. 2. Section 6. 4. 5.

126. Philip Mathew and Ajit Murican, eds., *Religion, Ideology and Counter-Culture*, his "*Non-Brahmin and Dalit Movements and their implications for Anti-Caste Struggle*," in Bangalore, Horizon book,1987, pp. 207-226.
127. Keer, Dananjay. *Dr Ambedkar*, p. 489; and D. R. Jatava, *The Political Philosophy of B. R. Ambedkar*, Phoenix Publishing Agency, Agra, 1965, p. 6.
128. Moon, Vasant, ed., *B. R. Ambedkar's Writings and Speeches*, Vol. III, p. 442; Ambedkar B. R, *The Buddha and His Dhamma*, Siddhartha Publications, 1991, pp. 169, 370, 388, 399, and 415.
129. Jatava, D. R, *The Social Philosophy of B. R. Ambedkar*, Phoenix Publishing Agency, Agra, 1965, p. 3.
130. *Ibid.*

Chapter – VI

Ambedkar's Views on Philosophy and Morality

The main objective of this chapter is to highlight Ambedkar's philosophy of morality. For Ambedkar, morality is the basic need of humanity, as it would create a just and powerful community. He believed that morality was necessary for the growth of a strong and powerful nation. He says that religion is a system of socio-cultural values, which would bring all the individuals and would create a spiritually powerful community. Ambedkar said that religion was a force which promises equal opportunity to all. He was also categorical that Buddhism alone could create a climate favourable to human equality and except Buddhism rest of the religions appeared to be false and unjust in their nature. As Hinduism already became corrupted and degenerated since it separated itself from the key element of morality. The critique is seen in operation in the rejection of religions and ideology, which clearly shows that without the existence of morality sufficient justice, cannot be promoted for the marginalised in the society.

The aim of this chapter is to explain the perception called 'new theology of morality' of Ambedkar who offered philosophical reasons to reject all religions and ideologies to prefer Buddhism as true dynamics of moral religion. He is of the opinion that morality is the central element for any religion. He has reinterpreted the Neo-Buddhism from the original teachings of Buddha that is purely based on the morality. Ambedkar emphasises on the transformation of the marginalised in the ideological terms as well as in the practice. In his view, morality is very much necessary for their 'spiritual ideology reforms' in the Hindu society. His quest and struggle for the liberation of marginalised had aimed to enter into the Hindu temples and consequently burnt the *Manu Smriti*, his ideological foundation for the egalitarian society remained as the core of his moral philosophy. Hinduism detached itself from morality so it degenerated and became corrupted. Hinduism has lost the three principles of liberty; equality, fraternity; and values necessary for the restructuring of Indian society based on Buddhism. This chapter explains the various reasons for his rejection of Hindu religion and its immoral ideologies; therefore he had decided to join Buddhism.

The underlying moral and logical assumptions of Ambedkar can be understood in terms of technical metaphysical concepts of liberty, equality and fraternity that associated with the philosophical notions of universality and rationality. Further, the inner essence of Ambedkar's intellectual development also can be understood as the attempt to realise his concepts of freedom and fraternity. Thus, Ambedkar's main concern shifts from proclaiming the philosophical nature of freedom to ever-deepening interests of the social and historical conditions that produce inequality, exclusion and alienation. Ambedkar's writings are full of moral judgements - implicit and explicit. From Ambedkar's early writings and also from his childhood experience made him to attack on the Hinduism. His analysis on the Hindu religious order with specific reference to the problem of the *caste* and *Untouchability* is potential of providing a viewpoint of liberation. Ambedkar made scathing attack on Hinduism as a philosophy and religious immoral order and how it paved way for a practice of *Untouchability* and social degradation. Ambedkar was fired by outrage, indignation and the burning desire for a better world through the establishment of true *Dhamma.*

According to Ambedkar, morality is a "form of social consciousness; it is a social institution which regulates the conduct of people in all spheres of their social life. Morality expresses the general social requirements and interests of society though generally recognised injunctions and evolutions that are supported by the people. Ambedkar says that an individual relaying on the moral conceptions produced by society, assimilating them in the process of education, the individual may independently regulates his behaviour to a considerable extent and judge about the moral significance of all developments that takes place around. Thus, Ambedkar says that the individual should not only act as the object of social control, but also as its conscious subject. Most of the philosophical, theological, religious, ethical writings of Ambedkar, along with his sociological writings are polemical in character."[1] Even, "*The Buddha and His Dhamma,* his most systematic book on religion, contains many passages which are polemic and apologetic, besides the dialectical disputes of the Buddha."[2]

Morality being a complex social formation is concerned with: what are rights, rightness, duty, responsibility, obligation, justice, punishment, virtue, conscience and wisdom? How are customs, public opinion, laws, contracts, authority, self-realisation and god or religion related to morality? What actions are accepted in a society, what norms of behaviour are adopted for the people to follow, what part do intentions play in determining rightness. Can practical moral problems be solved generally, or do specific problems like caste, race and religion require separate treatment? All these forms of moral consciousness are united into a logically ordered system which can prescribe, motivate and appraise moral actions. In addition to general human elements morality also incorporates historically transient and class, caste norms, principles and ideals. According to Ambedkar, morality is socially constructed, and says that, the morality and moral norms are formed in the moral consciousness of society.

Ambedkar says that the Hinduism is a religion, which is not founded on morality. Whatever morality Hinduism has is not an integral part of it. He argues that morality is not embedded in Hindu religion, for him, it is a separate force which is sustained by social necessities and not by the injection of Hindu religion. According to Ambedkar, the Hindu social order lacks the spirit of solidarity. Ambedkar says that, "the reasons for this want of solidarity is not far to seek. It is to be found in the system of graded inequality whereby the Brahmin is above every body; the *Shudra* is below the Brahmin but above the untouchables. If the Hindu social order were based on the inequality, it would have been overthrown long ago. But it is based on graded inequality so that the *Shudra* while anxious to pull down the Brahmin, is not prepared to see the untouchables raised to his level. He prefers to suffer indignities heaped upon him (rather than) to join the untouchables for a general levelling down of social order. The result is that there is nobody to join the untouchables in (there) struggle (against the oppressive caste system). He is completely isolated."[3]

Thus, Ambedkar argues very resplendently that Hindu social order is caste bound and rooted in a morality called *varnasramadharma,* hence, it no more remains to be a moral order or dharma. It turns out to be an *adharma* or immorality. While many of Ambedkar's arguments criticising the caste social order are embedded in the modernist enlightenment tradition of the west, equally important are his criticisms, which are hailing from his moral conscience. He evaluates the moralistic foundations of Hindu social order.

Ambedkar, in his thesis on the *Annihilation of Caste of 1936* provides a brief analytical summary of caste social order and the need for the total annihilation of it. While attempting to flatten the caste Hindu apologies for the prevalence of casteism, Ambedkar insisted that caste is not merely a division of labour but more truly it is a division of labourers. It attaches a value hierarchy. It is hegemonic in its structure. The division of labour is not based on choice ether; it is based on one's birth in a specified caste group. Thus, the Hindu social order is not a free order of human choice. It upholds a theory of the predetermination so as to evade or escape radical interrogation of the system. The function of Caste, Ambedkar observed, is to divide and disorganise the social groups for the social, cultural and political monopoly of the high caste Hindu. Caste, for Ambedkar, is an uncivilised social act about which the caste Hindu is not prepared to bring about any change. As a system of social organisation, caste performs the role of 'divide and rule' method of domination of the lower social groups.

The terrible suffering, pain and pathos of cultural deprivation, economic exploitation, social ostracism, and political domination caused by the ruthless monstrous caste-system, made Ambedkar whole-heartedly hate the caste system and anything or anyone related with its continuation. As he admits, such hatred for injustice is a must for the activists who wish to fight for a just and egalitarian order;[4] yet it should not, as it was in the case of Ambedkar, make one blind to the advantages, though few, of the jati/caste-system.[5] Here we are not referring to the *Brahminic Varna vavastha,* caste-social order, the inegalitarian hierarchical ideology, slave system, and the system of *Untouchability* which must be totally abolished. It is due to some advantages that caste system, in its present form of *jades,* still survives and is on the flourish, even in our modern times leading to gruesome atrocities and gaining political out.[6]

Ambedkar points out the intricacy cabled in the order of casteism. According to him, the social order of Hinduism does not contain any principle of social transformation. In the caste order, other than the Brahmins, those who occupy the higher caste order aspire to become higher and higher by 'infection by imitation' however in practice such an upward movement is not a possibility. In the order of its hegemonic hierarchy, the upper or middle caste groups do not and cannot have any inclination towards equilibrium or change towards equality and justice.

Ambedkar asserts that the Hindu is morally unconcerned about the untouchable. He had no conscience in this matter. By his absence of conscience, the caste-Hindu is a great obstacle to the removal of *Untouchability*. The untouchable does not belong to the society of the Hindu and the Hindu does not feel that he and the untouchable belong to one society. According to Ambedkar's observation, the Hindu social order is an outright denial of both spontaneity and a life of freedom for mankind. Instead it upholds the belief in the tradition of *manana* (transmission of the old knowledge to generation) and conformity of the past rules and regulations of tradition. It is infected with a strong sense of finality and fixity paving no way for any scientific progress and revolution in society.

Ambedkar observes that the Hindu social order tends to deprive moral life of freedom and spontaneity and to reduce it to a more or less anxious and servile conformity to externally imposed rules. There is no loyalty to ideas; there is only conventionality to command. The laws are inequities in that they are not the same for one class as for another. "The laws are made arranged to be the same for all generations. The laws made by certain persons called the lawgivers. This code has been invested with the nature of finality of fixity."[7] This passage in the writings of Ambedkar shows his deeper consideration of the dynamics of an ideal source of the society. It presupposes that a society must include in itself the sources of its own change and transformation without which it cannot promise its forward movement and growth. Ambedkar's assessment of the instant of spontaneity as one of the sources of social dynamics helps him to appraise the Hindu social order and come to the conclusion that it lacks such a basis.

From the previous discussion and analysis of Ambedkar, we can record a few and methodological structure of Ambedkar's observations about the theoretical backdrop of his analysis of the Hindu social order. For Ambedkar, the Hindu social order is grounded in immorality. It is against justice, liberty, equality and fraternity. It is a collection of closed units that enclose themselves leaving no room for relationship and social intercourse. It is an order of self-imprisonment that enslaves the human into the caste prisons. It segregates 'infection by imitation' which in turn affects every consecutive caste groups and eventually. The Indian society is a system that degrades and alienates human labour and labourers. It lacks any social conscience for being in union. Spontaneity and moral freedom are alien to the system of caste social order. Participation and communication for social living is methodically prohibited in it. Its social expression is the social exclusion whose increasing effect is laid very seriously on the shoulders of the broken people.

Therefore for Ambedkar, rebuilding of the identity of the broken people and through that restructuring Indian society on a moral basis becomes a life mission. Ambedkar's criticism of the caste social order is indivisible from his criticism of Hindu religion. This does not develop into his biased position but on the other hand the nature of the object of his study i.e., the caste social order itself objectively suggests this position. If he starts with evaluating the caste system inevitably, he ends up with the criticism of Hindu religion. If he starts with the assessment of Hindu religion he unavoidably ends up with the disapproval of caste social order. This predictability, we mean, is involuntary in the nature of the object itself. The interconnectedness of caste and religion in India seems to be one of the oldest facts of Indian society. It is notable to remind here that many of the native reform and complaint movements handled the Hindu religion and the caste order, united in the sense that one cannot be criticised without leaving the other. One can quote the examples of *Carvakas,* Buddhism in the ancient India as well as Phule, Periyar and Ambedkar in modern period. Perhaps, Ambedkar is the one who has provided a consistent hypothetical criticism of the Hindu social order and its caste basics.

Ambedkar has a strong backdrop of western clarification of thought that helped him to assess the Indian social structure from the point of view of liberty, equality, and fraternity. When he goes for assessing the structural elements of the Indian society, he looks up into the society from the point of view of individual, as the indispensable unit of the system on the one hand and from the point of view of social whole as the universal aspect of the society. Thus, the individual and the social are the two complementary vital elements in the theoretical frame of Ambedkar analysis. He is interested not only to define a society or to provide a theoretical discourse of society except basically his intention lies in indicating and providing necessary foundations of a humane society. And for this he strongly believes that that the sources of change and transformation for the forward movement of a society are essential. Such an approach of Ambedkar helps him to assess the Hindu *order* at a deeper level.

Another very significant facet of Ambedkar's method is the social democracy and democratic constitutional feature of his thought. Ambedkar powerfully holds that social democracy is an explanation to relocate the caste social order. Ambedkar criticises the Hindu social order from a moral point of view. For him, since the Hindu social order lacks any moral conscience and value basis, he gave advice that the Hindu society has to be reconstructed on the basis of an ethics of emancipation. For Ambedkar, liberty, equality and fraternity are the values that would offer a viable and humane Indian social order. From Ambedkar's study of the Hindu social order we could deduce the following projects of Ambedkar. The purpose of Ambedkar is to establish an alternative to the Hindu social order. Such a task in Ambedkar may be classified in two folds: On the one hand, Ambedkar wanted to establish the identity of the untouchables as an indigenous social religious '(Buddhism) group that resisted caste inequality from its very inception. And on the other, he ignited an ongoing social, educational, political movement, an action for liberation, which would continue to raise the cause of justice in the Indian society, irrespective of the pains and sufferings in its encounter with the orthodoxy.

Morality as Inclusive

Ambedkar as a humanist fights against untouchably or the evil of casteism his fight is not a simply a fight for the downtrodden people. Moreover, it is a fight for the moral redemption of the humanity. Existence of *Untouchability* may be only a direct challenge to the downtrodden only. But it is a moral challenge to all humanity. Caste and *Untouchability*, therefore it is crucial problems for humanity in general, rather than only problem of downtrodden. Deconstructing the identity of the untouchables, in the case of Ambedkar, is sill of reconstructing a society, which in turn conceives the possibility of building up a humanised world. Therefore, if the human society requisites to be really a social whole, then it should attend to the broken-particular, namely the discriminated. The universal to be universal needs to restore the broken particular if not what is claimed to be universal is pseudo. Such a task, he envisaged, needs to be carried on at two interlined levels. One at the level of the philosophical or theoretical, while the other at the level of the practical. At its philosophical level Ambedkar sets example for the need for a clear lucid and serious understanding and analysis of the theoretical foundations of an oppressive system. At the realistic level, he has suggested the need for a continuous discourse and a communication of resistance against any oppressive forces like caste and *Untouchability*.

The major theme of Ambedkars' analysis of morality is that the religious immorality is based on the philosophical and practice of social dominance. The Hindu religious philosophy and its socio-cultural appearances are grounded on the belief that human life is unequal and immoral, therefore cannot scream for religious and social equality. Those human beings are pre-determined to be born unequal and therefore cannot lay claim to equality either in terms of their religious-spiritual status or in terms of their social, economic, civic or political status in the community. Morality also played main role to survive religion to right path. The religion is survived in the wheel of morality in action and the Hindu religious moral ideology always hurting to the depressed people.

This shows the morality of the Hindu is purely social. This means that the level of his morality is merely traditional and customary. There are two evils of customary morality. In the first place there is no surety that it will always be charged with sincerity and purity of motive. For it is only when morality penetrates to the deepest springs of purpose and feeling in the individual that pretense will cease to find a place in human behaviour. In the second place customary morality is an anchor and a drag. It holds up the average man and holds back the man who forges ahead. Customary morality is only another name for moral stagnation. This is true of all cases where morality is only customary morality. But the customary morality of the Hindus has an evil feature that is peculiar to it. Customary morality is a matter of meritorious conduct. Ordinarily this meritorious conduct is something that is good from the general or public point of view. But in Hinduism the commendable conduct is not concerned with the worship of God or the general good of community. Meritorious conduct in Hinduism is concerned with the giving of presents, of good and of honour to the Brahmins. Hindu Ethics is worship of the superman.

The morality arises from the "direct necessity for man to love man."[8] Ambedkar makes it comprehensible that, "it is not to please God that man has to be moral, rather for his own good qualities that man is to love man."[9] In the struggle for existence the individual's rights may not be catered for, and at times his or her interests can be, rare by the group. Similarly, "a weak group may also be discriminated by a stronger group, hence the indispensability; ability of the *law of love*, fraternity and brotherhood, which is another name for morality."[10]

The norms devised by Ambedkar, as criteria to assess the ideal scheme of obligations, were mainly to deal a deathblow to Hinduism. He was persuaded that Hinduism badly needed reform, and wanted to expose the oppression it had unleashed and the slavery it had perpetuated on the depressed. He was one of the victims of the social system of Hinduism, and so he should know what Hinduism aimed at. Which of these was Ambedkar attacking? What Hinduism did he condemn and reject? After discussing, various meanings of the word 'Hindu' as denoting a religion, parentage, country and a race, Ambedkar points out that he is dealing with Hinduism in which caste has become indispensable as doctrine, ideology and sanctified social order. Hinduism that is object of his derisive attack is that Brahminic variety, a Hinduism who's 'care is the creed 'of caste',' and where "the *Manu Smriti* must be accepted as the Book of Religion."[11] Ambedkar quotes

Max Muller and affirms that his target is, "Modem Hinduism rests on the system of caste as on a rock which no arguments can shake."[12] Ambedkar sees that Hinduism is not a religion for individual justice with equality, fraternity and liberty and it fails to bring social utility of just, free and moral social order as the ideal scheme of divine governance. In the sense Hinduism has failed to lift the depressed.

Ambedkar arrives at the final judgment of Hinduism: The only answer is that Hinduism is overwhelmed with the fear of contamination. It has not got the power to purify. It has not the desire to serve and that is because by its very nature it is in human and unmoral. It is a misnomer to call it religion. Its philosophy is against the very thing for which religion stands.[13] Hinduism is destined for failing the trial by the first norm of justice. It is found advocating inequality as the dependable doctrine: "This brief analysis of the Philosophy of Hinduism from the point of view of justice reveals in an obtrusive manner how Hinduism is adverse to equality, antagonistic to liberty and opposed to fraternity. Indeed, inequality is the *Soul* of Hinduism."[14] The second norm of social utility equally fails to free from domination: "If these conclusions are sound, how can a philosophy which disconnects intelligence from labour, which expropriates the rights of man to comfort vital to life and which prevented society from mobilising resources for common action in the hour of danger, be said to satisfy the test of social utility."[15]

Ambedkar puts the rational and logical question that what difference would it have made if I had taken Hindu Ethics as the basis for deducing the philosophy of Hinduism? Most students of Hinduism do not remember that just as in Hinduism there is no difference between law and religion so there is no difference between law and ethics. Both are concerned with the same thing namely, regulating the conduct of the low class Hindus to *subserve* the ends of high Caste Hindus. The false pictures of Hinduism in as much as "I have omitted to take into account the *Upanishads* which are the true source of Hindu philosophy."[16]

Ambedkar reiterates that the Inequality is the *Soul* of Hinduism. The morality of Hinduism is only social. It is unmoral and inhuman to say the least. What is unmoral and inhuman easily becomes immoral, inhuman and infamous. This is what Hinduism has become. Those who doubt this or deny this proposition should examine the social composition of the Hindu society and ponder over the condition of some of the elements in it. It is essential to emphasise the great part played by crime in the general life of these peoples. A boy is initiated into crime as soon as he is able to walk and talk. No doubt the motive is practical, to a great extent, in so far as it is always better to risk a child in petty theft, who, if he were caught, would probably be cuffed, while an adult would immediately be arrested. Women, who, although they do not participate in the actual raids, have many heavy responsibilities, also play an important part. Besides being clever in disposing of stolen property the women of the Criminal Tribes are experts in shoplifting. The only answer is that Hinduism is overwhelmed with the fear of pollution. It has not got the power to purify. It has not the impulse to serve and that is because by its very nature it is *inhuman* and *unmoral.*

The concepts of rightness and wrongness lie close to the core of Ambedkar's moral thought. His explanation of rightness is in relation to duty, responsibility, oughtness, justice, virtue and wisdom. Acts are right because they produce good results for the most people. Rights consist in acting for the benefit of others; wrong action is one's own benefit. Self-seeking is selfish and selfishness is the root of all evils. The cure for this evil is to pursue the opposite course that is love others and promote their good. For Ambedkar democratic form of government is considered right because it is believed to produce the best results for the most people.

Ambedkar's morality is not only with rightness, but also with rights. This is more often associated with political and legal philosophy, since people seem to be more concerned about their legal than their moral rights. According to Ambedkar, "rights are real only if they are accompanied by remedies. It is no use giving rights if they aggrieved person has no legal remedy to which he can resort when his rights are invaded. Consequently, when the Constitution guarantees rights it also becomes necessary to make provision to prevent the Legislature and the Executive from overriding them. This function has been usually assigned to the Judiciary and the Courts have been made the special guardians of the rights guaranteed by the Constitution."[17] Ambedkar says that the "rights are protected not by law but by the social and moral conscience of society. If social conscience is such that it is prepared to recognise the rights which law chooses to enact, rights will be safe and secure. But if the fundamental rights are opposed by the community, no law, no Parliament, no Judiciary can guarantee them in the real sense of the word."[18] Thus, the right is the minimum claim upon the services of others, as a duty is the minimum claim of others upon us.

For Ambedkar fraternity is another name for morality. He says that the fraternity is nothing but another name for brotherhood of men and women which is another name for morality. Ambedkar concludes that the "fraternity is the name for the disposition of an individual to treat men as the object of reverence and love and the desire to be in unity with his fellow beings."[19] According to Ambedkar, "fraternity strengthens socialites and gives to each individual a strong personal interest in practically consulting the welfare of others. It leads him to identify his feelings more and more with their good or at least with an even greater degree of practical consideration for it. Ambedkar argues that with a disposition to fraternity, the individual comes as though instructively to be conscious of himself as being one who of course pays a regard to others. Thus, the good of others becomes to him a thing naturally and necessarily to be attended to like any of the physical conditions of our existence."[20]

For Ambedkar, morality and religion are inseparable and that morality has to be understood only in the context of religion and it has been at the center of his philosophical discussion. According to Ambedkar, religion must be essentially moral; religion cannot live unless it interacts with other forms of spiritual life as morality, beauty, and truth. Religion is thus when compared with morality turns out to be at once *infra* and *supra* ethical. Religion aims at harmonising human life, for this, it provides a life goal. Ambedkar says that the religion is not an end in itself. It is meant for the preservation of life and human welfare. Hence, religion is not the one that has the final say; it is not infallible, absolute, inflexible nor permanent. So also, Ambedkar stressed that religion is for humans and not humans for religion.[21] For him, "man and morality must be the centre of religion."[22] Humanist to the core, Ambedkar was ready to throw away any religion or religious practice; however, ancient and sanctified, that does not promote human welfare.

For Ambedkar, morality is based on love.[23] Morality is sacred and has taken the place of "God" in his Philosophy. It must not be desecrated even by the mighty, so that it is able to protect the weak in the society. He felt that the foundation of morality is love. The reason for this love is not anything mystical, it arises from man's natural condition, out of the necessity of peaceful coexistence, the need of protecting oneself and the weak, and to bear each other for a happy life on earth.

The ultimate vision and "goal of Ambedkar's liberative struggle is the Kingdom of Righteousness which, according to him, is the important purpose of *Saddhamma:* The Buddha by his *Dhamma* laid foundation to the Kingdom of Righteousness on earth and urged both the *Bhikkus* and the laypersons to strive for it."[24] The kingdom of righteousness consists of love, peace and justice for all.[25] It is the total and integral liberation of all, of every human being, every community and every nation on earth. Ambedkar's struggle all his life to liberate the oppressed community, which was the worst, affected by the caste system.[26] The liberation of the *Dalits* was not an end in itself, nor does it fulfil the ultimate goal of establishing the kingdom of righteousness, which entails the liberation of all peoples. Ambedkar urges the *Dalits* to work for the liberation of all at the first *deeksha* ceremony: "You must pledge today that you, the followers of Buddha, will not only work to liberate yourself, but will try to elevate your country and world in general... go forth to liberate people."[27] Dalit revolutions are for the liberation of all, to build the Kingdom of humanism.

The ideal of the kingdom of righteousness is realised in practice in a new society that is just and egalitarian, that is based on the principles of liberty, equality and fraternity.[28] The blueprint for the new society of Ambedkar's dream was drawn out by him from Buddhism that was incorporated in the Preamble of India's Constitution. All the members of this ideal society are assured of justice- social, economic and political; Liberty of thought, expression, belief, faith and worship; Equality of status and have opportunity. Fraternity is assuring the dignity of the individual and the unity of the Nation. In the new ideal society, "what is important is high ideals and not noble birth. No caste, no inequality; no superiority; no inferiority; all are equals."[29] Thus, the new society is socialistic in its economic structure; democratic in political structure and egalitarian in social structure. It is free from every form of exploitation, dictatorship, domination and the oppression of caste, class, gender, ethnic nationality and culture. The just society is where even the weakest group receives recognition, equal respect, dignity and identity, and is bequeathed with special affirmation, reservations and privileges to promote itself.

Ambedkar proposes that the "Cleansing the mind of it's impurities,"[30] "Training the mind to turn bad disposition into good disposition,"[31] awareness of the impermanence of all things, cultivation of detachment,[32] controlling of all passions[33] and cessation of all desires and craving.[34] Only armed with detachment and enlightenment an individual and society can strive for the Kingdom. This psycho-cultural revolution must precede and accompany the socio-political revolution. Ambedkar emphasises, "A good disposition is the only permanent foundation of and guarantee of permanent goodness."[35] To state it positively, the process of detachment and enlightenment unleashes the powers of love, which are the basis and the force of revolution. Unless one overflows with "an all-embracing love for the entire universe,"[36] one cannot worthily and effectively participate in the struggle for the Kingdom. None of the other means employed to attain realisation, "has a sixteenth part of the value of loving kindness. Loving kindness, which is the freedom of heart, absorbs them all, it glows, shines, it blazes forth."[37] The Kingdom of Righteousness can be made an historical reality only if both the monks as well as the lay-persons strive in practice to love and serve. Mere preaching "would not result in the creation of that ideal society based on righteousness. Compassion that is the essence of the *Dhamma* requires that every one shall love and serve, and the *Bhikkhu* is not exempt from it. A *Bhikkhu,* who is indifferent to the woes of mankind, however perfect in self-culture, is not at all a *Bhikkhu.*"[38]

Any religion that enslaves the minds of the people by fear or force, curtailing their liberation and freedom, that denies justice, equality and democracy that hinders universal fraternity, is no religion at all. Such religious practices, ceremonies and customs are to be rejected, and such doctrines are to be corrected. Even when a single person or small group is oppressed by a religion, a religious person or a religious class, that religion is in need of urgent reform. Domination of the clergy, exploitation of people in the name of devotions, superstitious and magical ceremonies, and outdated and irrelevant practices, over-spiritualisation of religious doctrines, and deification of religious figures and saints, distort religion. We need religion for the liberation of humanity, but from the religion that does not liberate humanity we need liberation.

Ambedkar urges the *Dalits* to free themselves of such superstitious and magical religion and the fatalistic attitudes inculcated by the enslaving doctrines of *karma* and *love.*[39] These not only impoverish and enslave, they also entrap the minds. While Ambedkar bequeathed the *Dalits* a religion of wisdom and compassion, a religion of loving service and self-sacrifice, and a religion of morality of love, to strive for the Kingdom of Righteousness, he condemned all superstitious practices. Ambedkar says that what is needed for salvation are not these but a critical, prophetic, liberative religion. Further, he reiterates that a liberative religion alone can inspire and inform the people with wisdom, and empower them with detachment and love, to struggle for the political power, to transform the unjust structures, and to usher in the *Dharma Raj*.

In short, the purpose of the liberative religion is to "teach the virtues of fellow feeling, equality and liberty"[40] and thus build the Kingdom of *Dhamma*. Hence, the urgency for all the religions to purge themselves of the magical practices, outmoded cults and ceremonies, irrelevant institutions and traditions, outdated doctrines and dogmas, and unleash the liberative elements and the revolutionary potential that is present in all of them. Only then can they be effective paths to the Kingdom.

Dhamma as a Scientific Morality

Ambedkar emphasised that the Buddhist ethics is not mere rules or guidelines for the individual purity and its sanctity. Certainly Buddhist ethics very much talk about the importance of minds to be cleansed. But that is not confined to itself. If we look on the morality of the all other religion we could have found out that all principles are directed towards the individual aspect of ethics. They are narrowed down as some kind of instruction to the individuals. One thing which we have to notice is that it does not mean that social aspects are totally excluded from it. But social aspects are also included in the frame work of individuality. The best example of this is Christian dictum

"Love thy neighbour as you love yourself."[41] The dictum which can be considered as the paramount of social concern is also exactly a preaching of individual oriented ethics. Actually that principle is also an advice to an individual to change his mind from the selfish motives. Other religions if we look we can find out that certain instruction to an individual which is quite appropriate to keep the current social order. Hinduism is the evident example. But only in Buddhist ethics we can find out the ethical aspects which address society as whole, which emphasises with the social concerns.

Ambedkar makes out this difference very clearly and emphasises the social-morality of the Buddhism in 'Buddha and His *Dhamma*'. "What is the purpose of religion? Different religions have given different answers. To make man seek after God and to teach him the importance of saving his *Soul* is the commonest answer one gets to this question. Most religions speak of three kingdoms. One is called the kingdom of heaven. The second is called the kingdom of earth and the third is called the kingdom of hell. All the religions preach that to reaching this kingdom of heaven should be the aim of man and how to reach it is the end of all." But Ambedkar emphasises that for Buddha, the purpose of religion was entirely different. To the question what is the purpose of religion Buddha's answer was entirely different. "He did not tell people that their aim in life should be to reach some imaginary heaven. The kingdom of righteousness lies on earth and is to be reached by man by righteous conduct."[42]

Ambedkar tries explains that the Buddhism is not related to the concept of God but morality. But what became now evident in Buddhism is that the purpose of morality is defined as to make the earth of righteousness. One should here note that many religions talks about the earth of love, but only Buddhism talks about the earth of righteousness. According to Ambedkar in Buddhism virtue is defined in social aspects. It is this which distinguishes Buddhism from all other religions.[43]

Moreover, what is appealing is that Buddhist ethics is not the denial of the Individual ethics, beyond it, the individual ethics and social ethics both are construed and formed in the critical engagement with each other. One wonders how we can categorically define certain values as social and individual. It is true that this division is not a watertight division. But in emphasis, one can define that certain values are socially oriented and certain others individual oriented. Certainly righteousness is social virtue. It is because righteousness is not merely a person's attitude towards others. This is a virtue which exists in the social relation only. This is not something which resides in one person and expressed towards other. But something which is only evolving in social relation. In certain sense we can distinguish both these kinds of values as follows: Social relation is quite necessary for the definition of the social value. Individual value also includes social relation to a large extent, but for the definition of it social relation is not a necessary one.

But at the same time Buddhist ethics is not the denial of individual aspects of ethics. But what we can see in Buddhist ethics is critical engagement between individual aspect and social aspects. In Buddhism both guides each other while in other religions it is only one-way relations. That is individual aspect determines the social aspects. But Buddhism offers the possibility of interaction of both. It is evident from following: "Only righteousness can remove this inequity and the resultant misery. That's why Ambedkar said that religion must not only preach but must inculcate upon the mind of man the supreme necessity for being righteousness in his conduct."[44]

Ambedkar proposed the ideal of *Saddhamma*. For Ambedkar: "*Dhamma* is *Saddhamma* when it makes learning open to all. *Dhamma* is *Saddhamma* when it teaches that mere learning is not enough. It may lead to pedantry. *Dhamma* is *Saddhamma* when it teaches what is needed is *prajna* (Pranya). *Dhamma* is *Saddhamma* only when it teaches that *Prajna* is not enough. *Sila* must accompany it. *Dhamma* is *Saddhamma* only when it teaches that besides *Prajna* and *Sila,* what is necessary, is *Karuna. Dhamma* is *Saddhamma* only when it teaches, that more than *Karuna* what is necessary is *Maitri, Dhamma* to be *Saddhamma* must break down barriers between man and man. *Dhamma* to be *Saddhamma* must teach that 'worth' and 'not' birth' is the measure of man. *Dhamma* to be *Saddhamma* must promote equality between man and man."[45] The functions of *Saddhamma* are in the first place to cleanse the mind of its impurities and in the second to make the world a kingdom of righteousness. In order to practice *Saddhamma,* however, *Dhamma* must promote *prajna* or insight, and this it does by making learning open to all, by teaching that mere learning is not enough as it may lead to pedantry, and by teaching that what is needed is *Prajna* or right thinking.

Moreover, *Dhamma* as *Saddhamma* only when it teaches that *Prajna* must be accompanied by *Sila* or right action as well as by *Karuna* or compassion for the poor and helpless and by *Maitri* or love for all living beings. It follows that, in the order to *Saddhamma, Dhamma* must break down the barriers between man and man, must teach the worth and not birth and must promote equality between man and man. According to Ambedkar, the practice of *Saddhamma* includes, to cleanse the mind of its impurities; to make the world kingdom of righteousness; to make learning (*knowledge*) open to all; to teach the relevance of what is learnt in education; to practice moral *virtues (Sila);* to promote mercifulness *(Karuna);* and to promote *Maitri* or fellowship. As part of negations, for the *Dhamma* to be *Saddhamma* it should involve in breaking away the barriers between men or among human beings. The *Dhamma* to be *Saddhamma* must teach worth and *not* birth as the measure of man. Buddha is against the theory of the supremacy of birth as described in the concept of *Chaturvarna.* Instead, he preached the idea of the worth of man. He says no one is an out-caste by birth- and no one is a *Brahmin* by birth and the most important element in the *Saddhamma,* more than *Prajna* is *Sila*. The *Sila* is *Karuna,* love of human beings and *Maitri* which is love of all living beings.[46]

According to Ambedkar, merits of Buddhist philosophy were as follows: Buddhism demanded living experience and a life divine, attainable there and now; not after death, it was realism and never idealism. It upheld liberty, equality, truth and justice; it emphasised humanity, love and peace. It was dynamic, scientific and all embracing. Its explanation of life and its meaning and purpose of birth and death and its aftermath were very clear, intelligible and logical. Above all, man was the center of his study and examination and not anything outside of him. Ambedkar tried to prove that the untouchables were Buddhists. In his thesis on the origin of *Untouchability* he made it clear that today's untouchables were once Buddhists.

"Buddhism was an Indian religion and the Buddha was nearer to the untouchable masses. Buddhism could withstand even the severest scientific test and had the power and capacity to direct destines of the modern world. The untouchables would join with the world Buddhist community and thus pave the way for world brotherhood."[47] Ambedkar said that, "Buddhism gives three principles in combination, which no other religion does. Buddhism teaches *prajna* (understanding) as against superstition and supernaturalism, *Karuna (love)* and *samata* (equality)... Neither god nor *Soul* can save the society,"[48] Referring to Marx's philosophy, Ambedkar observed that Man cannot live by bread alone. He has a mind, which needs food for thought. Religion instills hope in man and drives him to activity. Hindu religion has watered down the enthusiasm of the downtrodden. And "I found it necessary to change my faith and embrace Buddhism."[49] Ambedkar says that Religion emphasises, universalises social values and brings them to the mind of the individual who is required to be familiar with them in all his acts in an order that he may function as an approved member of the society.

Ambedkar's intervention in Hindu social order is considered as a Copernican revolution in the realm of morality and religion. Analysis shows that, Ambedkar's attempt to justify morality without reference to transcendental religious beliefs is a first step to make the realm of morality as an autonomous one. The concern for the universal well-being is the main consideration of Ambedkar's scheme of morality. Thus, external considerations are no longer above moral principles. Ambedkar makes such a morality the basis of religion, which he construed as *Dhamma*. In this construal, he redefines the centre of religion as morality rather than God. According to Ambedkar, Natural law is the basis of moral order of universe. *Dhamma* for Ambedkar is all-inclusive. The underlying meaning of the *Dhamma* is a message of equality and fraternity.

Ambedkar's position is that morality in religion would not be an effective one. In religion, morality is only a wagon which is attached to it. It is attached and detached as the occasion requires. Ambedkar notes that "Morality comes in only wherein man comes in relation to man. Morality comes into religion as a side wing to maintain peace and order....Be good to your neighbour because you are both children of God....The action of morality in the functioning of religion is therefore casual and occasional."[50] Ambedkar affirms that morality is *Dhamma* and *Dhamma* is morality that is inclusive. Further, analysis shows that, Ambedkar's attempt to justify morality without reference to transcendental religious beliefs is a first step to make the realm or morality as an autonomous one. The concern for the universal well-being is the main consideration of Ambedkar's scheme of morality. Thus, external considerations are no longer above moral principles. Ambedkar makes such a morality the basis of religion, which he construes as *Dhamma*.

Like the Lord Buddha, Ambedkar also insists that the purpose or religion and spirituality is not mere quest of notion or truth. His analysis shows that this is not a defensible claim. Buddha also analyses the metaphysical quest as follows; "Morality is justified in theistic religion in terms of reward and punishment give by God to the individual. Atheistic religions justify morality in terms of the doctrine of karma, according to which, morally good or bad lead to consequence, which are pleasant or painful to the agent. Therefore, the ethics in both theistic and atheistic religious lead to a kind of egoistic consequentialism."[51] This implies that the morality and its principles, roughly which can be considered as the benefit of all, is built on the egoistic basis. Morality is defined in most religions by looking on the consequence of violation or maintenance, which ego would face. Here, in Ambedkar's reconstruction of Buddhism, morality is justified in terms of universalistic consequentalism.

As we mentioned earlier Ambedkar extensively talks about the individual aspects of ethics through Buddhism. However, what one has to notice is that in this point also it differs from the other religions substantially. Through providing certain rule other religion advocates the suppression of certain aspects of individuality and life. Advocation of asceticism is the best example for it. And these individual ethical values are also construed as looking toward some heaven or other supernatural ideas. But Buddhism stands for the fullness of life and formulated ethical principles by looking on the face of reality. According to Ambedkar, to live in *Nibbana* is *Dhamma*. According to Buddha, nothing can give real happiness as *Nibbana*. Of all doctrines taught by the Buddha, the doctrine of *Nibbana* is the most central one. Brahmanic Upanishadic and Yogic traditions consider *Nibbana* as salvation of *Soul*. The three ideas underlie the Buddhist conception of *Nibbana*. "Of these the happiness of a sentient being as distinct from the salvation of the *Soul* is one. The second idea is the happiness of the sentient being in *Samsara* while he is alive. But the idea of a *Soul* and the salvation of the *Soul* after death are absolutely foreign to the Buddha's conception of *Nibbana*. The third idea which underlies his conception of *Nibbana* is the exercise of control over the flames of the passions which are always on fire."[52]

And for the individual Ambedkar said that the "Buddhism teaches social freedom, intellectual freedom, economic freedom and political freedom to man."[53] Ambedkar's approach to Buddhism thus, is social, philosophical and ethical rather than and mystical, as even a short account from *'The Buddha and His Dhamma'* will be sufficient to reveal. Ambedkar wanted to explain the teachings of Buddha by using the classification used by Buddha himself, namely the classification of *Dhamma* into the three categories *Dhamma,* Not-*Dhamma (Adhamma), and Saddhamma.* In the understanding of Ambedkar the concept of *Dhamma* in Buddhism refers: "To maintain purity of life is *Dhamma;* to reach perfection in life is *Dhamma;* to live in *Nibbana* is *Dhamma;* to-up craving is *Dhamma;* to believe the all compounded-things are impermanent is *Dhamma.* And to believe that *Karma* is to be an instrument of morality, it is *Dhamma.*"[54]

Ambedkar observes, "The religion of the Buddhism' is morality, it is embedded in religion. It is true that in Buddhism there is no God, in place of God there is morality. What God is to other refrains, morality is to Buddhism."[55] A morality, which was, based on the principles of truth and love. Hinduism, according to Ambedkar, did not recognise the principles of freedom and equality and had not succeeded in evolving a universal morality.

To explain what a *Dhamma* is, *not-Dhamma,* Ambedkar lists various negations or immoral activities that Buddha advocated in order to promote its social message. "Belief in the Supernatural is Not-*Dhamma (ADhamma). Beliefs in Ishwara (God)* is not essentially a part of *Dhamma* based on union with *Brahma* is a false *Dhamma.* Belief in *Soul* is *Not-Dhamma. Belief in Sacrifices is Not-Dhamma. Belief based on Speculation is Not- Dhamma.*"[56] *ADhamma* or *Not-Dhamma* consists in the belief in the supernatural as the cause of events, in the belief that the world is created by God, in the belief that *Dhamma* is based on union with *Brahma,* in the belief that sacrifices including animal sacrifices are a part of religion, in the belief that speculations regarding the origin of the self and the universe are a part of religion, in the belief that the reading of books is *Dhamma,* and in belief in the infallibility of sacred books like the *Vedas* as against *Adahmma.*

Morality is based on the Natural Order of the Physical world. It is evident from the natural phenomena that there is an order of the physical world. There is certain order for the movement of heavenly bodies, regularity for the seasons. These are called '*Niyamas*' in Buddhism. "Similarly there is a moral order in Human society. How is it produced? How is it maintained? Those who believe in God have no difficulty in answering the question. And their answer is easy. Moral order is maintained by Divined dispensation. God created the world and God is the supreme governor of the world. He is also the author of moral as well as of physical law. Such is the argument in support of the view that the moral order is maintained by Divine Dispensation."[57]

Ambedkar contests these arguments. He asks, "For if the moral law has originated from God and if God is the beginning and the end of the moral order and if man cannot escape from obeying God, why is there so much moral disorder in this world."[58] According to Ambedkar, Natural law is the basis of moral order of universe. "...God leaves it to Nature to work itself out in obedience to the laws originally given by him."[59] The moral order is maintained by Kamma Niyam and not God which maintains the moral order in the universe. "The moral order of universe rests on man and on nobody else. *Kamma* means man's action and *Vipaka* is its effect."[60]

The basic question is an action right or wrong because God commands or prohibits it, or God commands or prohibits the action because it is already right or wrong? A divine command ethicist takes the position that the standard of right or wrong is the commands and prohibitions of God. According to the divine command theory "an action or kind of action is right or wrong if and only if and because it is commanded or forbidden by God."[61] According to the Natural law theory, the basic principles of morals are objective, accessible to reason, and based on human nature. An action is right if it serves to fulfill human nature and wrong if it goes against human nature. Our human nature includes various inclinations and tendencies. The task of reason is to discover, sort out and order these inclinations in accord with appropriate human fulfillment.

However, in the analysis of Ambedkar's position one can find out that Ambedkar clearly counters the argument of the divine command ethics. Major divine command ethics' arguments are based on the conception that God is the first cause. That is God cannot be causally affected by anything. Therefore, it is difficult to claim that God chose which is already good, that is God is causally affected. All the similar positions already assume the supremacy of God in all senses. This presupposition which Ambedkar denies thoroughly throughout his theological positions and especially in his construal of Buddhism. If certain presupposition is accepted as certain, that itself is an obstacle to the critical engagement and analysis. Divine command ethics can be defended only on the ground that it follows from certain beliefs we have about God's nature and status and about the character of the relationship between god and human beings.

In Plato's *Euthyphro,* Socrates raises the question, "is a thing holy because the gods approve it, or do they approve it because it is holy."[62] According to Boyd and Vanarragon observe in their article 'Ethics is based on natural law" that "These questions, first posed in Plato's *Euthyphro* have for long troubled theists, because each of the obvious question carries with it unpleasant consequences. In other words, these questions appear to introduce a dilemma, as can be seen in the following argument:

- If God's command makes an act right, then morality is arbitrary.
- If God commands an act because it is right, then God's command is not essential to morality.
- Either God's commands make an act right, or God's commands an act because it is right.

Therefore,

- Either Morality is arbitrary or God's command is not essential to morality."[63]

Ambedkar's position was that the natural order of the universe is the basis of the morality. Ambedkar interprets the concept of *Karma* as, "the law of *Karma* has to do only with the question of general moral order. It has nothing to do with the fortunes and misfortunes of the world. It is concerned with the maintenance of the moral order in the universe."[64]

Dhamma for Ambedkar is social. *Dhamma* is social in the sense that it is all embracing and for all humanity. In other religions, a person leading a secluded life and performing certain rituals is considered to be a religious man but in Buddhism a man's behaviour towards his fellow-beings is the test of his being religious. *Dhamma* teaches righteousness which means right relations between man and man in all spheres of life. Society, therefore, cannot do without *Dhamma.* If *Dhamma* is not social and is not for the welfare of the people then it has no value for suffering humanity. Further, the underlying meaning of the *Dhamma* is a message of equality. Where there is equality, there is hope for individual initiative, progress and attainment of *Nirvana,* the supreme state of Bliss, the ultimate aim of every Buddhist.

Further, in most religions there is no place for morality but morality is the essence of the *Dhamma.* Without it, there is no *Dhamma.* In *Dhamma* morality takes the place of God although there is no God in *Dhamma.* Then Ambedkar discusses the principle of *Ahimsa* of Buddha. In Buddhism *Ahimsa* is a principle and not a rule. Buddha made a distinction between the 'need to kill' and the '*will to kill*'. Buddha denounced *Himsa* (Violence) and advocated a ban on the killing of animals for the sake of food, sacrifice, sport or pleasure; but it is wrong to interpret that He banned *Himsa* under all circumstances. But Buddha said that no one should run away from the Army with a view to join *Sangha.* This means that the Buddha was not against killing for the defense of the country. The principle of '*the need to kill*' and the 'will to kill' therefore is correct. To kill is entirely a matter of necessity and personal moral responsibility. Every act has to be guided by man's own *Prajna* and *karuna.* Buddhism in *Ahimsa* means non-aggressiveness; but in self-defense, if anyone needs to fight then he should fight.

Ambedkar tried to find the difference between *religion* and *Dhamma* in relation to their purposes and the way that different terminologies like *karma* and *Ahimsa* or non-killing are interpreted and used. Then he went to explore the relation between *Dhamma* and religion out of which he asserts that mere "Morality is not enough, but it must be sacred and universal."[65] Morality, he asserts, has no place in religion. Religion is concerned with the relation between man and God and morality is concerned with the relation between man and man. Though every religion preaches morality, morality is not the root of religion, it can be attached if it is needed or detached if it is not needed. The action of morality in the functioning of religion is not a serious one but casual and occasional. After describing the non-closeness of morality and religion Ambedkar takes *Dhamma* for his analysis and says that "Morality is *Dhamma* and *Dhamma* is Morality."[66]

In Ambedkar's understanding morality is the essence of *Dhamma* and the absence of it there is no *Dhamma.* Religion attaches every thing to God and man is expected to do every act to appease God. His responsibility is to serve and save the fellow beings. But *Dhamma* is not every thing man does, it is for his own self. He says that "Morality in *Dhamma* arises from the direct necessity for man to love man. Such morality does not require divine sanction. It is not to please God that man has to be moral. It is for his own good that man has to love man."[67] This morality, which is *Dhamma,* is not to satisfy a particular group but serves to protect the weak from the strong standards, and rules and which safeguards the growth of the individual. It is what makes liberty and equality effective, for if there is liberty for some but not for all and equality for few but not for the majority, what is the remedy? The only remedy lies in making fraternity universally effective. What is fraternity? It is nothing but another name for brotherhood of men, which is another name for morality.

That is the reason why Buddha said that *Dhamma* is morality and as *Dhamma* is sacred so is morality. As he begins writing the portion on the *Dhamma,* 'and his interpretation of "What the Buddha Taught", Ambedkar lists out "different views of the Buddha's *Dhamma*" on "What others have understood him to have taught": "What are the teachings of the Buddha?" This is a question on which no two followers of the Buddha or the students of Buddhism agree. To some *Samadhi* is his principal teaching. To some it is *Vippassana* (a kind of *Pranayam*). To some Buddhism is esoteric. To others it is exoteric. To some it is a system of barren metaphysics. To some it is sheer mysticism. To some it is a selfish abstraction from the world. To some it is a systematic repression of every impulse and emotion of the heart. Many other views regarding Buddhism-could be collected.'[68]

Ambedkar is justified in his reinterpretation of Buddhism; he has left a few gaps unfilled. Firstly, by not linking his community of Neo-Buddhists to any of the existing Buddhist *Sangha,* he fashioned a gulf between them. He refused to accept the existing forms of Buddhism, as they were not, he deemed, faithful to the original teaching of the Buddha.[69] This shortcoming has not only isolated the Neo-Buddhists depriving them of historical continuity, and a continuous tradition, it also deprived them of a *Sangha* and religious leadership to guide them.[70] The sudden demise of Ambedkar widened this gulf much more.

Ambedkar tried to turn to Buddha's original teachings and *Dhamma* and the social order advocated by him. He had preferred among the various Buddhist forms the original Hinayana rather than the Mahayana form. The society must have either the sanction of law or the sanction of morality to hold it together. Without either the society is sure to go to pieces. Religion, if it is to function, must be in accord with reason which is another name for science. It is not enough for religion to consist of a moral code, but its moral code must recognise the fundamental tenets of liberty, equality and fraternity. Religion must not sanctify or ennoble poverty.[71] Ambedkar's principles, for interpreting Buddhism are rationalism and utilitarianism coupled with socialism. He not only consciously employs them, also recommends them to those who are in doubt regarding the authenticity of the Buddha's teaching, as test-stones to clear the misunderstanding and confusion: One has therefore to be very careful in accepting what is said in the Buddhist canonical literature as being the word of the Buddha. There is, however, one test which is available. If there is anything that could be said with confidence that it is. He (Buddha) was nothing if not rational, if not logical. Anything therefore which is rational and logical, other things being equal, may be taken to be the word of the Buddha.

Usually science or reason is considered as in rival position of religion or religion bounded morality. The direct difficulty science could pose for religious belief would be direct scientific refutation of essential religious principles. But refutation can emerge only out of genuine conflict and that fact imposes some boundaries. For instance, many believe that science and religion operate in different domains or levels. If such positions are correct, there can be no genuine conflict. Any apparent conflict would represent trespassing or confusion. Further more, serious conflict between science and religion is possible only if both purport to be true. Consequently, if religious commitment is non-negative or non-propositional, genuine conflict seems impossible. That's why Ambedkar's position one who takes religion very seriously must approach it with a scientific attitude. Otherwise our religion would be a superstition. Making religion more active or creative or critical is making it scientific. Making it non-scientific is blocking the growth of religion; consequently it would become an ideology which advocates intolerance. And as per Ambedkar's position only through the critical engagement with science and reason one can draw the limits of religion. Drawing the limit is never deteriorating the system, it only corroborates it.

The second thing is that "the Buddha never cared to enter into a discussion, which was not profitable for man's welfare. Therefore, anything attributed to the Buddha, which did not relate to man's welfare couldn't be accepted to be the word of the Buddha."[72] This test for dealing with the teachings of the Buddha, Ambedkar offers, is to distinguish between those matters in which the Buddha was certain and those in which he was not and so gave only tentative views. Social relevance, that is making the *Dhamma* relevant to the present Indian context and to the unequal oppressive situation of the *Dalits*, should be considered the major principle and key to his interpretation. For, the above mentioned second test of the three prescribed by him, to clear the doubts that arise out of confusion and suspicion, again reiterates the use of the principle of existential social utility as important in interpreting the *Dhamma.* Ambedkar, with other *Dalits*, was in search of a religion with a revolutionary social message and the ideal of equality that enforces the moral social order of a class-casteless prosperous fraternal human society.

Ambedkar was also desperately in quest of and consciously trying to remake a religion, that is relevant for the independent, democratic, socialist, secular, sovereign Republic of India. He was strongly convinced that Hinduism with its Brahmin domination, and the ideology of inequality, that maintains with fear and force the hierarchical social order, of ascending power and descending contempt, as its ideal scheme of divine governance, was no more relevant to new India. As it is evident from his historic 1956 talk, he was seeking to revive a religion that is relevant and useful to the present world situation.[73] The *Dalit* critical principle, which is the key to Ambedkar's *Dalit* Hermeneusis, is at work, as was shown earlier, in his critique of all theistic religions, and the ideologies of Gandhism and Marxism that is the basis of Indian Communism. It is all the more effective in the reinterpretation of Buddhism. Ambedkar offers a revolutionary version of Neo-Buddhism to serve the cause of *Dalits*.

The gospel of Buddha according to Ambedkar is only a part of the religious revolution of Ambedkar, namely, "First to produce a Buddhist Scripture/ Bible, second, to make changes in the organisation, aims and objects of *Bhikkhu Sangha*, third, to set up a World Buddhist Mission,"[74] came to be realised. The Buddhist Bible that he authored was first titled as *Buddha and His Gospel* and was later on changed to '*The Buddha and His Dhamma.*'[75] Ambedkar consulted all the available sources on the Buddha to write this book, considered to be his *magnum opus.* It is a book of more than 400 pages, which was corrected again and again even as it was in print. Such was Ambedkar's concern to make it perfect, uptodate, and relevant to the contemporary social situation, that even on the night of his death he lay correcting the preface for the same book.[76] A few copies had been first printed by him and circulated for comments, and the final version was out of the press only in 1957, a few months after his death.[77]

As Ambedkar had originally intended, *The Buddha and His Dhamma* it reads like the Gospels with the biography of Compassionate Buddha interspersed with this teachings. The Buddha's inspiring life, noble mission, loving deeds, and the wise doctrine are combined to make the book a real Buddhist's Bible. Like the *Bible,* it is also broken down into books, chapters, and verses. It is rare to find a book on the Buddha and his *Dhamma* from which one can learn his teachings and life as much as one does from Ambedkar's gospel on the Buddha. It is in fact derived from Ambedkar's collection of hundreds of books on the Buddha.

The comments of Ambedkar on the original *suttas* and the biography are so inter-twined in, *The Buddha and His Dhamma;* at times it is difficult to distinguish who is talking. Ambedkar has also deliberately emphasised the social message of the Buddha. Ambedkar reinterpreted his teaching and projected his personality to bring out not only the enlightened Siddhartha Gautama full of wisdom, *prajna,* but also the compassionate one, full of *karuna* and *maitri.* It is indeed a social gospel of Buddhism. It lays more stress on love and service than wisdom and insight. What doctrines of Buddhism did Ambedkar hold and teach? In the central part of his Bible, Ambedkar dedicates a whole book to summarise the main teachings of the Buddha and the main doctrinal matters regarding the *Dhamma.* He candidly presents what are *Dhamma, Adhamma* and *Saddhamma* according to the Buddha. The main titles and points of the book' 'What the Buddha taught' are: What is *Dhamma*? "It is to maintain Purity of Life; to reach Perfection in Life; to live in *Nibbana*; to give up craving; to believe that all compound things are impermanent; to believe that *Karma* is the instrument of Moral Order."[78]

What is *Saddhamma*? His answer is that *Dhamma* is *Saddharma* when it makes learning open to all; teaches that mere learning is not enough and may lead to pedantry, that what is needed is *Pradnya*, that *Pradnya* is not enough, but must be accompanied by *Sila*, that besides *Pradnya* and *Sila* what is necessary is *Karuna*, and that more than *Karuna* what is necessary is *Maitri*. *Dhamma* to be *Saddhamma* must break down barriers between man and man, teach that worth and not birth is the measure of man, and must promote equality between man and man.[79]

Ambedkar's views of the Perfection in Ethical and spiritual life comes through (a) watchfulness, (b) mindfulness and (c) right understanding.[80] The virtue of liberally giving is essentially a product of compassion; compassion is the root of Bodhisattva's life. "His enlightenment is nothing but liberality or charity."[81] He thinks thus: "My neighbour suffers his pain just as I suffer mine; why should I be anxious about myself and not about him."[82] The perfection of charity leads to the equivalence of me and my fellow beings. When to me, as to others, pain and fear are unpleasant, there is no special to protect my own person and not others. Compassion is the only virtue to which a saint must apply himself; all other virtues will follow up naturally.[83] Nothing is superior to charity; even the vow of chastity. Liberality consists not only in giving material goods, things of enjoyment, but also in giving spiritual knowledge. Liberty born of compassion is the supreme means of conciliating creatures by alms giving, lovable speech, kind cooperation, and by sharing the joys and woes of beings.

The essence of Ambedkar's morality is self-preservation for the sole aim of benefiting creatures. It is, therefore, necessary to ensure good rebirths in order to undertake the career of a Bodhisattva. For this purpose morality must be observed. Without self-preservation, one cannot preserve others. This self-preservation is accomplished by the constant study of the scriptures.[84] In order to increase morality one must beware of Marv's evil deeds. Evil must be avoided, frivolity must be avoided; friendship must be cultivated with those established in the Doctrine. In order to protect against evil lapse, the following must be avoided: bad friends; forgetfulness of the idea of Enlightenment; despondency and lack of enthusiasm. Evil must be discarded by active service of man, and of the *Sangha*.[85] Confession of sins before Buddha's and Bodhisattvas also contributes to moral growth.

Mind control, the Essence of Morality: since all actions are preceded by thought, all feelings, sensations and desire proceed from the mind.[86] When the mind is unfree from attachment and hatred, keep quiet like a wooden piece; whenever it becomes noisy, jovial, critical, self-praising, wicked and deceptive, keep quiet like a wooden piece.[87] When my mind runs after gain, honour, fame, and wants family and servants, "I sit idle like a wooden piece; my mind has turned away from the supreme good, has become selfish, wishes association and conversation, therefore, I am lying like a wooden piece; I do likewise when it becomes intolerant, indolent, fearful, wicked, talkative and partial. These are the ways by which a brave *Soul* brings about the control of vain and soiled minds. Self-possessed in the lap of truth and free from pride, I hold the mind as a created thing; I have rendered my body completely inactive, it does not react to the objects of sense."[88]

Love thy foe: Pain is disliked by all; those that are in the grip of passions and torture themselves, may torture others as well. Fire will burn wherever it is; anger rises out of this fire of passion and don't out of the objects. It is a pity that I dislike pain but like the body, the house of woe. It is unwise to be angry with men who injure us, for they are only acting under the influence of causes and conditions; and the foremost of these causes are our wicked deeds of previous existence. "My enemy takes a stick to beat me, and I have assumed this body, liable to be wounded, and destined to be beaten. Far from being angry with my enemy I ought to consider him almost as beneficial as the Buddhas, for he affords me the opportunity of practicing patience and forgiveness of wrongs, which blots out my sins. Am I to make this principle of salvation the cause of my condemnation? Let us rather pity our enemies who ruin themselves by their anger, and let us think of means of saving them in spite of themselves as the Buddhas do."[89]

Further, he says that, it is because of anger that "I have suffered in hells a thousand times, but have always sought after my own good. It befits my career of patience that I should welcome such pain as would help removal of the miseries of the world. Never grudge the joy of others, rather be happy by the happiness of others."[90] He who wants Enlightenment wants everything for every body; he who is jealous of the property of others has no thought of Enlightenment.[91] Do not be misled by praise, honour or gain, they are false and deceptive. The living beings are the proper field of spiritual career even as the Buddhas; worship of beings is the worship of Buddha; friendliness towards beings in fact amounts to Buddha-worship. Ambedkar has strong belief that all beings have the seed of Buddha-qualities.

References

1. Keer, Dananjay, *Dr. Ambedkar: A Memorial Album*, Popular Prakashan, Bombay, 1982, p. 3.
2. Ambedkar, B. R, *The Buddha and His Dhamma*, Siddharth Publications, Bombay, 1984, pp. 156-157, 159, 351-364, and 370-371.
3. Moon, Vasanth, ed, *Babasaheb Ambedkar's Writings and Speeches* Vol. V, Government of Maharashtra, 1989, p. 116.
4. Moon, Vasant, ed., Ambedkar's preface to his, Ranade, Gandhi and Jinnah (1943), *Writings and Speeches*, Vol. V, Government of Maharashtra, Bombay, 1991, pp. 208-209.
5. Murdoch, J. *Review of Caste in India*, Prem Rawat, Jaipur, 1977, p. 216.
6. Rajni Kothari, *Caste in Indian Politics*, Orient Longman. New Delhi, Section 1. 1.
7. Moon, Vasant, ed., *Dr. Babasaheb Ambedkar's Writings and Speeches*. Vol. V, Government of Maharashtra, Bombay,1989, p. 118.
8. Jatava, D.R. *The Social Philosophy of B. R. Ambedkar*, Agra, Phoenix Publishing Agency,1965, p. 231.

9. *Ibid.* and A. Thumma, *Prema Yoga*. Oxford University Press, New York, 1974, p. 232.
10. *Ibid*, pp. 233-234.
11. Keer, Dananjay and Dr. Ambedkar, *Babasaheb Ambedekar's Writings and Speeches*, Vol. III, p. 336. and Vol. IV, pp. 5-8, *The Buddha and His Dhamma*, Which was being written at the same time, Sangan Books, London, 1987, p. 487.
12. *Ibid*, p. 488.
13. Keer, Dananjay, *Dr. Ambedkar: A Memorial Album*, Popular Prakashan, Bombay, 1982, p. 92.
14. *Ibid*, p. 66.
15. *Ibid*, p. 71.
16. *Ibid*, p. 73.
17. Moon, Vasant, ed., *Dr. Babasaheb Ambedkar's Writings and Speeches*, Vol. I, Government of Maharashtra, Bombay,1989, p. 406.
18. *Ibid*, p. 222.
19. Moon, Vasant, ed., *Dr. Babasaheb Ambedkar's Writings and Speeches*, Vol. III, Government of Maharashtra, Bombay,1989, p. 97.
20. *Ibid*, pp. 97-98.
21. Jatava, D. R. *The Social Philosophy of B. R. Ambedkar*, Phoenix Publishing Agency, Agra,1965, Section 3. 3. 3. 2.
22. Moon,Vasant, ed., *B. R. Ambedkar's Writings and Speeches*, Government of Maharashtra, Bombay, 1989, Vol. III, p. 442.
23. Jatava, D.R, *The Social Philosophy of B. R. Ambedkar*, Agra, Phoenix Publishing Agency, 1965, p. 267.
24. Moon, Vasanth, ed. *Babasaheb Ambedkar's Writings and Speeches*, Vol. V, Government of Maharashtra,1991, pp. 318-319.
25. Ambedkar, B. R, *Buddha and His Dhamma*, Siddhartha Publications, Bombay, 1991, p. 79.
26. Keer, Dananjay, ed., *Babasaheb Ambedkar's*, *Writings and Speeches*, Vol. II, 1982, pp. 609, and 655-656; pp. 449-500; G. S. Lokhande, B. R. Ambedkar – *A Study in Social Democracy*, Intellectual Publishing House, New Delhi, 1977, pp. 143-156.
27. Moon, Vasant, Thus Spoke *Ambedkar's, Writings and Speeches,* Government of Maharashtra, Bombay, Vol. II, 1982, pp. 164-165.
28. Ambedkar, B. R., *The Buddha and His Dhamma*, pp. 318 – 319; *Writings and Speeches*, Vol I, pp. 57 – 58; Jatava D.R., *The Social Philosophy of B. R. Ambedkar*, pp. 86 – 93 and 231 – 269; G. S. Lokhande, Ambedkar B. R.– *A Study in Social Democracy*, Intellectual Publishing House, New Delhi, 1977, pp. 50 – 63; Section, 3. 4. 2.

29. Moon, Vasant, *Thus Spoke Ambedkar*, Vol. II, 1982, pp. 164 – 165; D. R. Jatava, *The Political Philosophy of B.R. Ambedkar*, Agra, Phoenix Pub. House, 1965, pp. 81 – 160.

30. Ambedkar, B. R, *The Buddha His Dhamma*, Siddhartha Publications, Bombay, 1991, p. 166.

31. *Ibid*, p. 202.

32. *Ibid*, p. 170.

33. *Ibid*, pp. 156 and 165.

34. *Ibid*, p. 296.

35. *Ibid*, p. 202.

36. *Ibid*, p. 301.

37. *Ibid*, p. 214.

38. *Ibid*, pp. 318 – 319.

39. Keer, Dhananjay, *Dr. Ambedkar, Life and Mission*, Bombay, Popular Prakashan, 1991, pp. 233 – 235.

40. *Ibid*, p. 273.

41. Dr. Billy Graham, "*The bible is a book*", ed, The Bible, *New Testament Gospel According to Luke*, Chapter X, verse, 27.

42. Ambedkar, B. R, *Buddha and His Dhamma*, Siddharth Publications, Bombay, 1987, p. 283.

43. *Ibid.*

44. *Ibid*, p. 284.

45. Kuber, W. N, *B.R. Ambedkar*, Ministry of Information and Broadcasting, Govt. of India, New Delhi, 1978, p. 96.

46. Jatava, D.R. *The Social Philosophy of B. R. Ambedkar*, Agra, Phoenix Publishing Agency,1965, p. 301.

47. Ambedkar, B. R, *Buddha and The Future of His Religion*, Bheem Patrika Publication, Jalundur, 3rd Edn. 1968, p. 5.

48. *Ibid.*

49. Rob Peter, ed, *Dalit Movements and the meaning of labour in India,* Oxford University Press, New Delhi, 1993, p. 18.

50. Ambedkar, B. R, *The Buddha and His Dhamma*, Siddhartha Publications, Bombay, 1991, p. 322.

51. Pradeep, P. Gokhale, *Reconstructing the World*, '*Universal Consequentilism: A Note on Ambedkar's Reconstruction of Buddhism*. Sri Satguru Publicatiions, New Delhi, 1993, p. 127.

52. Ambedkar, B. R, *Buddha and His Dhamma,* Siddhartha Publications, Bombay, 1991, p. 234.

53. Shashi, S. S, ed., *Ambedkar and Social Justice,*Vol. I and II, Ministry of Information and Broadcasting, Govt. of India, New Delhi, 1992, pp. 92 – 93.
54. Kuber, W. N, *B.R. Ambedkar,* Ministry of Information and Broadcasting, Govt. of India, New Delhi, 1978, p. 93.
55. Busi, S. N, *Mahatma Gandhi and Babasaheb Ambedkar*, Saroja Publications, Hyderabad, 1997, p. 325.
56. *Ibid*, p. 95.
57. Ambedkar B. R., *Buddha and His Dhamma*, Bombay, Siddhartha Publications 1991, p. 242.
58. *Ibid*, p. 243.
59. *Ibid.*
60. *Ibid*, p. 244.
61. Frankena, W.K, *Ethics*, 2nd edn, Oxford University Press, New York, 1989, p. 28.
62. Janine Marie Idziak, *Divine Commands are the Foundation of Morality*, Oxford Clarendon Press, Oxford, 1978, pp. 290-299.
63. Boyd, Craig A and Vanarragon, Raymond. J '*Ethics is based on natural law*" Francis Printer, London, 1987, p. 94.
64. *Ibid*, p. 95.
65. Kadam, K. N, *Dr. Ambedkar The Emancipation of the Oppressed*, Sangam Books, London,1993, p. 105.
66. *Ibid.*
67. *Ibid.*
68. Ambedkar, B. R, *Buddha and His Dhamma*, Siddhartha Publications, Bombay, 1991, p. 158.
69. Asgar Ali Engineer, ed., *Religion and Liberation*, Delhi, Ajanta Publications, 1989; Stan Lourdusamy, *Religion as a Political Weapon*, Calcutta, Multi Book Agency, 1990; and Paul Puthanangady, *Towards an Indian Theology of Liberation*, Bangalore, NBCLC, 1986, Section 5. 2.
70. Michael Mahar J, ed., *The Untouchables in Contemporary India*, Tucson, The University of Arizona Press, 1972, pp. 122 – 123.
71. Keer, Dhananjay, *Dr. Ambedkar: Life and Mission*, Popular Prakashan, Bombay, 1991, p. 421.
72. Keer, Dhananjay, *Dr. Ambedkar: Life and Mission*, Popular Prakashan, Bombay, 1987, pp. 254 – 255.
73. *Ibid*, p. 490.
74. Paradkar, "*The Religious Quest of Ambedkar*,"Ajay Prahaghan, New Delhi 1968, p. 66.

75. Keer, Dananjay, *Dr. Ambedkar: Life and Mission*, Popular Prakashan, Bombay,1987, p. 489.
76. *Ibid*, pp. 488 and 513.
77. Bhole's R. R, ed, *Introductory Writings*,and Ambedkar B. R, *The Buddha and His Dhamma*, Siddhartha Publications, Bombay, 1991, pp. 105 – 108.
78. Ambedkar, B. R, *The Buddha and His Dhamma*, Siddhartha Publications, Bombay, 1991, pp. 229-233.
79. Paradkar, "*The Religious Quest of Ambedkar*," Ajay Prahaghan, New Delhi,1968, p. 69.
80. Joshi Lal Mani, *Studies in the Buddhistic Culture of India*, Motilal Banarasidass, New Delhi, 1977, p. 101.
81. *Ibid*, p. 102.
82. *Ibid.*
83. *Ibid.*
84. *Ibid*, p. 103.
85. *Ibid*, p. 104.
86. *Ibid*, p. 105.
87. *Ibid.*
88. *Ibid.*
89. *Ibid*, pp.106 - 107.
90. *Ibid*, 107.
91. *Ibid.*

Conclusion

The present study tries to explain Ambedkar's views on philosophy, religion and morality. It started with discussing Ambedkar's comments on the place of religion and morality in Semitic and Indic traditions. Ambedkar while commenting on the Semitic traditions, he considers that the altruistic nature of Judaism was under suspicion because of its special preference to Israel. He understood that, the preference may be because of the Jew community has been under slavery for long time. In that sense, he appreciates the notion of Lord with the Oppressed. Ambedkar was very much enthusiastic and appreciative on the life of Jesus and the principles of Christianity. However, he disagrees with them mainly on the affirmation of speculative ideas of the religion and other superstition in the practice. Moreover, his main criticism has been that the principles of equality and other valuable things withered by church in its practices. His complaint against another Semitic religion the Islam was mainly for its intolerance, which develops from the persistent affirmation of only one true God.

Ambedkar's analysis and criticism mainly concentrates on the nature of Indic tradition particularly the Hinduism. He criticises Hinduism for its attempts to provide justification to the present hierarchical order of the society. Ambedkar says that the Hindu religious philosophy and its socio-cultural appearance grounded on the belief that human life is unequal and immoral therefore cannot scream for religious and social equality. According to Ambedkar human beings, in Hindu tradition pre-determined to be born unequal and therefore cannot lay claim to equality either in terms of their religious-spiritual status or in terms of their social, economic, civic or political status in the community. The major theme of Ambedkar's' analysis of religious immorality based on the philosophical and practice of social dominance thus, the Hindu religious moral ideology always hurting to the depressed people.

Ambedkar appreciate the democratic, equalitarian aspect of Buddhism and its realistic and scientific attitudes. Ambedkar says that the Buddhism is a true religion guided by the three principles of knowledge, right path and compassion. Ambedkar provided a message that the change from Hinduism to Buddhism only can provide, honour, respect, status, standard civilised life and freedom from slavery. Ambedkar said, it is impossible for humanity to live peacefully and righteously without Buddha and his *Dhamma.* Ambedkar adopted Neo-Buddhism as the means to annihilate caste. Since Ambedkar rejected all other religions as theistic superstition, he chooses to revive Buddhism. His scientific rationalism was also too strong. This religious approach to the whole problem, we must admit, has led Ambedkar to give more importance to socio-religious reform and the caste struggle.

Ambedkar persuaded that Hinduism badly needed reform, and wanted to expose the immorality and oppression it had unleashed and the slavery it had perpetuated on the depressed. He was the victim of the social system of Hinduism. After discussing, various meanings of the word 'Hindu' as denoting a religion, parentage, country and a race. Ambedkar points out that he is dealing with Hinduism in which caste has become indispensable as doctrine, ideology and sanctified social order. Ambedkar sees that Hinduism is not a religion for individual justice with equality, fraternity and liberty and it fails to bring social utility of just, free and moral social order as the ideal scheme of divine governance.

Ambedkar arrives at the final judgment of Hinduism: The only answer is that Hinduism is overwhelmed with the fear of contamination. It does not have the power to purify. It has not the desire to serve and that is because by its very nature it is in human and unmoral. It is a misnomer to call it religion. Its philosophy is opposed to the very thing for which religion stands. Hinduism is destined for failing the trial by the first norm of justice. It advocates inequality as the dependable doctrine. In his brief analysis of the Philosophy of Hinduism from the point of view of justice reveals in an obtrusive manner how Hinduism is adverse to equality, antagonistic to liberty and opposed to fraternity.

Indeed, inequality is the soul of Hinduism. Secondly, its norm of social utility equally fails to free from domination. If these conclusions are sound, Ambedkar asks the questions how can a philosophy that disconnects intelligence from labour, which expropriates the rights of man to comfort vital to life and which prevented society from mobilising resources for common action in the hour of danger, said to satisfy the test of social utility.

The relation of religion and morality is important in Ambedkar thought process. Ambedkar perhaps the one who has set forth most clearly the way in which the relation between specifically religious belief and the ideal of the good life should prevail in specific social formation. Ambedkar's thesis is that morality must be autonomous and that it must not be held in the leading strings of religion, theology or dogmatic metaphysics. Ambedkar adopts uncompromising position that the morality is not maintained by the Divine dispensation but it rests on the individual. That the action of right and wrong depends upon God is repugnant to Ambedkar.

Ambedkar takes recourse to the classical argument to disprove the existence of God who allows evil and suffering in the world. According to him, the notion of God as good and the existence of evil and suffering are incompatible. Ambedkar develops a series of arguments for the futility of the notion of the existence of God taking recourse to Buddha's arguments. Ambedkar questions the integrity of God. He is basically raising the ontological question on the nature of God. If God is the answer to everything then he should take the responsibility for the evil also? The God who sanctions social discriminations cannot be said to exist. If God is omnipotent, man must be passive and in the final analysis, the freedom of the will is under question. If at all god existed, then why there is so much evil why his hand so rarely spread to bless? *Man is only responsible to his own mistakes and creations, not applying for unknown God, whether God supposes to exist or not.*

This means that the idea of religion is abhorrent for Ambedkar. According to him what is loosely referred as the religious morality is thought to be authoritarian in spirit and antagonistic to the freedom of an individual. However, the possibility that morality might be the need of religious foundations but its authoritarian character is not considered.

It is the opposition to religious authority in the matter of motives and norms which alienates the fellow human beings rejected by Ambedkar. In this context Ambedkar says that the morality and the religion are inseparable and that morality is able to be understood only in the context of religion and it has been at the center of his philosophical discussion. According to Ambedkar, religion must be essentially moral; religion cannot live unless it interacts with other forms of spiritual life as morality, beauty, and truth. Religion is thus when compared with morality turns out to be at once *infra* and *supra* ethical. The fact that the religion takes as its point of departure human life, for this it provides a goal. Without such a destiny in sight religion cannot exist, provided with its faith passes on far beyond the realm of morality.

It must be remembered that Ambedkar categorically defends the autonomy of morality. Like Spinoza, Ambedkar says that the good life is not a means to something else but is itself a supreme end. Hence according to Ambedkar morality must be autonomous in the sense that, no alien considerations, like the fear of tyrannical God or deity from an absolute Hindu religious *Dharma* should be admitted as valid in determining the conduct of human persons. Again he says that any consideration of earthly gain or worldly reward and success should not determine the truly moral conduct. The good is to be chosen for its own sake, just as the good life is to be lived for its own sake. Thus, in any respect according to Ambedkar the morality is truly autonomous. However, Ambedkar's persistent question still remains. Which morality is dependent for its content on the norms and concepts derived from which religion? Here, Ambedkar makes clear difference between Buddhism and Hinduism and takes the position that the Hindu social order is immoral and it is against the human freedom and fraternity.

Ambedkar's model of theology on religion is a good model available for us in India to emulate. We need to follow Ambedkar's methodology not only to learn from the great master and achieve what he did, also to carry forward his struggle, and the liberation of all. It is quite clear that Ambedkar's intervention in the philosophical realm is clearly guided by the socio-political reason. Ambedkar holds a perception that religion is a vital force, a scheme of moral governance and foundation for human society. In Ambedkar's sense, religion is necessary as a system of values and as a science of social reconstruction.

He looked at religion not as an instrument for the individual salvation but as the basis for social interaction. And Ambedkar focuses on the notion of Liberative religion. Through this notion what he emphasises that notion of religion is quite essential to social transformation. But for him, all the factors in the social transformation are self-subsistent in itself (i.e. social structure, individuals, religion etc). Ambedkar redefines the notion of religion also on the basis of reason and scientific method. He redefines the purpose of the religion. This redefinition is what makes him to embraces of Buddhism. Ambedkar equates *Dhamma* with morality.

The morality of love arises from the direct necessity for man to love man. He makes it comprehensible that it is not to please the God that man has to be moral but for his own good qualities, man has to love man. In the struggle for existence the individual's rights may not be catered for, and at times his or her interests can be, reared by the group. Similarly, a weak group may also be discriminated by a stronger group, hence the indispensability of the *law of love*, fraternity and goodwill, which is another name for morality. The most important in, *Saddhamma,* more than *Prajna* and *Sila, Sila* is *Karuna,* love of human beings and *Maitri* that is all living beings.

Ambedkar stressed that religion is for humans and not humans for religion. For him, man and morality must be the centre of religion. Humanist to the core, Ambedkar was ready to throw away any religion or religious practice however ancient and sanctified if that does not promote human welfare. According to Ambedkar, Buddhism demands living experience and it was realism and never idealism. It upheld liberty, equality, truth and justice; it emphasised humanity, love and peace. It was dynamic, scientific and all embracing. Its explanation of life and its meaning and purpose of birth and death and its aftermath were very clear, intelligible and logical. Above all, man was the center of his study and examination and not anything outside of him.

Buddhism which was an early Indian religion and the Buddha was nearer to the untouchable masses. Buddhism could withstand even the severest scientific test and had the power and capacity to direct destines of the modern world. The untouchables would join with the world Buddhist community and thus pave the way for world brotherhood. Ambedkar said that, Buddhism gives three principles in combination, which no other religion does. Buddhism teaches *prajna* (understanding) as against superstition and supernaturalism, *Karuna (love)* and *samata* (equality). Neither god nor soul can save the society, referring to Marx's philosophy, he observed, man cannot live by bread alone. He has a mind, which needs food for thought. Religion instills hope in man and drives him to activity. Hindu religion has watered down the enthusiasm of the downtrodden. And I found it necessary to change my faith and embrace Buddhism Ambedkar says that Religion emphasises, universalises social values and brings them to the mind of the individual who is required to be familiar with them in all his acts in an order that he may function as an approved member of the society.

Ambedkar's intervention is considered as a Copernican revolution in the realm of morality and religion. Analysis shows that, Ambedkar's attempt to justify morality without reference to transcendental religious beliefs is a first step to make the realm of morality as an autonomous one. The concern for the universal well-being is the main consideration of Ambedkar's scheme of morality. Thus, external considerations are no longer being above moral principles. Ambedkar makes such a morality the basis of religion, which he construes as *Dhamma*. In this construal, he redefines the centre of religion as morality rather than God. According to Ambedkar, Natural law is the basis of moral order of universe. *Dhamma* for Ambedkar is all-inclusive. The underlying meaning of the *Dhamma* is a message of equality.

Ambedkar's position is that morality in religion would not be an effective one. In religion, morality is only a wagon which is attached to it. It is attached and detached as the occasion requires. Ambedkar notes that the morality comes in only wherein man comes in relation to man. Morality comes into religion as a side wind to maintain peace and order....Be good to your neighbour because you are both children of God....The action of morality in the functioning of religion is therefore casual and occasional. Ambedkar affirms that morality is *Dhamma* and *Dhamma* is morality.

The terrible suffering, pain and pathos of cultural deprivation, economic exploitation, social ostracism, and political domination caused by the ruthless monstrous caste-system, made Ambedkar whole-heartedly hate the caste system and anything or anyone related with its continuation. As he admits, such hatred for injustice is necessary for the activists who wish to fight for a just and egalitarian order. Towards the end of his life, Ambedkar had to stand lone most of his life, with no support from other ideologie, parties, and religions, because of his non-compromising attitude. His strong critique of them all and avoidance, made them also shun him. The adoption of Buddhism further isolated him. However, he refused to accept the existing forms of Buddhism, as they were not, he deemed, faithful to the original teaching of the Buddha. This shortcoming has not only isolated the Neo-Buddhists depriving them of historical continuity, and a continuous tradition, it also deprived them of a *Sangha* and religious leadership to guide them.

Study on Ambedkar reveals that his address towards religion is not a mere craving towards addressing a religion as a social institution but it was very deep that concentrated on the structure of social system in its wholeness. Ambedkar holds a perception that the religion is a vital force, a scheme of moral governance and foundation for human society. In Ambedkar's sense, religion is necessary as a system of values and as a science of social reconstruction. He looked at religion not as an instrument for the individual salvation but as the basis for social interaction. He redefines the purpose of the religion. This redefinition is what makes him to embraces of Buddhism.

Religion is not an end in itself. It is meant for the preservation of life and human welfare. Hence, religion is not the one that has the final say; it is not infallible, absolute, inflexible nor permanent. Ambedkar stressed that religion is for humans and not humans for religion. For him, man and morality must be the centre of religion. Religion instills hope in man and drives him to activity. Hindu religion has watered down the enthusiasm of the downtrodden. Ambedkar says that religion emphasises, universalises social values and brings them to the mind of the individual who is required to be familiar with them in all his acts in an order that he may function as an approved member of the society. The concern for the universal well-being is the main consideration of Ambedkar's scheme of morality.

According to Ambedkar, merits of Buddhist philosophy were as follows: Buddhism demanded living experience and a life divine, attainable there and now; not after death, it was realism and never idealism. It upheld liberty, equality, truth and justice; it emphasised humanity, love and peace. It was dynamic, scientific and all embracing. Its explanation of life and its meaning and purpose of birth and death and its aftermath were very clear, intelligible and logical. Above all, man was the center of his study and examination and not anything outside of him. Ambedkar tried to prove that the untouchables were Buddhists. In his thesis on the origin of Untouchability, he made it clear that today's untouchables were once Buddhists. Buddhism was an Indian religion and the Buddha was nearer to the untouchable masses. Buddhism could withstand even the severest scientific test and had the power and capacity to direct destines of the modern world. The untouchables would join with the world Buddhist community and thus pave the way for world unity. Ambedkar said that, Buddhism gives three principles in combination, which no other religion does. Buddhism teaches *prajna* (understanding) as against superstition and supernaturalism, *Karuna (love)* and *samata* (equality)... Neither god nor soul can save the society.

Thus, external considerations are no longer being above moral principles. Ambedkar makes such a morality the basis of religion, which he construes as *Dhamma.* In this construal, he redefines the centre of religion as morality rather than God. *Dhamma* for Ambedkar is all-inclusive. The underlying meaning of the *Dhamma* is a message of equality. Ambedkar's position is that morality in religion would not be an effective one. Ambedkar notes that morality comes in only wherein man comes in relation to man. Morality comes into religion as a side wind to maintain peace and order....Be good to your neighbour because you are both children of God....The action of morality in the functioning of religion is therefore casual and occasional.

Buddhism is the truly civilised earliest ethical system where man called upon to have himself governed by him. The Buddha alone has the glory of having rightly judged the intrinsic greatness of man's capacity to workout his salvation without extraneous aid. No other religion insists upon the values of knowledge and evil of ignorance so much as they are in Buddhism. No other religion lays so much stress upon keeping one's eyes open. No other religion has formulated such deep-laid plans for mental culture. The Buddhist moral ideal, the *Arhat,* had to be both normally and intellectually great. The Buddha is not essential to salvation, and ignorance is one of the two main causes of failure to attain it (craving or attachment being the other) and always stressed knowledge. If there were any religion that would cope with modern scientific and spiritual needs, it would be Buddhism.

The teachings of a religion which is competent with modern science is essential for the future human race, the higher teachings on ultimate realities by Lord Buddha, that is known as *Abhi-Dhamma*, should be studied in schools and universities as "*Mental Science*" or "*Ultimate Science*". The Buddha's *Middle way* is the only way, which can systematically eliminate all the defilements of the mind and thus offer total inner peace and eternal happiness.

Bibliography

Abraham Joshua Heschel, (1965). Who is Man, Stanford University Press, California, London.

Adhar Das, (1934). *Sri Aurobindo and the future of Mankind,* University of Calcutta Press, Calcutta.

Ahir, D.C. (1996). "*The Pioneers of Buddhist Revival in India*", Blue Moon Books, New Delhi.

Ahir, D.C. (1995). (ed.), *Ambedkar on Christianity.* Blue Moon Books, New Delhi.

Alasdair Macintyre, (1976). *A Short History of Ethics*, Routledge & Kegan Paul, London, and Henley Press, Oxford.

Alban G. Widgery and R.D. Ranade, (1929). *The Indian Philosophical Review*, Vol. 38, No. 5. Vedic Books Publishers, New Delhi.

Alexander Lyon Macfie, (1988). *Eastern, Influence on Western Philosophy*, Edinburgh University Press, Edinburgh.

Alexander, (1920). *Space, Time and Deity*, Vol. II, The Gifford Lectures at Glasgow, 1916-1918, MacMillan & Co., London.

Allen W. Wood, (1999). *Kant's Ethical Thought*, Cambridge University Press, Cambridge. London.

Ambedkar B.R,(1987). *Why Go for Conversion*? Dalit Sahitya Academy, Bangalore.

Ambedkar, B. R.(1950). *The Buddha and the Future of His Religion*, The Mahabodhi, Bombay.

Ambedkar, B.R, (1991). *The Buddha and His Dhamma.* Siddharth Publications, Bombay,

Ambedkar, B.R, (1946). *Who were Shudras?,* Thacker & Company, Bombay.

Anand,Teltumbde, (2003). *Ambedkar on Muslims (Myths and Facts)*, VAK Publications, Mumbai.

Annemarie, (1978). *Islamic Principles; Mystical Dimensions of Islam*, The University of North Carolina Press, Carolina.

Arjun Dangle, (1992).(ed)., *Poisoned Bread*, Orient Longman, New Delhi.

Khare, R. S.(1984).*The Untochable as Himself; Ideology Identity, and Pragmatism among the Lucnow Chamars*, Cambridge University Press, New York.

Anthoniraj, Thumma, (1999). *Prema Yoga,* ISPCK, New Delhi.

Arthur J. Arberry, trans, (1983). *The Koran*, Oxford University Press, U. K.

Arvind Sharma, (1995). *The Philosophy of Religion- A Buddhist Perspective*, Oxford University Press, New Delhi.

Asghar Ali Engeneer,(1989).(ed)., *Islam and Revolution*, Ajanta Published, New Delhi.

August Cruises, (1990). A Guide to Rational Living; *Moral Philosophy from Montaigne to Kant*, Cambridge University Press, Cambridge.

Augustine, (1963). *The City of God Against the Pagans*, University Press, Harvard.

Aurobindo Sri, (1947). *Heraclilus,* Arya Public House, Calcutta.

Aurobindo Sri, (1985). *Human Cycle the Ideal of Human Unity War and Self determination*, Sri Aurobindo Ashram, Pondicherry.

Aurobindo Sri. (1971). *The Life Divine,* Book II, Sri Aurobindo Ashram, Pondicherry.

Bhattacharya, Hari Mohan, (1975). *The Principles of Philosophy*, Oxford University Press, Calcutta.

Bhattacharya, H. S. (1976). *Jain Moral Doctrine*. Jain Sahitya Vikas Mandal. Mumbai.

Bharathi K.S, (1990). *Foundations of Ambedkar Thought,* Dattsons Publications, New Delhi.

Bhasam, A. L, (1968). *The Wonder that was India*, Taplinger Press, New York.

Billy Graham. Dr, (1983). "*The Bible is a Book*", American Bible Society, New York.

Bhole's R.R,(1946).(ed), *Introductory Writings, and B. R. Ambedkar,* posthumously published, Bombay.

Bouquet, A.C, (1941). *Comparative Religion,* Harmondsworth, Penguin Books Ltd., Middlesex, New York.

Bowes Pratima, (1976). *The Hindu Religious Tradition; A Philosophical Approach*, Allied Publishers Private Limited, Bombay.

Boyd, Craig A and Vanarragon, Raymond. J. (1887). '*Ethics is based on natural law,* Francis Printer, London.

Bradwell L. Smith, (1978). (ed)., *Religion and Legitimation of Power in South Asia*, Leiden, E.J. Brill.

Burrell David C, (1979). *The Islamic Contribution to Medieval Philosophical Theology*, Routledge, New York.

Chalmers, (1986). *What is this thing called Science?* Oxford University Press, London.

Chanda Chakraborty, (1977). *Common life in the Rig – Veda and Atharvana Veda,* Punthi Pustak, Calcutta.

Charles Taylor, (1995). *Religion Today,* Cambridge Mass, Harward University Press, Harward.

Charles, T. Gorham, (1986). *Ethics of the Great religion; Judaism & Christianity,* PRIRUP Prakashan, New Delhi.

Charlesworth, M. J. (1998). *Philosophy of Religion*; *Kant's religion and practiced reason.* Cambridge University Press, London.

Chattopadyaya, D. P. (1975). *Indian Philosophy, A popular introduction*, People Publishing House, New Delhi.

Chatterjee and Datta, (1984). *History of philosophy Eastern and Western*, (Ed), Radhakrishnan S, George Allen & Unwin Limited, Vol. I, London.

Christian W. A, (1964). *Meaning and Truth in Religion,* N. J. Princeton University Press, Princeton.

Cohen Arthur. A, (1928). *The Jews*, The University of Alabama University Press, Alabama.

Dandekar R. N, (1979). *Insights into Hinduism,* Ajanta Publications, New Delhi.

Dasgupta, (1974). *Religion and Rationalism - Religion and the rational outlook,* Motilal Banarasidass, New Delhi.

David Waines, (1995). *An Introduction to Islam*, Cambridge University Press, Cambridge (London, UK).

Descartes René, (1981). *New Essays on Human Understanding*, University Press, Cambridge, London.

Dev Raj Bali,1989. *Introduction to Philosophy*, Sterling Publishers Private Limited, New Delhi.

Dinesh Anand. (2002). *Origin of Scriptures*, Blumoon Books, New Gyan Offset Press, New Delhi.

Donald E. Smith, India, (1963), 1967 *As a Secular State : Hinduism and Indian Culture,* chapter- 13, Princeton University Press, Princeton.

Donald H. Bishop, (1975). *Indian thought*, Wiley Eastern Private Limited, New Delhi.

Douglas J. Davies, (1999). (ed)., *Christianity: A companion to Religious Studies and Theology*, Edinburgh University Press, London.

Ducasse, C. J, (1953). *A Philosophical Scrutiny of Religion,* The Ronald Press Company, New York.

Durant Drake, (1967). *Problems of Religion*, Washington Square, New York.

Edward Conze, (1982). *Buddhist thought in India*, The University of Michigan Press, United States.

Edward Craig, (1998). *Encyclopedia of Philosophy*, Routledge, New York.

Flanagan, Kieran and Jupp, Peter. C (1996). (eds)., *Post Modernity, Sociology and Religion*, McMillan, London.

Foucault Michel, (1991). "*Truth and Power*," Prentice Hall Publishers, New Jeresy.

Frankena W.K, (1989). *Ethics*, 2nd edn, Oxford University Press, New York.

Frederick Soatag and M. Darrol Bryant, (1982). *The Concept of God*, The Rose of Sharon Press Incs New York.

Gail Omvedt, (2003). *Buddhism in India*, Sage Publications, London.

Gauri Viswanathan,(1998). *Outside of the Fold: Conversion, Modernity and Belief*, Princeton University Press, New Jersey.

Geoffrey Thomas, (1987). *The moral philosophy of T. H. Green*, Clarendon Press, Oxford.

George C. Kerner, (1990). *Three Philosophical Moralists: Mill, Kant, and Sartre: An Introduction to Ethics*, Clarendon Press, Oxford.

George Schler Singer, (1946). *Religion and Scientific Method*, Reidel Publishing Company Inc, Boston, USA.

George Wilhelm Friedri Hegel, (2004). *The Philosophy of History*, Barnes & Noble Publishing House, New York.

Gerhard Böwering, (1998). *God and his Attributes, Islam: The Straight Path*, Oxford University Press, Oxford.

Gilbert Harman, (1977). *The Nature of Morality; An Introduction to Ethics*, Oxford University Press, New York.

Giriraj Gupta, (1978). *Religion in Modern India,* Vikas Publishing House Private Limited, New Delhi.

Goddard, Hugh, (1999). (ed)., *Islam: A Companion to Religious Studies and Theology,* Edinburgh University Press, USA.

Goodman, Lenn E, (1999). *Judaism: A companion to Philosophy of Religion*, Edinburgh University Press, USA.

Gordon H. Clark, (1992). *Biblical Doctrine of Man*, Trade paperback, Maryland, 2nd ed.

Gore, M.S, (1993). *Social Context of an ideology: Ambedkar's Political and Social Thought*, Sage Publications, New Delhi.

Gould, Harold A, (1987). *The Hindu Caste System*, Vol. I, Chanakya Publications, New Delhi.

Guenter Lewy, (1974). *Religion and Revolution*, Oxford University Press, New York.

Habermas, Jürgen, (1984). *Reason and the Rationalisation of Society : The Theory of Communicative Action*, Volume I, English translation by Thomas McCarthy, Beacon Press, Boston.

Hajime Nakamura, (1992). *A Comparative History of Ideas*, Motilal Banarsidass Publishers, New Delhi.

Helen. K. Bond, Seth D. Quinn and Francesca Aran Murphy, (1999). (ed)., *A Companion to Religious Studies and Theology*, Edinburgh University Press, London.

Hari Mohan Bhattacharya, (1985). *The Principles of Philosophy*, Oxford University Press, Calcutta.

Harold A. Durfee, (1952). *The journal of religion*, vol. 32, No.3. University of Chicago Press, Chicago.

Harold B. Smith, (1954) .*The Muslim World*, Vol. 44 American Religious Society, NewYork.

Heidegger, M. (1975). *Poetry, Language, Thought*, translated by Albert Hofstadter, Harper & Row Co Publications, New York.

Heidegger, M. (1978). *Being and Time/* translated by John Macquarrie and Edward Robinson, Basil Blackwell Publication, Oxford.

Hiriyanna, (1978). *Outline of Indian Philosophy*, George Allen & Unwin Limited, London.

Hobbes, Thomas (1968). *Leviathan*, Edited by Thomas Hobber and C.B. Macpherson, Penguin Books, Baltimore.

Hume David, (1976). *Enquiry Concerning the Principles of Morals*, Oxford University Press, London.

Husain M, (1989). *Islamic Principles*, Mehra Offset Press, (Reference Press), New Delhi.

Iqbal, Mohammad, (1993). *Reconstuction of Religious Thought in India*, Oriental Publishers and Distributors, New Delhi.

Jagtiani G. M. (1988). *Burning Question on Hindutva* , Self- Help Housing Society, Bombay.

Jaini, J.L. (1916). *Outlines of Jainism*, Cambridge University Press, London.

James Rachels, (1993). *The element of moral philosophy,* 2nd ed, Mc Graw-hill, Inc. New Delhi.

Janine Marie Idziak, (1978). *Divine Commands are the Foundation of Morality*, Clarendon Press, Oxford.

Jatava, D. R. (1998). *Ambedkar's Philosophy of Religion*, Shree Publishers, INA, Jaipur.

Jatava D. R, (1965). (ed)., *On contextuality of Ambedkar's thought, The Political Philosophy of B. R. Ambedkar*, Phoenix Publishing Agency, Agra.

Jatava, D. R. (1965). *The Social Philosophy of B. R. Ambedkar*, Phoenix Publishing Agency, Agra.

Jatava, D.R. (1993). The Critics of Dr. Ambedkar, Surabhi Publications, New Delhi.

Jayatillek K.N, (1975). (ed)., Ninian Smart, *The Message of the Buddha*, George Allen and Unwin, London.

Rousseau, Jean-Jacques, (1994). *The Social Contract*, Chapter- I, Oxford University Press, Oxford.

Jerome B, (1990). *A Guide to Rational Living*: *Moral Philosophy from Montaigne to Kant*, Schneewind Published, New York.

John A. Hutchison, (1957). *Biblical Foundations of Democracy*, Published by the National Association of Biblical Instructors to Foster Religion, UK.

John A. Hutchison, (1962). *Journal of Bible and Religion*, Vol. 30, No. 1, Oxford University Press, Oxford.

John Deway, (1977). *The essential writings*, Edited by David Sidorsky, Harper & Row Publications, New York.

John E. Hare, (ed)., Bryn Mawr, (1985). *Plato Euthyphro*, Commentaries by Plato, Bryn Mawr Commentaries Publishers, PA.

==John E. Smith, (1949). *Religion and Morality, The Journal of Religion,* No. 2. Vol. 29,

John Hick, (1978). *Philosophy of Religion,* Part - II Prentice-Hall of India Private Limited, New Delhi.

John Hick, (1983). *The philosophy of Religion,* third edition; Englewood Cliffs, Prentice-Hall Inc, New Jersey.

John Paul II's, (1979). *The Acting Person,* D Reidel Publishers Complex, Germany.

John R. Burr and Milton Goldinger, (2007). *Philosophy and Contemporary Issues*, V. K. Batra, Pearl Offset Press Private Limited, New Delhi.

Joseph Kenny, (2003). *Philosophy of the Muslim World*, Library of congress cataloging-in- publication, USA.

Joshi Lal Mani, (1977). *Studies in the Buddhistic Culture of India*, Motilal Banarasidass, New Delhi.

Julian Young, (2006). *Nietzsche's Philosophy of Religion*, Cambridge University Press, USA.

Kadam K.N, (1993). *Ambedkar: The Emancipator of the Oppressed,* Sangam Books, London.

Kadam, K.N, (1991). *Babasaheb Ambedkar and the Significance of His Movement,* Popular Prakasan, Bombay.

Kant Immanuel, (2002). *Critique of Practical Reason*, Hackett Publishing, London.

Kant Immanuel, (1998). *Religion Within the Boundaries*, Cambridge University Press, Cambridge.

Keer, Dhananjay, (1982). *Ambedkar: A Memorial Album,* Popular Prakasan, Bombay.

Keer, Dhananjay, (1987). *Dr Ambedkar: Life and Mission,* Sangan Books, London.

Kellner, Menachem, (1999). *Jewish Ethics: A companion to Ethics*. Edinburgh University Press, Edinburgh.

Kieran Flanagan and Peter C. Jupp, (1996). (ed)., *Postmodernity, Sociology and Religion*, St. Martin's Press, Inc, New York.

Knitter, F. Paul, (1995). *One Earth and Many Religions: Multi Faith Dialogue and Global Responsibility,* Orbis Books, New York.

Krishna, Iyer, V.R, (1991). *Ambedkar Centenary: Social Justice and the Undone Task,* B. R. Publishing Corporation, New Delhi.

Kuber, W.N, (1991). *Ambedkar: A Critical Study,* People's Publishing House, New Delhi.

Kuber, W.N, (1990). *B.R. Ambedkar,* Publication Division, Ministry of Information and Broadcasting, Government of India. New Delhi.

Lal B.K, (1987). *Contemporary Indian Philosophy*, Motilal Banarsidass, New Delhi.

Lederle, M, (1976). "*The Untouchables' Claim to Human Dignity*," Journal of the University of Poona, Humanities Section, Off-Print, Pune.

Leibniz, (1981). *New Essays on Human Understanding*, Cambridge University Press, Cambridge.

Leszek, Kolakowshi, (1982). *Religion*, Oxford University Press, New York.

Levi, Reuben, (1969). *Social Structure of Islam*, Cambridge University Press, Cambridge.

Locke, John (1988). *Treatises,* Edited by Peter Laslett, The Cambridge University Press Publishers, USA.

Lokhande, G.S, (1977). *Bhimrao Ramji Ambedkar A Study in Social Democracy,* Intellectual Publishing House, New Delhi.

Louis Green Span and Stefen Andersson, (2006). (ed)., *Russell on Religion*, Routledge, New York.

Ludwig Andreas Feuerbach, (1957). *The Essence of Christianity*, Harper Collins Publishers, New York.

MacIntyre, Alasdair, (1998). *Short History of Ethics : A History of Moral Philosophy from the Homeric Age to the Twentieth Century*, Routledge and Kegan Paul Publisher, London.

Mahadevan, T.M.P, (1981). *Contemporary Indian Philosophy*, Sterling Publishers Private Limited, New Delhi.

Mahadevan, T. M. P, (2006). *The Philosophy of Advaita*, Published Bharatiya Kala Prakashan, New Delhi.

Majumdar, A.K. (1997). *Ambedkar and Social Justice,* Radha Publications, New Delhi.

Malickal, John, (1991). *Caste in India Today.* Centre for Social Action, Bangalore.

Martin Luther, (1990). *The Bondage of the Will*, Fleming H Revell & Co, New York.

Matilal, B.K. (1977) . *Nyaya-Vaisesika*. Otto Harrassowitz, Weisbaden.

Massey, James, (1996). *Dalits in India: Religion as a Source of Bondage or Liberation with Special Reference to Christians,* Manohar Publishers, New Delhi.

Michael Mahar J, (1972). (ed)., *The Untouchables in Contemporary India*, Tucson, The University of Arizona Press, Arizona.

Michael, L. Peterson and Raymond, J. Vanarragon, (2004). (ed)., *Contemporary Debates in Philosophy of Religion*, Blackwell Publishers Inc, Oxford, U.K.

Michael Walzer, (2006). *Law, Politics, and Morality in Judaism,* Princeton University Press, U.K.

Michael Woods, (1986). (ed)., *Aristotle: Eudemian Ethics,* Oxford University Press, New Delhi.

Mill, J.S, (1998). *Three Essays on Religion: Nature, the Utility of Religion, and Theism,* Libri. Amherst, New York.

Mohapatra, A.R. (1985). *Philosophy of Religion*, Sterling Publishers Private Limited, New Delhi.

Moitra, S.K, (1945). *The Philosophy of Sri Aurobindo*, Banaras Hindu University Press, Banaras.

Monior Williams, (1995). *Buddhism*, Munshiram Monoharlal Publication Pvt Ltd, New Delhi.

Moon,Vasant,(1989). (ed.)., *Babasaheb Ambedkar's Writings and Speeches,* Vol. I, Dept. of Education, Govt. of Maharashtra, Bombay.

Moon, Vasant, (1989). (ed.)., *Babasaheb Ambedkar's Writings and Speeches,* Vol. III, Dept. of Education, Govt. of Maharastra, Bombay.

Moon, Vasant, (1991). (ed.), *Babasaheb Ambedkar's Writings and Speeches,* Vol. V, Dept. of Education, Govt. of Maharashtra, Bombay.

Moon, Vasant, (1990). (ed)., *Babasaheb Ambedkar's Writings and Speeches,* Vol. VII, Dept. of Education, Govt. of Maharashtra, Bombay.

Moon, Vasant, (1987). *Why go for Conversion?*, trans, Dalit Sahitya Akademy, Bangalore.

Moore, C.A, (1953). (ed)., "*The Indian Approch to the problem of religion*", *Philosophy and Culture-East and West*, George Allen & Unwin, London.

Moore, C.A. (1953). (ed)., "*Relation of Philosophical Theories to the Practical Affairs of Men,*" *Philosophy and Culture –East and West,* George Allen & Unwin, London.

Moore, C.A. (1953). (ed)., "The *Realistic Aspect of Indian Spirituality,*" *Philosophy and Culture –East and West,* George Allen & Unwin, London.

Nakamura Hajime, 1992. *A Comparative History of Ideas*, Motilal Banarsidass Publishers, New Delhi.

Murdoch, J. (1977). *Review of Caste in India*, Prem Rawat, Jaipur.

Nanji, Azim, (2000). *Islamic Ethics: A Companion to Ethics,* Blackwell Publishers, Massachusetts, U. K.

Narain A.K and Ahir D.C (1994). (eds.), *Dr.Ambedkar, Buddhism and Social Change.* B. R. Publishing Corporation, New Delhi.

Narain, A.K, (1994). *Ambedkar, Buddhism and Social Change,* B.R. Publishing Corporation, New Delhi.

Nathumal Tatia, (1952). *Studies in Jaina Philosophy*, P. V. Research Institute, Jainashram, Hindu University Press, Varanasi.

Nietzsche F, (1956). *On the Genealogy of Morals*, Double-day Publications, New York.

Nietzsche Friedrich, (1956). *Birth of Tragedy and the Genealogy of Morals*, Double-day Publications, New York.

Otto Maduro, (1982). *Religion and Social Conflicts*, Orbis Books, New York.

Paley William, (1979). *The Principles of Moral and Political Philosophy*, R. Faulder Publishers, New York.

Paliwal, K. V. (2005). *Untouchability Alien to Hindu Dharma*, Hindu Writers Forum, New Delhi.

Pandyan, David K. (1996). *Dr. B. R. Ambedkar and the Dynamics of Neo-Buddhism*, Gyan Publishing House, New Delhi.

Panikar and A. Koothothil, (1981). *Man and Religion*, Jeevadhara Publications, New Delhi.

Paradkar, B. A. M. (1968). *The Religious Quest of Ambedkar*, Ajay Prahaghan, New Delhi.

Parkinson, G.H.R. (1988). *An Encyclopedia of Philosophy* (ed), *The Nature of Moral Philosophy*, Richards Lindley, Routledge, UK.

Patric, G. T. W. (1925). *Introduction to Philosophy*, George Allen & Unwin, London.

Paul, Davis. (1983). *God and the New Physics*, Simon and Schuster, London.

Paul, Edwards, (1967). *The Encyclopedia of Philosophy,* Collier Macmillan Publishers, New York.

Paul, Tillich, (1951). *Dynamics of Faith,* Harper & Row, Publishers, New York, 1957.

Paul, Tillich, *Systematic Theology,* Chicago University Press, Chicago.

Paulos Mar Gregorios, (1989). *Enlightenment East and West: Pointers in the Quest for India's Secular Identity*, Simla, IISA.

Perston, Ronald. (1993). *Christian Ethics: A Companion to Ethics*. Blackwell Publishers Inc, Oxford, U.K.

Peter Singer, (2000). *A Companion to Ethics*, Blackwell Publishers, USA

Peter Vander Veer, (1996). *Conversion to Modernities: The Globalisation of Christianity,* Lagos, Evangelical Publishers, Germany.

Philip, Mathew, (1987). (ed)., *Non-Brahmin and Dalit Movements and their implications for Anti-Caste Struggle*, Horizon Book, Bangalore.

Philip, L. Quinn and Charles Taliaferro, (1999). (ed)., *A Companion to Philosophy of Religion,* Blackwell Publishers Inc, Oxford, U.K.

Pieris, A. (1988). *Love Meets Wisdom: A Christian Experience of Buddhism*, Orbis Books, New York.

Pradeep P. Gokhale, (1993). *Reconstructing the World. 'Universal Consequentlism: A Note on B.R. Ambedkar's Reconstruction of Buddhism'*, Sri Satguru Publications, New Delhi.

Paul, Puthanangady, (1986). *Towards an Indian Theology of Liberation*, Bangalore, NBCLC.

Puligundla, (1975). *Fundamentals of Indian Philosophy*, Mahabodhi Publishers, Mumbai.

Puligundla, (1975). (ed)., *The Heart of Jainism, Fundamentals of Indian Philosophy*, Mahabhodi Publishers, Mumbai.

Pushpendra Kumar Sharma, (1979). *Hindu Religion and Ethics*, Asain Publication Service, New Delhi.

Qanauji Lal Gautama, (2002). *Dr. Baba Saheb Ambedkar and Brahmanism*, B.R. Publishing Corporation, New Delhi.

Qa Deeruddin, Ahmed, (1989). *Islam in outlives*, Saddar Royal Book Company, Karachi.

Quinn, Philip. L and Taliaferro, Charles, (ed)., and Goodman, Lenin E, (1999). *Judaism; A Companion to Philosophy of Religion*, Blackwell Publishers Inc, USA.

Radhakrishnan, Sarvepally and Charles A. Moore, (1967). *A Source book in Indian Philosophy,* Princeton University Press, New Jersy.

Radhakrishnan, S, (1947). *Religion and Society,* George Allen & Unwin Ltd., London.

Radhakrishna, S. (1960). *Brahma Sutra, The Philosophy of Spiritual Life*. Greenwood Press, New York.

Raghavendra Rao, K. (1993). *Babasaheb Ambedkar*, Naveen Shahadhara Publishers, New Delhi.

Rajasekhar Setty, V.T.(1983). *Ambedkar and His Conversion*, Dalit Sahitya Academy, New Delhi.

Rajni Kothari, (2004). *Caste in Indian Politics*, Orient Longman. New Delhi, Section 1. 1.

Rao, Katti Padma, (1995). *Caste and Alternative Culture,* Gurukul Theological Institute, Chennai.

Ramaiah, Sundara, G. (1995). *Nature and Destiny of Soul in Indian Philosophy,* Oxford University Press, New Delhi.

Rhys Davids, (1971). *Buddhist India,* Motilal Banarasidass, New Delhi.

Rhys Davids, (1976). *Buddhist Psycology and Ethics*, Oxford University Press, Oxford.

Rhys Davids, (1978). *Out-lines of Buddhism*, Oriental Books Reprint Corporation, New Delhi.

Richard, Dworkin, (1972). *Religion and Morality*, Macmillan Publishing Co., Inc. Canada,

Richard Hope, (1960). (translated) *Aristotle, Metaphysics.* Columbia University Press, New York.

Richard Norman, (1983). *The Moral Philosophers, An Introduction to Ethics*, Clarendon Press, Oxford.

Richards Swinburne, (1977). *The Coherence of Theism,* Clarendon Press. Oxford, London,

Robert Appleton, (1915). *The Elementary Forms of the Religious Life*, George Allen & Unwin Ltd., London.

Rob Peter, (1993). (ed)., *Dalit Movements and the meaning of labour in India,* Oxford University Press, New Delhi.

Roderick Hindery, (1978). *Comparative Ethics in Hindu, Buddha Tradition*, Motilal Banarasidass, New Delhi.

Roger Scruton, (1981). *A Short History of Modern Philosophy, From Descartes to Wittgenstain*, Routledge & Kegan Paul, New York.

Roger Scruton, (1981). *From Descartes to Wittgenstein: A Short History of Modern Philosophy*, Routledge & Kegan Paul, New York.

Rouseau, Jean-Jacques, (1994). *The Social Contract*, Chapter-I, Oxford University Press, Oxford.

Rudavsky, Tamar, (1998). *The Jewish Contribution to Medieval Philosophical Theology.* Edinburgh University Press, London.

Runzo, Joseph and Nancy, M. Martin, (2007). (ed)., *Ethics, the World Religions*, One World Publications, New York.

Sangharakshita,(1986). *Ambedkar and Buddhism,* Windhorse Publications, Glasgow.

Saral Jhingran, (1989). *Aspects of Hindu Morality*, Motilal Banarasidass Publishers Pvt Lmt, New Delhi.

Shankar Srivastava Rama, (1984). *Contemporary Indian Philosophy,* Sarda Publications, Ranchi.

Sartre, Jean-Paul, (1984). *Existentialism and Human Emotions*, Citadel Place: Secaucus, New Jersy.

Schopenhauer Arthur, (1958). *The World as Will and Representation* / Translated by E.F.J. Payne, Dover Publications, New York.

Segundo, J. L. (1977). *Faith and Ideologies*, Orbis Books, New York.

Seth, A. Pringle Pattison, (1967). *The Idea of God*, Academic Publishers, Oxford University Press, Calcutta.

Sharma, Aravind, (1990). *A Hindu Perspective on Philosophy of Religion*, Macmillan.

Sharma, C.D., (1987). *A Critical Survey of Indian Philosophy*, Motilal Banaraidass Publishers, New Delhi.

Shashi, S.S. (1992). (ed.), *Ambedkar* and *Social Justice:* Vol. I and II, Ministry of Information and Broadcasting, New Delhi.

Shivesh, Chandra Thakur, (1969). *Christian and Hindu Ethics*, George Allen and Unwin Ltd, London.

Shukla, J.J. (1993). *Ambedkar on Hinduism,* Globe Books and Periodicals, Ahmedabad.

Sidgwick Henry, (1981). *The Methods of Ethics: Indianapolis*, Hackett Publishing Company, London.

Sister Nivedita, and Ananda, K. Coomaraswamy, (1972). *Myths of the Hindus and Buddhists*, Sagar Publications, New Delhi.

Smith, Mark S. (2002). *The early history of God: Yahweh and the other deities in ancient Israel.* Wm. B. Eerdmans Publishing Co.; 2nd ed., Philippines.

Spinoza, (1977). *Ethics and on the Correction of the Understanding* / translated by Andrew Boyle, (1992). *Everyman's* Library Publishers, New York and J M Dent & Sons Ltd, London, United Kingdom.

Srinivas, M.N. (1988). *Social Change in Modern India,* Orient Longman, Hyderabad.

Srivastava, (1974). *Comparative Religions*, Ramsankar Mushiram Monoharlal Publishers, New Delhi.

Srivastava, (1984). *Contemporary Indian Philosophy*, Sarda Publications, Ranchi.

Stace, W. T, (1990). *Time and Eternity*, IGNCA, New Delhi.

Stan Lourdusamy, (1990). *Religion as a Political Weapon*, Calcutta, Multi Book Agency.

Surendra, Ajnat, (1993). *Letters of Ambedkar.* Bheem Patrika Publications, Jalandhar.

Swami Vivekananda, (1987). *Complete Works, II*, ed, Lal B.K., *Contemporary Indian Philosophy*, Motilal Banarasidass, New Delhi.

Tara Sethia, (2004). (ed)., *Ahimsa, Anekanta and Jainism*, Motilal Banarasidass Publishers Pvt Ltd, New Delhi.

Tatai Natumal, (1951). *Studies in Jaina Philosophy*, P. V. Research Institute, Jainashram, Hindu University,Varanasi.

Taylor, Chales, (1995). *Religion today*, Cambridge Mass, Harward University Press, Harward.

Thomas St. Aquinas, (1947). *The Summa Theological,* Benziger Bros. Edition Publishers, London.

Thomas V. Morris, (1987). ed., *The Concept of God*, Oxford University Press, Oxford.

Thumma Anthony Raj, (2000). *Wisdom of the Weak: Foundations of People's Theology*, ISPCK, New Delhi.

Thumma, Anthoniraj, (1974). *Prema Yoga, Religion and Revolution*; *Religion and and Social Conflicts*; Oxford University Press, New York.

Uma Gupta, (1987). *Materialism in the Vedas*, Classical Publishing Company, New Delhi.

Vernon Pratt, (1970). *Religion and Secularisation*, Macmillan & St. Martin Press, London,

Wagner, F. Michael, (1991). *An Historical Introduction to Moral Philosophy*, Prentice Hall, New Jersey.

Walter Kaufmann, (1958). *Critique of Religion and Philosophy*, Harper and Row, Publishers, New York.

William Barnard, (1991). *Morality and Introduction to Ethics*, Cambridge University Press, Cambridge.

William L. Reese, (1975). *Dictionary of Philosophy and Religion*, Humanities Press, New Jersey.

Wittgenstein, L., (1976). *Philosophical Investigations*, Translated by G.E. M. Anscombe, Basil Blackwell Publishers, Oxford.

Zelliot Eleanor, (1969). "*Religion and Legitimation in the Mahar Movement*," Princeton University Press, Princeton.

Index